THE POETRY OF SEARCH
AND
THE POETRY OF STATEMENT

AND OTHER POSTHUMOUS ESSAYS ON LITERATURE,
RELIGION AND LANGUAGE

by

DOROTHY L. SAYERS

Eugene, Oregon

Wipf and Stock Publishers
199 W 8th Ave, Suite 3
Eugene, OR 97401

The Poetry of Search and The Poetry of Statement
and other Posthumous Essays on Literature, Religion and Language
By Sayers, Dorothy L. and Reynolds, Barbara
Copyright©1963 The Estate of Anthony Fleming
c/o Watkins Loomis Agency acting in association with David Higham Associates
ISBN: 1-59752-493-X
Publication date 1/1/2006
Previously published by Victor Gollancz, Inc., 1963

Errata

Dorothy L. Sayers, *The Poetry of Search and the Poetry of Statement* (Victor Gollancz, 1963)

p. 7, line 1: the *a* in "As" should be lowercased
p. 22, line 5: "share's" should read "shares"
p. 30, line 13: "*che 'elle*" should read "*che 'ella*"
p. 34, 5 lines from end: "quello" should read "quelle"
p. 36, line 17: omit "the"
p. 38, 13 lines from end: "*liberio*" should read "*libero*"
p. 35, line 9: align
p. 65, line 10: "creto" should read "certo"
p. 65, line 16: "de" should read "del"
p. 65, line 17: "se" should read "me"
p. 65, line 18: "ch'i," should read "ch'io"
p. 78, line 15: "Diomede" should read "Diomedes"
p. 82, 3 lines from end: "sonnet" should read "*canzone*"
p. 89, 2nd quotation, line 3:   insert "of" after "opposite"
p. 97, line 20: "Tich" should read "Titch"
p. 142, line 13: "Vöglein" should read "Vögelein"
p. 144, line 6: w.f.
p. 150, 5 lines from end: "volier" should read "voler"
p. 150, 4 lines from end: "volier" should read "voler"
p. 161, 4 lines from end: "stands" should read "stand"
p. 177, Italian quotation: "*Dizò*" should read "*Dirò*"
p. 216, 10 lines from end: insert "no" before "different"
p. 217, last line: insert a period after "*King*"
p. 218, first line: "whch" should read "which"
p. 269, line 17: "officialses" should read "officialese"

Series Foreword

It is now sixty years since Dorothy L. Sayers gave her first lecture on Dante. Few people were then aware of her new interest and the audience of three hundred who attended the Summer School of Italian at Jesus College, Cambridge, in August 1946 did not know what to expect. They were attracted by her fame as a detective novelist and as the author of the radio plays on the life of Christ, *The Man Born to be King.*

She had been drawn to Dante by Charles Williams, whose book *The Figure of Beatrice* appeared in 1943. A year went by before she acted on her resolve to read the *Commedia* right through and when she did the whole direction of her work was changed. At the same time, it fulfilled and completed all that she had done. I have told the story of her discovery of Dante in my book *The Passionate Intellect: Dorothy L. Sayers' Encounter with Dante,* of which a second edition has now been made available by the present publishers.

Her first lecture, entitled "The Eighth Bolgia," was a highlight. It led to a series of lectures, given mainly to subsequent summer schools. They were published in two volumes, *Introductory Papers on Dante* and *Further Papers on Dante,* and, posthumously, in *The Poetry of Search and the Poetry of Statement,* which contains lectures on several other subjects besides Dante. All three have long been out of print and in demand. It is with great pleasure that I welcome their reprint.

It should be remembered that these lectures were written during and immediately after World War II, at a time when the collapse of European civilization was imminent. Dante's message concerning sin and virtue seemed, to Dorothy Sayers, startlingly relevant to the current situation and she made it part of her war work to explain and interpret it from this point of view.

The first volume contains the most profound of her lectures. They also show the extent to which she felt she could rely on an audience to follow her argument, a situation that has changed in the ensuing sixty years. The most challenging is "The City of Dis," a lecture written for a group of mature undergraduates, recently returned to academic work after their experience of war. They knew the realities of evil and the state of the world and were a particularly responsive audience. So were the civilians who listened to her explanations of the Christian truths she perceived in Dante's allegory as well as the public who bought her translation, *Hell*, one of the early Penguin Classics.

The second volume, *Further Papers on Dante*, is more literary in quality and represents her talent as an entertainer. It contains the first lecture, "The Eighth Bolgia," on the subject of the famous canto concerning Ulysses and offers for the first time a solution to a mystery that had not been solved for six and a half centuries. The volume also contains the contribution she had previously made to *Essays Presented to Charles Williams*, in which her appreciation of Dante's talent as a storyteller is vividly presented.

The third volume, *The Poetry of Search and the Poetry of Statement*, was published after Sayers' death. It contains three lectures on Dante, one of which, "The Beatrician Vision in Dante and Other Poets," indicates the direction her work would have taken had she lived. She was convinced that Dante's vision had been shared by many poets before and after him and she was planning to write a work entitled "The Burning Bush" to show his connection with the mystic tradition.

In "The Meaning of Purgatory," one of the lectures contained in the first volume, Dorothy L. Sayers wrote:

> To appreciate Dante it is not, of course, necessary to believe what he believed, but it is, I think, necessary to *understand* what he believed, and to realise that it is a belief which a mature mind can take seriously.

The vibrant voice that first communicated these lectures has long been silent but the children, grandchildren, and great-grandchildren of the generations that first heard them now have the opportunity of reading them. They will discover that their relevance to the modern world has not diminished.

Barbara Reynolds
Cambridge 2006

CONTENTS

CHAPTER		PAGE
I.	The Poetry of Search and the Poetry of Statement	7
II.	Dante the Maker	21
III.	The Beatrician Vision in Dante and Other Poets	45
IV.	Charles Williams: A Poet's Critic	69
V.	On Translating the *Divina Commedia*	91
VI.	The Translation of Verse	127
VII.	The Lost Tools of Learning	155
VIII.	The Teaching of Latin: A New Approach	177
IX.	The Writing and Reading of Allegory	201
X.	The Faust Legend and the Idea of the Devil	227
XI.	Oedipus Simplex: Freedom and Fate in Folklore and Fiction	243
XII.	Poetry, Language and Ambiguity	263

NOTE

This selection from the numerous talks and lectures delivered by Dorothy L. Sayers between 1946 and 1957 includes six that have never been published and six that have already appeared in print, either independently or in the publications of the learned societies to which they were addressed (see p. 287). These latter may be regarded as having been passed for press by the writer herself, with the exception of Nos. III and V which appeared shortly after her death in *Nottingham Mediaeval Studies* in 1958, with an appreciation by the Editor commemorating her distinguished work as a mediaevalist. The six new items have been printed from the typescripts she used: any corrections she had made have been incorporated and the quotations have been checked. Her two volumes of Dante studies are widely known, but this is the first collection to represent her all-round scholarship.

CHAPTER I

THE POETRY OF SEARCH AND THE POETRY OF STATEMENT

EMERGING (AS I occasionally do) from the Middle Ages to survey the contemporary scene, I have discovered that there is an argument going on about what kind of thing poetry ought to be. From an article by Mr. Dennis Donoghue in *The London Magazine*, I gather that there is on both sides of the Atlantic a movement towards what is called a "New Conservatism". I do not care for this phrase, which has been chosen for its political association, and is—if I understand the point at issue—rather misleading. Here are a few of the opinions that Mr. Donoghue quotes. Mr. Robinson Jeffers has said that the "great poet of the immediate future" would turn away from the obscure and self-conscious poetry that has recently been fashionable; he would "have something new and important to say, and just for that reason he would wish to say it clearly. He would be seeking to express the spirit of his time (as well as of all times), but it is not necessary, because an epoch is confused, that its poet should share its confusion". Professor Dobrée asks: "Why should we, the readers, have to share in the poets' gropings? Why should we have to pry? The moment we hear singing, we respond." Mr. Kingsley Amis suggests, rather tartly, that "perhaps the modern practitioners of a chop-fallen Romanticism may give up exhibiting themselves before their readers and at last set about telling them something". Mr. Donald Davie has expressed a desire for "a poetry of urbane and momentous statement", and has been rash enough to opine that "a public exists" for didactic poetry, which he defines as "poetry that openly asserts conclusions drawn from experience"; while Mr. Peter Viereck has advocated a return to "the hardwon simplicity that resolves spiritual tensions and literary complexities. Difficult simplicity is the tragic affirmation that follows the dark night of the soul, not the crass and jovial affirmation that precedes it".

Mr. Donoghue, on the other hand, says that "as long as contemporary society remains to a large extent confused, desperate and chaotic, the poetic announcement of 'conclusions' will be a gratuitous and unnatural gesture"; and he implies that even if there is a public which is eager for simple statements, it would be a corrupt weakness in the poet to try and establish communication with it. He goes on:

> Surely poetry that achieves the result of spiritual tensions and literary complexities, if it is not deliberately to exclude those tensions from view, must reveal them in the poem : it must show the strains, the sweat and the scars, and if it does so it cannot be a simple poem in any sense of that adjective. Poems are difficult... precisely because they show the whole fight, round and round between the poet and the materials of his work (experiences personal, imaginative, intuitive, credal).... The alternative is the total concealment of the struggle and the mere "lucid" announcement of the poet's victory : surely that is a fair description of most bad poems.

He declares that he "can see no future for didactic poetry", and concludes: "Who wants the poet to philosophize?" He is speaking, of course, of today; otherwise one would have to remind him that there have been long periods when nobody wanted or expected the poet to do anything else.

Having examined the arguments on both sides, I am tempted to put forward one of those generalizations which (though open to many modifications in detail) are sometimes helpful in clearing the ground. I think there are two kinds of poetry, one of which appeals more strongly to this age, and another to that age, though both can be good poetry. They correspond roughly to the categories of Romantic and Classical; but those words have been much abused. I would rather call them the Poetry of Search and the Poetry of Statement. Or one may say, if that is a better way of putting it, that there are two kinds of poet : the one writes in order to find out what he feels, the other in order to tell what he knows. Both are concerned with personal experience; but the poetry of Search concentrates on the "gropings", whether or not they succeed in reaching any goal; the poet writes the diary of his journey as he goes along, describing for their own sake all the false steps, blind alleys, and pits of confusion into which he may fall by the way. The poetry of Statement, on the other hand, is not written till the journey is ended : it maps the true route from tentative beginning to triumphant arrival. If it mentions the false wanderings it is only to warn people off them; but it is concerned to get somewhere and to show other people the way. The poet must of course have plodded every step of the journey himself: he must not merely announce other people's conclusions—that is indeed a sure recipe for bad poetry. But the poet is concerned with the truth he has dicovered about things in general, not merely with the workings of his own mind. Mr. Donoghue, in the manner of the schoolmaster, requires that "all rough workings should be shown in the margin". That is all right: but the mathematics master is not interested in the answer to the sum—he knows that already; he is interested only in seeing how Jones minor got there, or failed to get there. But when a mathematician sets out a theorem, he is interested in the proof; he sets down only the correct and most elegant working that leads to a right conclusion; for, having wrestled with the problem himself, he desires to exhibit it to the world in all its "hardwon simplicity". Where Mr. Donoghue seems to me to be mistaken is in suggesting that the sole alternative to setting down all the "gropings" is to present and announce the conclusion without showing any workings at all.

I do not wish to make a polemical issue of all this. Nothing is more distasteful than the more-than-theological odium with which literary critics pursue one another, as though it were positively wicked to write poetry of a kind which does not appeal to them. There are bad poets, and there are good and even supreme poets, in both kinds. It is possible to argue that the poetry of Statement is more mature than the poetry of Search. It is only when we have known how to profit by much experience that we learn for ourselves the truth of all the great commonplaces; and the poetry of Statement is often the reaffirmation of some great commonplace, with all the weight and all the intellectual excitement which comes of having tested a thing by living it and found it true. There are men who begin as poets of Search and end as poets of Statement: Dante is one of them. His Ode, *Voi che 'ntendendo il terzo ciel movete*, is a typical poem of Search: he was distracted between the old love and the new, and he wrote down that distraction while he was undergoing it, and was still not fully assured of the end. But the *Divina Commedia* records his personal rediscovery of all the greatest commonplaces in the world: "God is love." "The first love is always the best." "It's love that makes the world go round." He had made the journey and reached his conclusion; and having done so, he made a Statement of his conclusions. His, not another man's: for he had made them his by discovering them.

A typical poet of Search is Keats. One of the things for which he was passionately searching was the true meaning of the poet's nature and calling. He started to examine this in *Hyperion,* but he changed his mind as he went along, broke off, and started again with *The Fall of Hyperion.* That, too, was never finished. He himself admitted that he had been trying to write in an unsuitable style—the style of Milton. It is unreasonable to deduce from this that Milton's style is vicious, or that Keats thought it so. But it was the wrong style for that particular poem. Keats was trying to write a poem of Statement in the style of the poetry of Statement; but he was not really ready to issue a statement, because he was still engaged in the search. The two kinds of poetry cannot use the same style. Neither can they be stretched side by side on the same Procrustean bed of criticism: "one law for the Lion and the Ox is oppression."

We must remember that Keats died young. Had he lived to maturity, he might have found a permanent statement to make, in spite of his *obiter dictum* about "negative capability" which appears to look forward to a chronic unsettlement. We have perhaps built too towering a critical structure on the basis of that single observation: a sentence addressed to a familiar correspondent, which may be the expression of a passing mood or a kite flown to test the other man's reaction, ought not to be erected into an *ex cathedra* pronouncement merely because it happens to suit us. It does, I think, represent a permanent truth about the poetic imagination; but the imagination is not the whole man, and it does not necessarily represent the whole truth about the will and judgement, if I may use those old-fashioned expressions. About Keats it is, I think, only safe to say that at the time of his death he was still writing to find out what he felt, and that sometimes, as in the case of Hyperion, his feelings changed in the course of writing—or rather, perhaps, the act of writing convinced him of the instability of his feeling—so that he was unable to finish the poem.

More paradoxical is the case of Tennyson, in some ways the most sensitive and uneasy of all the Victorians. To the end of his life his poems express a desperate search and groping among the afflicting disturbances of his era. His *In Memoriam* is a typical poem of search—a poetic diary, exploring his inner events as they occurred, and fumbling its way from point to point as it proceeds, without any clear foresight of the end in view. Because it is clearly this, we are able partially to accept it, even today, though we do not much like the other-worldly conclusion—the reconciliation out of time—towards which it is painfully struggling. We forgive more readily the poets of the period between the two wars, who, in a period of even greater confusion, pinned their hopes on a this-worldly and Marxian triumph of the "somehow good". This vision, too, Tennyson saw; he gave expression to it in *Locksley Hall, Sixty Years After*; and, in expressing it, explored himself, and found that he could not fully commit himself to it. So, too, in *The Princess,* he explored a new relation between the sexes and then, finding his will unable to give full assent to his imagination, became troubled and warned his audience that the whole thing must be received as a fantasy. The subject has ceased to interest us—partly because the battle for women's education has ceased to be a living issue and we are no longer capable of thinking the question out on those particular lines—and we are better able to sympathize with the lyric portions of *Maud* and their exploration into emotional instability. This is the easier for us, now that we know how terribly close Tennyson himself lived under the shadow of congenital madness, and because—once again—the poem wears its inconclusiveness plainly written upon its structure. What is surely ironical is that the most tragic and terrible of all Tennyson's dark journeyings— that long poem-cycle which took some forty years in the making and ends in a confession of total doubt and almost total despair —should be pilloried today as a typical example of Victorian smugness and complacency. *The Idylls of the King* is not, as it is too readily taken to be, the history of good temporarily overthrown by evil—which would be distressing but not tragic— followed by a glib assurance that everything will come out all right in the end: there is no such assurance. It is the history of the defeat of that idealism which had nourished men's minds ever since the beginnings of the Romantic Movement—a defeat caused not by pressure from without, but by decay from within, due to the inherent inability of idealism to come to terms with the powers which alone can make it practically effective. If ever Tennyson made a statement, this is it: for the conclusion of

The Passing of Arthur is that very same *Morte d'Arthur* which he had written as a young man, without a word changed; only the steps that lead to that conclusion are now displayed in all their inevitability. It is not a comforting statement. The good must perish because not only does it contain in itself the seeds of its own corruption, but because it is a danger to society—

> Lest one good custom should corrupt the world—

yet its perishing lets in the jungle:

> all my realm
> Reels back into the beast, and is no more.

It perishes without any of the martyr's clear certainty of himself or his mission:

> For all my mind is clouded with a doubt;

and, although we may feel confident that:

> Arthur will come again, he cannot die,

we can have no confidence that the same tragedy will not happen all over again. Even the Epilogue, which does its best to introduce a little light into this haunting gloom, can do no more than urge the nation to do its best, with the aid of "saving common-sense", to cope with the immediate situation.

The puzzle is, not that a man so temperamentally vulnerable as Tennyson, and unequipped with any very strong intellectual philosophy or theology, should have failed to escape from the tension of his time, but how his contemporaries should have found any comfort in this agonizing cleavage of the spirit, and still more, how we should have come to mistake these unhappy searchings for a statement, and above all for a statement of smug complacency. We may perhaps suggest a few reasons which will throw light on the whole question of poetic search and statement.

First of all: we are apt to find what we look for. The traditional conception of the poet as a prophet and an authority was still alive up to the end of the last century. A statement of some kind was expected: the poet was greater than other men, inspired by virtue of his office and thus speaking out of a knowledge that was not his own. Even the Enlightenment, nurtured on the classics, never failed to pay at any rate lip-service to the

Muses; and when Coleridge is found urging Wordsworth at the age of thirty-five or thereabouts to "assume the character" of an aged Recluse and write a great philosophical poem, he is asserting his friend's duty, as a poet, to "tell what he knows". We find Coleridge and Wordsworth a little absurd in their earnestness, as we do not find Isaiah or Lucretius, or Dante, or even Milton; but it is only when we come down to the time of our immediate ancestors that we find the prophetic claim unendurably pompous and irritating. Sometimes one wonders whether the calculated indignity of the modern male costume has not something to do with it. But the Victorians were robustly enough within tradition to accept a *vates,* even if he were as well-dressed as Robert Browning: the cause of our discontents lies deeper. Tennyson and his fellow-poets could still be accepted as prophets: therefore a statement was expected from them and, being expected, was found, even where it did not really exist. It was the general doubt and fear that were voiced, and the hearers were rather too ready to be self-deceived in supposing that a solution was being offered them; but I doubt whether their poets deceived them. And there is less excuse for us to be deceived about it.

There is, however, some excuse. We are deceived, to a considerable extent, by the language and the metre, which have a stately movement calculated to disguise the agitated emotions which it clothes. It is again, as in the case of *Hyperion,* a poetic medium fitted for the statement. The violent revolt against it, characteristic of our century, was justified; for it presently became obvious that subversive opinions and cries of spiritual bewilderment could not be expressed in it without an appearance of hypocrisy. The same thing applies to a whole vocabulary belonging to a background of received religious opinion that was coming to be, in fact, no longer generally received. Words like "God", "spirit", "infinite", "immortal" and so on, in whatever context they were used, produced a numbing effect upon the hearer that prevented him from understanding, or even noticing, what was being said. The phrase:

> God fulfils Himself in many ways,
> Lest one good custom should corrupt the world—

is startling, and even shocking, if one can listen to it. But the three words "God fulfils Himself" had soothing associations which rendered the hearer completely deaf to the end of the sentence, both then and now. To the modern ear the whole thing sounds like a plaster of religious clap-trap slapped on to cover up whatever might be festering beneath. With the great poets, I am sure that this accusation is untrue. The danger, however, is a real one, and it was time that there should be such an upheaval both of metre and vocabulary that the underlying realities should be shaken to the surface, so that it should become impossible either to use the language of faith unless it was made quite clear what one believed, or to use the form of the poetry of statement unless one actually had a statement to make. It will be noticed that today a similar fate is overtaking the whole vocabulary of the religion of democracy. The sacred words are uttered, the heads of the hearers are bowed, and the liveliest doubts, or even the most alarming heresies, pass without examination.

I have been speaking of the effect of language upon the hearers, and this naturally brings up the whole problem of "communication". There is a school of criticism which asserts roundly that art and communication have nothing to do with one another. A work of art can only be assessed by that which it is in itself, and not by its effect upon the audience or spectators. That pronouncement might be answered philosophically, in the manner of the schoolmen, by saying that, unfortunately, we cannot know anything "as it is in itself", but only in its effects; or empirically, by saying that if works of art are to be assessed at all, somebody must do the assessing, and that therefore a communication of some kind has to be made to the assessor if to no one else. Moreover, all artists, even the most intransigent, intend their works as a communication; otherwise, as someone has drily observed, "Why do they publish?" I will not pursue this controversy, because—though discussion is the aim of this assembly—I do not want to start too many hares at once. I will only draw attention to Mr. David Daiches' recent definition: "Poetry, in the largest sense of the word, is a unique method of making a unique kind of communication, and it is the real or potential effectiveness of the communication which justifies the method, not vice versa."[1] The word "potential" is important, because it excludes what Mr. R. H. Wilenski calls "the absurd conclusion that a great work of art is valueless if it happens to be

[1] *Literary Essays*, pp. 173-174.

produced in a society so poor in aesthetes that nobody reacts to it".[1] Communication can only be made to those who have ears to hear.

There is, however, a distinction which we must make, if what Mr. Donoghue calls "didactic poetry", and the "poetry of statement" generally, is not to be confused with something very different. It is a distinction extremely clear to any honest writer or artist, but one that is for some reason extremely difficult to make clear to anybody else: I mean the distinction between writing *to* an audience and writing *for* an audience. The communication which it is intended to convey must be of something which the artist desires or delights in for its sake and his own and wants to tell people about; he must not *primarily* want to give his audience either what they want or what is good for them—otherwise he will produce, not art, but what R. G. Collingwood called "pseudo-art"; that is, commercial entertainment or didactic writing in the bad sense of the word. He may indeed hope that his own exciting experience, whatever it is, will either please or instruct those to whom he communicates it, but that hope is incidental. The important thing is the expression and communication of an experience which has fired his own imagination.

An example will put the thing plainer than this collection of abstract nouns. Let us consider the woman in the parable who had lost one of the ten pieces of silver from her necklace. She lights a candle and sweeps the house diligently till she finds it. And when she has found it she calls her neighbours together saying, "Rejoice with me, for I have found the piece which was lost".

The woman, in that instance, was a poet of statement. She found the missing piece first, and then, unable to contain her excitement, she called in the neighbours and, no doubt, related to them the whole story of her search. She desired to communicate her experience and hoped for their pleasure and sympathy: "Rejoice with me."

Had she, on the other hand, been a poet of search, she would have called the neighbours in the moment the piece was lost. She would have made them spectators of the search, and entertained them with a running commentary as it went on, calling for their interest and sympathy every time she hit her head

[1] *The Modern Movement in Art*, p. 151.

against the sink or found a nest of mice under the boiler; nor would they have been spared her disappointment over every glittering fragment which looked promising, but turned out only to be a bit of broken glass or tinfoil. And she would have made this communication whether or not the search was in the end successful.

But in either case, the end and aim of the whole operation is the missing piece of silver. The woman was not putting on a show to amuse the neighbours, and she was not giving a demonstration in house-cleaning. The search was for the sake of the silver, the communication for the sake of the joy.

That being so, it is obviously useless for anybody to demand that poets should "tell us something" if they have nothing to tell, or "make a statement" if the search is still proceeding; for the poet cannot, if he is to retain his integrity, pay the slightest attention to what the audience wants to hear. If the audience are weary of assisting at a search which seems doomed to endless frustration, all they can do is to drift away quietly, and refuse to listen any longer to the laments of the searcher.

What is difficult to condone is the attitude of those who seem to regard with a kind of rancour *all* poetry of statement, as though they thought it disgraceful that any search should come to a successful conclusion. The people who accompanied Mr. T. S. Eliot with approving cries on his search through *The Waste Land* were horribly disconcerted when he emerged clutching his recovered piece of silver, and his invitation to "rejoice with him" found little response from that particular set of neighbours. Some even went so far as to say that *The Four Quartets* were inferior *as poetry* to the earlier works (which was manifestly untrue), while the critical reception of *The Family Reunion* was a notorious scandal. Expressions like "retreat" and "stagnation" begin to be used, and the old epithets "smug" and "complacent" crop up again. This might be put down to the fact that Mr. Eliot's statement is Christian and traditional; but the same kind of antagonism is apt to display itself even to statements about other religions, such as Mr. Aldous Huxley's eclectic Buddhism, the Marxian millennium, and even the resignation to pure pessimism. It may be that the evolutionary myth of endless progress is not so dead as we had supposed, and that the mere notion of rest and fulfilment has come to be regarded as something undesirable—a kind of treason to the universe. The demand that poets should "tell us something" comes up against a very strong reluctance to accept anything that we are told. It is clear that our whole attitude to the poet has changed. We no longer look up to him as a greater than ourselves, inspired by an authority which is not his own. Any apparent inspiration he may get is presumed to derive—if from anywhere—from his own unconsciousness; and there seems little reason to suppose that his unconscious is any more authoritative than our own. We are by no means sure that it is in touch with the eternal things—and probably it is not the eternal things that we wish to hear about, even if we were persuaded that any things are eternal. If not, then the only thing that the poet can tell us about is himself; and indeed, the modern trend of criticism is, very largely, to disregard the work itself, except in so far as it throws light upon the workings of the writer's mind. We do not care whether the man writes truth or not; we care only for the hidden process which caused him to suppose his conclusions to be truthful. This is all very well for us, but it is death to the poet, in whom it is bound to produce not only a self-consciousness amounting to inhibition, but a desperate sense of frustration, since what he intends as statements will be accepted only as what Mr. I. A. Richards has called "pseudo-statements". Mr. Stephen Spender, in an essay which poignantly expresses the extreme discomfort of the poet under contemporary conditions, has voiced the dangers which attend this kind of attitude both as regards the poets of the past and those of the present. As regards the poets of the past, it falsifies our criticism. He is speaking primarily of poets such as Wordsworth and Yeats, who "expressed in their poetry mystical experiences which they believed to be true and to which they bore witness", but his protest applies equally, I think, to all poets who have made statements which they believed to be universally true. He says:

> To accept or interpret all such statements as being only "psychologically true", is to understand them in a sense the opposite of that in which they were intended. The effect of this kind of acceptance of the past on terms which those who lived then would regard as their rejection, may be justified by science, but to the poetic mind, which has its own kind of literalness, it is an extremely dubious proceeding. There is always the danger of turning the present into a kind of prison of our own science and ideologies and analyses where every idea that enters from outside

is doctored and treated with our modern medicine that renders it—in its own historic terms—meaningless.[1]

The effect upon the living poet is even worse; he "finds himself shut out from God and the past, and inside the cage of contemporary attitudes".

> The picture ... of the poet devoted entirely to creating order amongst purely human complexities locks poetry completely within psychology, and bars it out from any contact with spiritual purpose in the universe outside humanity. The poet is put in the position of having to project patterns of experience in which man is outside everything but himself, expelled from God and the past by the contemporary state of scientific knowledge.[2]

And again:

> He is in a cage with bars that are mirrors reflecting only himself, and there is no possibility of entering through the imagination into the factual realities outside.[3]

It would seem unreasonable, under the circumstances, to expect a statement of any kind from a poet—unless, indeed, from a poet with the religious faith. But in that case, the poet will find it difficult to establish communication with anybody except his co-religionists, and he will be accused, as Mr. Spender in fact accuses the Christian poets, of "weakening their hold on the idiom of contemporary life". Nevertheless, in the face of all this, we find the demand that poets should "tell us something", and "make a statement". It begins to look like a demand for the impossible.

A final question suggests itself. Does the rejection of the traditional religions, of the great archetypes, of the universal values imply a more far-reaching claim for the myth of progress than any we have yet considered? Is it felt that the psychological and scientific techniques of the nuclear age are about to result in a fundamental alteration of human nature itself, and that the "poetry of search" should be addressing itself to the analysis of a totally new set of physical, mental, and emotional experiences? This suggestion seems to be adumbrated in some of the more disturbing imaginations of the science fictionists. If this is so, the poet is going to find himself "cut off from God and the past" in an even more drastic manner; that past from which he draws his

---

[1] *The Making of a Poem*, p. 24. [2] *Ibid*, p. 23. [3] *Ibid*, p. 26.

nourishment will dry up, and history will in fact become altogether meaningless both for him and for us.

Now, I am not here to make any statement of my own. I do not pretend to know, of my own knowledge, the answers to any of these questions. I wish only to direct your attention to a situation that appears to have come about, and to invite your comments upon it. To start the discussion off, I might suggest two questions:

1. Is it a fact that some of the younger poets today are trying to make statements—i.e. to "tell what they know" and not only to "find out what they feel"? Because, if they are not, it is clearly useless for you or me or the critics to issue directives to them. (This is a question for *you*; I cannot help you because I do not know enough about contemporary poetry.)

2. If the answer to the first question is "Yes", then what type of criticism will be fruitful in dealing with the results? Because it is evident that the type which treats all statements as "pseudo-statements", valuable only as a key to the poet's psychology, is a wrecking instrument which, applied to statements in the past, may only destroy our understanding of them, but, applied to the living poet, may distort, or even destroy, the poet.

CHAPTER II

DANTE THE MAKER[1]

It may be true that, in confused times like our own, when one can count upon no common background of belief or feeling, the poetry of Statement, however truthfully it may reflect the poet's personal achievement, is not likely to win much critical approval. (To say it has no future is scarcely justifiable—who are we to consign the whole future to permanent confusion of mind?) But in the periods where the poetry of Statement is at home, we shall find in it, at its greatest, two characteristic qualities: on the large scale, a massive simplicity of outline, combined with a closely articulated complexity and lucidity of speech, and an astonishing richness of hidden allusion. This is what we should expect: the poet can be lucid and precise because he knows what he intends to say; his structure can be massive in outline and intimately related in all its parts because it is planned, and he knows, while writing, exactly what every word and line bears to the whole poem; he can afford to leave many things unexpressed, because, using the language of a common belief and feeling, he can rely on his reader to fill in for himself all the implications latent in an apparently simple phrase. The poet of this type is a "maker" in the strict sense of the word: his poem is a *made* thing, a true creation, possessing a proper, though derived, being of its own, so that we can, in Mr. Donald Davie's words, "move out of the poet's mind into the poem" and deal directly with what we find there. Dante is the great master of the poem of statement, and this (as we shall see presently) is precisely what he understands by "creation".

I propose to look at two examples of the work of "Dante the Maker": to see, first, how the whole of the *Paradiso* is built like

---

[1] As originally delivered, this address opened with a passage identical with the opening paragraphs of the preceding essay, *The Poetry of Search and the Poetry of Statement,* up to the words: " 'One law for the Lion and the Ox is oppression.' "

a bridge between the first and the last terzains, and how roads from all the other parts of the poem run together to one point from which to pass over that bridge; to see, secondly, how, from a single unadorned statement in the seventh canto, the reader who share's Dante's background may construct a whole labyrinth of associated imagery, turning and returning perpetually upon the central affirmation of fact in which a whole complex of meanings lies implicit.

In the opening terzain of the *Inferno*, Dante introduces himself immediately, intimately, and in a tone so casual that he might be merely conversing with us, as an actor in his own comedy:

> Nel mezzo del cammin di nostra vita
> mi ritrovai per una selva oscura
>
> *Inf.* i. 1–2.

(In the middle of the journey of our life I came to myself within a dark wood.)

In the opening terzain of the *Purgatorio*, he steps aside for a moment from the action, and speaks with a little more distance and formality, as the author of the poem:

> Per correr migliori acque alza le vele
> omai la navicella del mio ingegno
>
> *Purg.* i. 1–2.

(To course over better waters the little bark of my wit now lifts her sails.)

In the opening terzain of the *Paradiso*, he withdraws his own personality altogether, and sets before us the naked fact of Godhead:

> La gloria di colui che tutto move
> per l'universo penetra e risplende
> in una parte più e meno altrove.
>
> *Para.* i. 1–3.

(The glory of Him who moves all things penetrates the universe and shines in one part more and in another less.)

This is the first and, I think, the only passage in the *Commedia* where he uncompromisingly confronts us with this stark Aristotelian abstraction of the unmoved Mover. He has, of course, used various titles and periphrases for God: *"il sommo bene"*, *"sommo Giove"*, *"l'alto lume"*, *"il Rege etterno"*, and so forth, ranging from the Scriptural tenderness of *"Padre nostro"* among the penitents of the first Cornice to the austerely impersonal word of power—a will without a name—which Virgil invokes to command Charon and Pluto:

> vuolsi così colà dove si puote
> ciò che si vuole
>
> *Inf.* iii. 95–96.

(It is so willed where will and power are one.)

Now, with his feet on the very threshold of Heaven, he deliberately strips off every anthropomorphic and every specifically Christian attribute, in order to present us with this bare intellectual concept.

It has been said that the most difficult task of Christian philosophy, and one which it has never yet perfectly succeeded in fulfilling, is the reconciliation of the abstract, mathematically static First Cause, which it took over from classical Greece, with the actively personal God whom it inherited from Jewish prophecy. The one concept is necessary to its theological reason; the other, fundamental to its revelation and indispensable for its interpretation of history. They meet us, already indissolubly welded, in the first Epistle of St. John: "That which was from the beginning ... which we have looked upon and our hands have handled." The fact and the manner of their welding are Dante's preoccupation in his final vision of God, and his intuition of it forms the climax of the vision and of the poem. His intention is defined and proclaimed in the first and last lines of the *Paradiso,* which balance and echo each other with so subtle and so important a change of wording:

> La gloria di colui che tutto move
>
> *Para.* i. 1.
>
> L'Amor che move il sole e l'altre stelle.
>
> *Para.* xxxiii. 145.

"In my beginning is my end"; the opening line contains the two great seminal words out of which the whole articulated structure of the cantica is built up.

The first is *"gloria",* with its attendant and corresponding *"risplende". "Gloria, lume, luce"*—these, as we know, are Dante's words for direct light, proceeding from its source in the *"eterna fontana"; "splendore"* and its derivatives are the reflected light which, being received by the creation, returns from it to its source. Dante has already taken pains to make us acquainted with the word "*splendore*" used in this sense, when in *Purg.* xv. 7–21 he described the double brilliance of the western sun and of the angel beating up into his face from the rocky surface of the Cornice. He then expounded the behaviour of reflected light and the angle of incidence with a wealth of scientific detail, "*sì come mostra esperienza ed arte*". Now, in *Para.* i. 49–50 he is careful to mention it again—

> E sì come secondo raggio suole
> uscir del primo e risalire in suso,

(And as a second ray will issue from the first and mount up again),

dragging it in, indeed, by the heels, in the course of a rather awkward simile, in his anxiety to keep the phenomenon of reflection constantly in our minds.

The second key-word *"move"* is even more important, because it defines the nature and activity of God, and looks forward to the culmination of the whole poem. Dante emphasizes its significance by throwing it to the end of the line and giving it the rhyme—thus, incidentally, setting a frightful technical trap for the English translator, whether in prose or verse. For it is in practice almost impossible to stress the word "moves" as Dante does and at the same time preserve the symmetry of the first and final lines intact. Still, however we decide, our understanding of the problem has made some progress since the day (1840) when the Rev. Ichabod Wright could blithely set down:

> The glory of the Lord, to all things given, ...
> Pervades creation.

Not only does he leave the key-word untranslated, but by turning Aristotle's "Mover" into the Hebraic "Lord", he makes confusion of Dante's serene progress from the abstract to the personal. No modern translator could be at once so inaccurate and so insensitive; though indeed, as late as 1927, the eccentric American, John Jay Chapman, had the face to perpetrate:

> The glory of the Universe is He
> Whose glory beats and shines through every sphere,
> With less or greater visibility.

Not only is the "Mover" lost, but also that necessary distinction between *"gloria"* and *"risplende"*, on which point, as we shall see, a number of very important conclusions hang. But Chapman, as all his comments show, never had any sure grasp of what Dante was driving at; and he was writing in a bad period, when lyrical effects were considered more "poetical" than architectural structure.

"Gloria" and *"move"* being thus the key-words of its theme, we find that the whole *Paradiso* is presented in images of light and motion. The fact needs no dwelling on: perhaps the first thing that strikes us about the book is the absence of any sort of chiaroscuro or perspective, of landscape or picture or event. Except for Dante and Beatrice themselves, no human form appears between the second heaven and the tenth; and of these the dwellers in the Moon appear faint as reflections in clear water—

> debili sì, che perla in bianca fronte
> non vien men tosto alle nostre pupille,
> *Para.* iii. 14–15.

(so faint that a pearl on a white brow does not come less quickly to our eyes)

while those in Mercury only gleam out for a moment from the light of joy which partly shrouds them and in which all the dwellers in the heavens above them are wholly hidden *"quasi animal di sua seta fasciato"*. All the variety is provided by the changing colour and intensity of the lights, and by the abstract patterns they trace against a background, itself of pure light, in which they move *"come in fiamma favilla si vede"*. Dante's heaven is the despair of illustrators: what, one wonders, looking at the Sistine Last Judgement, did Michelangelo make of it in those marginal sketches with which he adorned his copy of the *Comedy*, lost, alas, with all his luggage in the Bay of Genoa? If we lay the *Paradiso* beside *Paradise Lost* or the *Apocalypse*, we see how strictly, for reasons that seemed good to him, Dante excluded the Hebraic element from the imagery. Only the scripture names and the reiterated hosannas sounding through the verse keep this heaven of intellectual light in touch with the vigorously anthropomorphic figure of "the Lord high and lifted up, [whose] train filled the Temple". The four Beasts and the four-and-twenty Elders were last shown us with Beatrice in the Earthly Paradise, and do not reappear. The forms of men and angels are veiled, only to be displayed at length in the Empyrean, as in eternity they are, and in time shall be "at the Resurrection", when form shall be restored along with the restoration of all things. Last of all, the Humanity of the Incarnate is revealed, inextricably coinherent in the changeless light of the Godhead. There is, after a fashion, an ascent through a naughting of the images and a "cloud of unknowing"; but the cloud is not a darkness but an excess of light, and the images are not extinguished but eclipsed in their own brilliance.

> Come subito lampo che discetti
> li spiriti visivi, sì che priva
> dall'atto l'occhio di più forti obbietti,
> così mi circunfulse luce viva;
> e lasciommi fasciato di tal velo
> del suo fulgor, che nulla m'appariva.
> *Para.* xxx. 46–51.

(Like sudden lightning that scatters the visual spirits and deprives the eye of the action of the clearest objects, a vivid light shone round about me and left me so swathed in the veil of its effulgence that nothing was visible to me.)

The whole cantica is full of these pictures of light shining through light, emotion expressed and communicated by changes of light, form at the point of disappearing into or bursting out of the light that swathes it:

> quant'esser convenia da sè lucente
> quel ch'era dentro al sol dov'io entra'mi,
> non per color, ma per lume parvente!
> *Para.* x. 40–42.

(How shining in itself must have been that which was within the Sun as I entered it, showing not by colour but by light!);

> L'altra letizia, che m'era già nota
> per cara cosa, mi si fece in vista
> qual fin balasso in che lo sol percuota.
> Per letiziar là su fulgor s'acquista,
> sì come riso qui;
> *Para.* ix. 67–71.

(The other joy, which was already known to me as precious, became in my sight like a fine ruby on which the sun is striking; there above brightness is gained by joy, as laughter here);

> Dinanzi alli occhi miei le quattro face
> stavano accese, e quella che pria venne
> incominciò a farsi più vivace,
> e tal nella sembianza sua divenne,
> qual diverrebbe Giove, s'elli e Marte
> fossero augelli, e cambiassersi penne.
>
> *Para.* xxvii. 10–15.

(Before my eyes the four torches stood flaming; and the one that had come first began to grow brighter, and its aspect became as would Jupiter's if it and Mars were birds and exchanged plumage);

> Talvolta un animal coverto broglia,
> sì che l'affetto convien che si paia
> per o seguir che face a lui la 'nvoglia;
> e similmente l'anima primaia
> mi facea trasparer per la coverta
> quant'ella a compiacermi venìa gaia.
>
> *Para.* xxvi. 97–102.

(Sometimes an animal that is covered up stirs so that its impulse is made to appear by the wrappings that follow its movement; and in like manner the primal soul showed me through its covering how gladly it came to do me pleasure.).

As this visual music proceeds through its shimmering variations upon the theme of light, to resolve itself finally into one great harmony of recovered form, we begin to see the outline of a single over-riding pattern impressed on the whole poem, which is the pattern of salvation. In Dante's personal revelation it stretches from the first image of the earthly Beatrice, through the loss of that image, to the recovery of the image in the heavenly Beatrice; in the ascent of contemplation, which is the *Paradiso*, it stretches from the faint lunar images of the first Heaven, through the overwhelming of the images, to the return of the images in the celestial Rose, clear and distinct in the light without addition or subtraction by distance; in the life of man, it stretches from the birth of the flesh, through the death of the flesh and the luminous persistence of the substantial form, to the triumphant resurrection of the flesh. The pattern is defined by Solomon in the fourteenth Canto of *Paradise*:

> .... "Quanto fia lunga la festa
> di Paradiso, tanto il nostro amore
> si raggerà dintorno cotal vesta.

> La sua chiarezza seguita l'ardore;
> l'ardor la visione; e quella è tanta,
> quant'ha di grazia sovra suo valore.
> Come la carne gloriosa e santa
> fia rivestita, la nostra persona
> più grata fia per esser tutta quanta;"[1]
>
> "Ma sì come carbon che fiamma rende,
> e per vivo candor quella soverchia,
> sì che la sua parvenza si difende;
> così questo fulgor che già ne cerchia
> fia vinto in apparenza dalla carne
> che tutto dì la terra ricoperchia;
> nè potrà tanta luce affaticarne;
> chè li organi del corpo saran forti
> a tutto ciò che potrà dilettarne."
>
> *Para.* xiv. 37–45, 52–60.

(As long as the feast of Paradise shall last, so long our love shall radiate this vesture about us. Its brightness answers to our ardour, the ardour to our vision, and that is in the measure each has of grace beyond his merit. When the flesh, glorified and holy, shall be put on again, our person shall be more acceptable for being all complete.... But like a coal that gives flame and with its white glow outshines it so that its own appearance is preserved, so this effulgence that now surrounds us will be surpassed in brightness by the flesh which the earth still covers. Nor will such light have power to trouble us, for the organs of the body shall be strong for all that can delight us).

It would be difficult to assert more emphatically that fundamental earthiness and particularity, that sanctity of the individual creature and of the "holy and glorious flesh", which marks Christianity off so sharply from the Gnostic heresies, as prevalent in Dante's day as in our own. The body, by its very nature, implies difference—the Many over against the One. The "far-off divine event to which the whole creation moves" is not absorption into, but union with, the Absolute. Consequently, there was never any such thing as a "fall into matter": the creation of the Many is a deliberate divine act.

The phrase *"risplende in una parte più, e meno altrove"* not

---

[1] "After the affirmations we may have to discover the rejections, but we must still believe that after the rejections the greater affirmations are to return." Charles Williams: *Figure of Beatrice*, pp. 10-11.

only announces to us that Dante intends to deal with this question but indicates the lines along which he means to answer it. And in fact he wastes no time, but in Canto ii gets down to the job by asking Beatrice what those dusky marks are which were known to his contemporaries as "Cain with the thornbush", but to us as the "Man in the Moon". She replies by hinting that where the senses can give no help reason may find itself in difficulties, adding: "What do you think yourself?" Dante offers a scientific explanation, saying (and mark the form of the words he uses, for it is important):

> .... "Ciò che n'appar qua su diverso
> credo che fanno i corpi rari e densi."
> *Para.* ii. 59–60.

("That which appears to us diverse up here I suppose to be caused by rare and dense matter").

The *diversity* which we see is due, he supposes, to the rarity or density of the bodies involved. Beatrice counters this by saying reasonably enough that, if the dark patches were thin places, the light of the sun would show through them in an eclipse. She then proceeds to dispose of the suggestion that the patches look darker because they are depressions in the Moon's surface; and this brings us to the famous experiment of the three mirrors.

Somebody must have actually made this experiment, and it seems to have taken Dante's fancy. Unhappily, though the scientific method is perfectly sound, the experiment is vitiated by an error of observation, due to a lack of instruments of precision for measuring the intensity of reflected light. The passage stands as an awful warning to poets not to embellish their works with fashionable scientific theories—nothing dates them so fatally. In making merry over this little misfortune, and in deriding as "fantastic" the explanation which Beatrice then offers as the true one, the modern critic is apt to overlook what Beatrice is really doing. She is not, as he supposes, propounding an alternative scientific explanation of the "how"; she is showing Dante that he has asked the wrong question. To know whether the difference is one of rare and dense, or of near and far, does nothing to solve the real problem, which is not *how*, but *why* there should be any difference at all. Virgil said: "Content you with the *quia*, sons of Eve"—but we have passed beyond Virgil now; we are moving from the *quia* to the *quid*. Why are there many different things rather than just one thing? Why is the universe manifold? For what reason has the undifferentiated prime matter individualized itself into what Professor C. S. Lewis has called "this astonishing cataract of bears, babies, and bananas: this immoderate deluge of atoms, orchids, oranges, cancers, canaries, fleas, gases, tornadoes and toads"?[1] Why the Man in the Moon? Why the Moon itself? Why anything?

Beatrice then goes on to say that all differences are caused by the Intelligences who indwell and move the spheres as the indwelling soul moves the body, and who, uniting their diverse power (*virtù*) to the *"prezioso corpo ch'elle aviva"*, produce different combinations (*diversa lega*); or, as we might say, they are caused by the forces of nature bringing energy to bear in various ways on the irreducible basic stuff of the universe and thus organizing it into the various atomic patterns out of which the material world is built up—

> così l'intelligenza sua bontate
> multiplicata per le stelle spiega,
> girando sè sovra sua unitate.
> *Para.* ii. 136–138.

(so the Intelligence unfolds its bounty, multiplied through the stars, itself wheeling on its own unity.).

The Intelligence in question is that of the sphere of the Fixed Stars, where difference begins and from which the *virtù* is diffused downward through all the lower spheres to the earth. This Intelligence itself derives its *virtù* from the Primum Mobile above it "in whose virtue lies the being of all that it contains"; and the Primum Mobile, in its turn, is contained in and derives its virtue from, the "Heaven of the divine peace"—that is, the Empyrean.

The peculiarities of Dante's cosmology need not trouble us. What he is saying is that all diversity, together with all movement (or change), proceeds ultimately from the still Heaven, which knows neither change nor motion—from, in fact, the Unmoved First Cause *"che tutto move"*. It is distributed by the angelic Movers (God works by secondary causes), and the attributes of the Movers are intelligence, power, and goodness (*intelli-*

[1] *Miracles*, p. 81.

genzia, virtù, and *bontate*). We have not yet reached the answer to our new question, "why?" but we are approaching it. And as readers we do now at any rate know *why* our arrival in the moon's sphere has plunged us into this rather tedious and apparently inconsequent argument about the Man in the Moon. We may of course feel that Dante might have allowed himself to ask a more direct and grown-up question to start with. I feel that it is, on the whole, more true to human nature that he should not. It is very difficult to think up really searching and intelligent questions to ask when one is being shown over a cathedral or a ship or a cotton-factory, let alone the Universe. Beatrice "smiled a little" at this guileless inquiry, and proceeded, as a good teacher should, to give it a better answer than it deserved.

We now have some idea about "*in una parte più, e meno altrove*"; Dante has next to unfold the implications of "*risplende*" and "*splendore*". The theme of diversity in unity is further expounded in a famous passage by Piccarda. Those in the lower heavens are not envious of those above them, because, though souls are unequal in their capacity for beatitude, each soul enjoys as much bliss as it is capable of experiencing, and all are united in God's will, which is their peace. She goes on to explain that all, in fact, dwell in one and the same Heaven; and here again we notice the persistent play with the phrase "*più e meno*":

> De' Serafin colui che più s'india,
>   Moïsè, Samuèl, e quel Giovanni
> che prender vuoli, io dico, non Maria,
>   non hanno in altro cielo i loro scanni
> che questi spirti che mo t'appariro,
>   nè hanno all'esser lor più o meno anni;
> ma tutti fanno bello il primo giro,
>   e differentemente han dolce vita,
> per sentir più e men l'etterno spiro.
>
> *Para.* iv. 28–36.

(Not he of the Seraphim that is most made one with God, not Moses, Samuel, or whichever John thou wilt—none, not Mary herself, have their seat in other heaven from these spirits that have now appeared to thee, nor for their being have more years or fewer; but all make fair the first circle and hold sweet life in different measure as they feel more and less the eternal breath).

The theme of light continues. As we mount through sphere on

sphere filled with *splendori*, and slowly approach the Heaven which "most receives the light" of the First Mover, the smile of Beatrice grows more dazzling, and we remind ourselves that "light" there, and a smile "down here", are equivalent. The lights of the Eighth Heaven are experienced as *"un riso dell' universo"*. It is the arduous task of the reader never to forget anything, for Dante, that "miser with words", never wrote a word idly, and the whole poem is a gigantic system of cross-correspondences and interlocked allusions,

> sì ch'ogni parte ad ogni parte splende—

and merely to say this is to remember that the *"splendore"* theme was first given out as early as the seventh canto of the *Inferno*.

But we must leap over now to the twenty-ninth canto of the *Paradiso*, where the "why?" that was asked in the second receives its answer:

> Non per avere a sè di bene acquisto,
>   ch'esser non può, ma perché suo splendore
>   potesse, risplendendo, dir: *"Subsisto"*,
> in sua etternità di tempo fore,
>   fuor d'ogni altro comprender, come i piacque,
>   s'aperse in nuovi amor l'etterno amore.
>   *Para.* xxix. 13–18.

(Not to gain any good for Himself, which cannot be, but that His splendour, shining back, might say *Subsisto*,—in His eternity, beyond time, beyond every other bound, as it pleased Him, the Eternal Love revealed Himself in new loves.)

Why are these different things? In order that the divine splendour, shining back (*risplendendo*) in innumerable facets from the face of the finite creation, should be able to stand up before its Creator and say, "Look! this is me. I really exist. I am something. I am myself. *Subsisto*". It can add nothing to the Source from which it derives—God gets nothing out of it; but it has pleased Him that every creature—angel, man, beast, beetle or buttercup—should be able, in its small way, to enjoy itself, to enjoy being a self of some sort, dependent on God and yet distinct from Him. We are, in a sense, back where we began:

> La gloria di colui che tutto move
>   per l'universo penetra, e risplende
>   in una parte più, e meno altrove—

but the language has changed. The All-Mover has now become "*il primo Amore*", and the "splendours" have become "loves".

The pattern of light and splendour has brought us thus far; we must now examine the pattern of motion.

It is curious, and may or may not be significant, that, as we pass from the *Inferno* through the *Purgatorio* to the *Paradiso*, the pattern of motions becomes increasingly complex. In Hell— if we exclude the movements of Dante, who does not belong there, and Virgil who, as his guide, enjoys a special privilege— there is only one kind of movement. The souls are fixed in their eternal abode, and their only motion is a vicious circularity. Once they have arrived at their place of punishment, there they stay, and their guardian demons with them:

> chè l'alta provedenza, che lor volle
> porre ministri della fossa quinta,
> poder di partirs' indi a tutti tolle.
> *Inf.* xxiii. 55–57.

(for the high providence which willed to set them as ministers of the fifth ditch deprives them all of power to leave it.)

Upward or downward they cannot pass, to all eternity: free movement through the circles indicates invasion from without the dreadful gate:

> Sopr'essa vedestù la scritta morta:
> e già, di qua da lei, discende l'erta,
> passando per li cerchi, sanza scorta,
> tal che per lui ne fia la terra aperta.
> *Inf.* viii. 127–130.

(Over it thou sawest the deadly writing, and already within it one descends the steep and passes without escort through the circles, by whom the city shall be opened to us.)

At the appalling sound of those unfettered feet, all Hell is shaken.

In Purgatory, the pattern of movement acquires a new dimension. Purgatory is not eternal; it is a temporal process, and therefore allows of progress in a right line. So long as the soul's desire remains "set toward the pain as once 'twas toward the sin", it moves, if at all, only to circle the Cornice. But the moment it feels itself free from the taint of sin, it is free also to turn through the Pass of Pardon and ascend the stair. At that free movement the whole Mountain shakes and resounds with the *Gloria in Excelsis*.

In Heaven, the movement is threefold: the new dimension that is added is the intricate patterning of the celestial dance, which varies from Heaven to Heaven, and is accompanied with song. It appears to be a free and spontaneous expression of a communal joy. The "compulsive" pattern of circling is transferred from the spirits themselves to the *magne rote*, the wheeling spheres within which they trace their proper evolutions. We will return in a moment to consider the nature of the compulsion by which the Movers, in their moving, move the spheres. The third movement is, like the characteristic movement of Purgatory, a linear movement; but it is not an actual physical ascent since, as we have seen, all the Heavens are one Heaven and, being out of space and time, it does not include anything that we could call progress. There is, nevertheless, a movement upward and downward which expresses itself in a kind of tension, like the movement of an electric current. We hear of it in that magnificent twenty-eighth canto which describes the Heavenly hierarchies:

> Questi ordini di su tutti s'ammirano,
>   e di giù vincon sì, che verso Dio
>   tutti tirati sono, e tutti tirano.
> *Para.* xxviii. 127–129.

(These orders all gaze above and so prevail below that all are drawn and all draw to God.)

Each angelic order, with the sphere that it governs, draws up the order and sphere below it; each order and sphere in its turn strains up to those immediately above it; the power descends in *agape* and ascends in *eros*, vibrating as it were between anode and cathode. At the positive pole is God, who is pure act; at the negative pole is the prime matter, pure potentiality; between them lies the whole creation, compounded of act and potentiality mingled in varied proportions:

> Concreato fu ordine e costrutto
>   alle sustanze; e quello furon cima
>   nel mondo in che puro atto fu produtto;
>   pura potenza tenne la parte ima;
>   nel mezzo strinse potenza con atto
>   tal vime, che già mai non si divima.
> *Para.* xxix. 31–36.

(With it, order was created and ordained for the spirits, and these were the summit of the universe in whom was produced pure act; pure potency had the lowest place; between, potency and act were held together with such a bond as never is unbound.)

That which thus passes from sphere to sphere is the power of love, which (once again we cast our minds back to the *Purgatorio*) is defined by Virgil as a "spiritual motion".

We have spoken of the circular motion of the spheres as "compulsive"; but we must now modify that phrase. The circling of the souls in Hell is compelled in the strictest sense of the word: it is imposed from without. The circling of the souls in Purgatory is compulsory only in so far as it is imposed upon the absolute will-to-ascend by the "desire" or conditioned will which holds the soul back until its purgation is accomplished. To will the end is to will the means; therefore the "desire" is ultimately conditioned by the true will against which it only seems to contend. The compulsive movement is not imposed from without; it is a discipline accepted from within. This being so, we should be astonished to discover less freedom in Heaven than in Purgatory. But Heaven and the Heavens are not the same thing—or are they? We recall the long arguments in which man's free will seems to be contrasted with the mechanical operation of the stars. The movement of the spheres—that is, the observed order of nature—exerts upon Man an influence which may be resisted. He is a free agent for good or for evil. The *diversa lega* produced by the action of the Intelligences creates difference and provides opportunity; in that part of a man which comes directly from the First Cause resides free will. But what of the Intelligences themselves? Do the powers of Nature work blindly and mechanically? Does freedom cease at the very apex of the scale of creation?

It is here that Dante's thought appears most alien to us. This is partly because—though it may seem an odd thing to say—we are much more anthropocentric in our outlook than the men of the Middle Ages. We are apt to assign no value to Nature, except as she can be made to subserve human ends. That God and Nature should enjoy each other and themselves, without continual reference to us, is an idea which we find it hard to stomach. Moreover, like Dante with the moon-spots, we tend to suppose that when we know the *how* we know the *why*. Anything that works predictably we dismiss at once as irrational; it is all very well for poets like Wordsworth to suggest that the stars are kept in their courses by devotion to duty: we know that they are kept there by gravitation, and have no choice in the matter, having indeed no will to choose with. For us, the question does not arise—our habit of thought prevents us from asking it. But for Dante, who believed that the spheres were informed by Intelligences, it was obviously bound to arise. We notice, all through the *Commedia,* that it is sometimes difficult to know whether he is speaking of the material spheres or of their Intelligences. That is because of yet another difference between modern and mediaeval habits of thought. We make a rigid distinction, which they did not. Dante did not think of a sphere pushed about by an exterior Intelligence as a man kicks a football, but of a sphere indwelt by a spirit, as a man's spirit indwells his mind and body. Nor does he think, even of man, as a spirit imprisoned in a body, but as a single complex—a body-soul (he makes this clear in the Statius's discourse in the twenty-fifth canto of the *Purgatorio*). In the same way, there is not a sphere *and* an Intelligence, but a sphere-Intelligence—indeed a whole order of Sphere-Intelligences. These are the Angels whom he sees in the Primum Mobile, for ever circling about that Point "on which Heaven and all Nature hang".

What, then, keeps them circling about that still point which, having no motion, yet moves all things? Dante says that it is love. When we lightly observe that "O 'tis love, 'tis love that makes the world go round", we usually mean no more than that when Boy meets Girl things become a good deal livelier. But when a mediaeval man said the same thing, he meant it for a serious statement about cosmology. And Newton, when he demonstrated that the revolutions of the planets were due to their tendency to fall inwards towards the sun, used exactly the same metaphor: he said that they were moved by attraction. And incidentally it is interesting to see how much better Dante would have been suited by a Newtonian astronomy than by the Ptolemaic system with which he had to do his best. The daily motion of the spheres about the earth was a real trouble to him, for it meant that the furthest sphere must needs move the most swiftly, whereas a sound instinct assured him that the nearer to the centre of attraction the swifter the movement should be. And so in his vision he sees the Movers move. But he is worried because his analogy between the world of divine order and the world of sense cannot be directly made.

> La donna mia, che mi vedea in cura
> forte sospeso, disse: "Da quel punto
> depende il cielo e tutta la natura.
> Mira quel cerchio che più li è congiunto:
> e sappi che 'l suo muovere è sì tosto
> per l'affocato amore ond'elli è punto."
> E io a lei: "Se 'l mondo fosse posto
> con l'ordine, ch'io veggio in quelle rote,
> sazio m'avrebbe ciò che m'è proposto;
> ma nel mondo sensibile si pote
> veder le volte tanto più divine,
> quant'elle son dal centro più remote.
> Onde, se 'l mio disio dee aver fine
> in questo miro e angelico templo
> che solo amore e luce ha per confine,
> udir convienmi ancor come l'essemplo
> e l'essemplare non vanno d'un modo,
> chè io per me indarno a ciò contemplo."
>
> *Para.* xxviii. 40–57.

(My Lady, who saw me eager and perplexed, said: "From that point hang the heavens and all nature. See that circle that is closest to it, and know that its motion is thus swift from the burning love by which it is impelled." And I answered her: "If the universe were disposed in the order I see in these wheels I would be satisfied with what thou has set before me; but in the world of sense we can see that the orbits are more divine the farther they are from the centre. Therefore if my desire is to gain its end in this wondrous temple of the angels which has only love and and light for bounds, then I still have to hear why the pattern and the copy do not follow the same plan; for by myself I meditate on this in vain".)

Beatrice gets over this difficulty by explaining that the innermost order of Intelligences governs the outermost sphere, and so onwards in order. But had Dante known about the rotation of the earth, which makes the hypothesis of the spheres unnecessary, he would have found that the proper motion of the planets (which he knew all about) was the only motion he need take into account, and that this obeyed precisely the law which he had ascribed to the Intelligences. Type and ectype would then (so far as the solar system goes) have fitted perfectly; particularly as he was accustomed to use the Sun as a type of God. But we cannot always contrive to be born at the most convenient moment.

The compulsion of the Movers is, then, from within—their immutable order is their immutable will; they have made necessity their choice. Or, in Hegel's words: "The stars are not pulled this way and that by mechanical forces; theirs is a free motion. They go on their way, as the ancients said, like the blessed gods." Relativity physics may be invoked to support this point of view. But this is not really our present business. What we call "gravitation", Dante calls "love"—and if we object to his nomenclature it is not so much because we know better as because we are more conscious of our own ignorance. We do not know what gravitation is; possibly we do not know very well what love is, either. In any case, both for the physicists as for Wordsworth, and for Hegel as for Dante, the motion of the Heavens would appear to be one of the regions in which freedom and necessity coincide. And of this free compulsion, the circling of the spheres is Dante's symbol and image.

Let us pause here to make another link with something that went before. It is Nature—symbolized always by the circling of the spheres—that implants in us those primary impulses from which all our behaviour derives. They are *given*—and therefore, as Marco Lombardo points out, we deserve neither merit nor blame for them, but only for what we do with them. In themselves, Virgil adds, they are always good—love is the mainspring of all our actions, and natural love is "*senza errore*": it is only our "rational love" that errs, because man's reason is corrupted by sin. Hence, our *liberio arbitrio*—free will or (better) free judgement—is given to us in order (and this at first seems strange) that our will may be conformed to our instinct (*la prima voglia*). This is a hard saying, both for those who have been taught to distrust instinct, and for those who have been taught that the Schoolmen despised Nature; but Dante's intention is made clear by this vision of the Movers, in whom instinct and will are at one.

The threefold pattern of motion in the *Paradiso* is thus the line, the circle, and the dance; but in the thirtieth canto the pattern is transformed. The onward and linear motion of time is seen as a river of light, which, when Dante has bathed his eyes in it, becomes the still circle of the Rose: time and eternity are known as one; the stillness and the dance are the same; and in the light of that simultaneity, form is restored.

We must pass quickly over the earlier stages of Dante's vision of God, noting only two things. First: the simultaneous apprehension of the whole complex of the created universe is represented in terms of the light-theme and the love-theme:

> O abbondante grazia, ond'io presunsi
> ficcar lo viso per la Luce etterna,
> tanto che la veduta vi consunsi!
> Nel suo profondo vidi che s'interna,
> legato con amore in un volume,
> ciò che per l'universo si squaderna;
> sustanze e accidenti e lor costume,
> quasi conflati insieme, per tal modo
> che ciò ch' i' dico è un semplice lume.
> Para. xxxiii. 82–90.

(O abounding grace, by which I dared to fix my look on the Eternal Light so long that I spent all my sight upon it! In its depth I saw that it contained, bound by love in one volume, that which is scattered in leaves through the universe, substances and accidents and their relations as it were fused together in such a way that what I tell of is a simple light.)

Secondly: up to the very instant of Dante's perceiving the human form and image within the nature of the Godhead, that Godhead is presented to us under the same impersonal aspect that it had in the opening lines: the vision of the three distinct spheres of equal dimensions and occupying the same space is an abstraction of multi-dimensional geometry. It does not appear like an object of love: the Aristotelian All-mover and the Living God of the Bible are held apart, as it were, for a vibrating moment, until in the flash of a single line they are fused into a single identity.

And then the wheel turns.

Long ago, Love—the lord of terrible aspect—had said to young Dante: "*Ego tanquam centrum circuli, sui simili modo se habent circumferentiae partes; tu autem non sic.*" It seemed to Dante, who was then still engaged in the search for himself, that Love had spoken very darkly. But at that time Love—who was then known to him only as the Amor who governs the hearts of human lovers—discouraged further questioning. Some thirty years have passed, and Dante now knows both who Love is, and what happens at the circumference of the circle of which all-moving Love is the centre: it must move as the great wheels move. The simile of the wheel in the last terzain is not simply that of an earthly mechanism. It takes up the image of the *magne rote*, which has appeared at intervals all through the poem: the will and desire, purged from eccentricity, are now conformed to the *prima voglia* and free to move with the Movers:

> All'alta fantasia qui mancò possa;
>   ma già volgeva il mio disio e 'l *velle*,
>   si come rota ch'igualmente è mossa,
> l'amor che move il sole e l'altre stelle.
> *Para.* xxxiii. 142–145.

(Here power failed the high phantasy; but now my desire and will, like a wheel that spins with even motion, were revolved by the Love that moves the sun and the other stars.)

We have spent a long time upon the function of the two key-words in the first terzain of the *Paradiso*, and are still far from exhausting their significance. My second example of Dante's "art of making" also turns upon two key-words, but can be examined much more briefly. The passage occurs in the great exposition of Atonement Theology in *Paradiso* vii. Beatrice is explaining that when Adam sinned, God might have reacted in either of two ways. He might have chosen the way of pure mercy—simply annulling the effects of the Fall. Or He might have chosen the way of unmitigated justice—demanding from Man the full penalty of the crime—a penalty which, in the nature of things, Man could not possibly pay. The one way would have made Man's freewill meaningless, since it would have rendered his power of choice ineffective; the second way would have left Man eternally and hopelessly, as it were, in prison for debt. God therefore chose "to go by both His ways at once": by becoming Man, He took Man's debt upon Himself, and thus satisfied justice and mercy alike. That is the argument—it is necessary for the understanding of the passage: you are not called upon to agree with it. Here, then, are Beatrice's words at this point:

> la divina Bontà, che 'l mondo imprenta,
>   di proceder per tutte le sue vie
>   a rilevarvi suso fu contenta.

> Ne tra l'ultima notte e 'l primo die
> sì alto o sì magnifico processo,
> o per l'una o per l'altra, fu o fie:
> chè più largo fu Dio a dar sè stesso
> per far l'uom sufficiente a rilevarsi,
> che s'elli avesse sol da sè dimesso;
> e tutti li altri modi erano scarsi
> alla giustizia, se 'l Figliuol di Dio
> non fosse umiliato ad incarnarsi.
> Para. vii. 109-120.

(the Divine Goodness which puts its imprint on the world was pleased to proceed by all its ways to raise you up again; nor between the last night and the first day was or will be a procedure by the one way or the other so lofty or so glorious. For God was more bounteous in giving Himself so as to make man able to raise himself again than if, simply of Himself, he had pardoned; and all other means came short of justice save that the Son of God should humble Himself to become flesh.)

That is, on the surface, as plain and dry a theological statement as you could well have. Even so, there is something about the second terzain which, by its tone and rhythm, warns us that not all the meaning is on the surface. The arresting effect is largely due to the emphatic distribution of the balanced antitheses: *ultima notte/primo die; alto/magnifico; per l'una o per l'altra; fu o fie.* Dante is fond of these antithetical effects—they form the most Augustan element in his style. Here they serve, so to speak, as signposts, pointing to where the direct statement opens out into the "place of the images". And the images are evoked by a simple play on the ambiguous significance of two words: *via* and *processo.* Most fortunately for the translator, these ambiguities are exactly reproduced in the corresponding English, which I will venture to render thus:

> Nor between final night and primal day
> Was e'er proceeding so majestical
> Or high, nor shall not be, by either way.

The word *via,* like the word *way,* can mean either, literally, a *road* or, figuratively, a *method.* The word *processo,* like the word *proceeding,* can mean no fewer than four things. By derivation it is a *going forth*: a literal "going-forth" or progress along a road, as in "the royal cortège was *proceeding* along the Mall"; and also, theologically, a going-forth of the Godhead: as in "the

Holy Ghost *proceeding* from the Father". It also may mean a *process*, as in: "during the course of these *proceedings*"; or, by a further transference, a process at law, as in: "*legal proceedings*". It is by a play on all these meanings that Dante calls up the images.

"Primal day" is the Creation—the first "going forth" of the One to express Itself in otherness and in space and time. "Final night" is the last "going forth", when God will return at the end of time in Judgement (*processo*) by the way of justice. Behind both these, and out of time altogether, lies the eternal begetting of the Son—the "going-forth" from the Father; *between* them lies that "going-forth" of the Son into history, which we call the Incarnation. Than this, says Dante, no greater "proceeding" ever was or shall be. Further; this great "process" of salvation is ushered in and ushered out by literal "goings" upon literal roads—each more majestical than any imperial "progress" —the feet of the ass going up to Bethlehem, and there the "going forth" from the womb by the way of mercy; the feet of the ass going up to Jerusalem, and there the surrender to "process of law" by the way of justice. And after this: the "way" of the Cross—*via dolorosa*; the "going forth" of the human soul of Christ, at death, into the place of death, and the "bringing forth" of the blessed dead from Limbo; the "going forth" again out of time into eternity at the Ascension. But this is not all: for this "high and magnifical", unrepeatable and unsurpassable, archetype of the "process" of salvation has its ectype in the continually repeated "going forth" of the eternally-Begotten into the Holy Host at the Eucharist: and it is here that our minds are gathered and brought back again to Dante and his poem. For we remember that, after his slow and painful "progress", begun "in the middle of life's way", and leading through Hell and Purgatory, he is shown the triumphal "progress" or "procession" of the car which is the Church, drawn by the Gryphon which typifies the Incarnation, and that on the car he beholds Beatrice, who is herself the image of the Host.

Now, this great procession of imagery is not in the passage I have read: the images are *evoked* by Dante by the juxtaposition of two ambiguous words. They involve no alteration of the direct statement which those words convey in their context; yet univocal words, such as "method" and "operation", would have left the images unsummoned. With an astonishing economy of means, the poet simply speaks his two words of power, and leaves the rest to our own imagination, helped out by the knowledge which we possess of the Christian context in which he is speaking.

It will be seen that Dante's method here is the exact opposite of the method used in the symbolist poetry to which we have grown accustomed. In the symbolist tradition, to quote Mr. Davie again, "images or symbols are ranged about, and the meaning flowers out of the space between them". Dante also uses this method on the grand scale—the meaning of many incidents in the *Commedia* is only to be ascertained by watching the movement of the images; we understand, for instance, Dante's judgement of all that Virgil stands for by observing what happens to Virgil. But in the passage we have just been examining, the poet states the meaning, and the images flower from within the statement. Neither is the ambiguity of the Empsonian kind: there is no dislocation of syntax, and the plain sense of the words is as lucid and unambiguous as the poet can make it. The working of the spell relies upon the associations that the words call up, but it is not "free association" in the psychologist's sense: it is a controlled association—controlled by the strong intellectual cords which bring every called-up image firmly back to the historic act which the statement affirms. And finally, the passage does not, I think, invite us to speculate about "Dante's attitude to religion"; it simply confronts us with Atonement doctrine and leaves the rest to us. Dante, to be sure, has reached a conclusion, and he shows us the working of the problem; but to talk of his "attitude" is no more relevant than to talk of Euclid's "attitude" to the square on the hypotenuse.

When Archimedes cried out "Eureka!" he was transported with joy at having found the answer to his problem. It is a commentary upon our preoccupation with the personal that most of us have forgotten both the problem and the solution—we remember only the attitude of Archimedes—he was in his bath at the time. His attitude was, in fact, relevant, because it was the overflowing of the bathwater when he got in that suggested the solution of the problem. *We* are liable to be interested in the human weakness displayed by Archimedes in running the bath too full; but to Archimedes and to his scientific posterity the important thing was and remains the mathematics of displacement, and his delight was in having found the right experiment for his purpose. The delight of the poetry of Statement is a delight of the same kind—in the experiment which has proved fruitful; not in the various experiments which failed, or in the cogitations which failed even to suggest an experiment—which Archimedes did not record. It would be entertaining to know what these fruitless speculations were; they would tell us a great deal about Archimedes; but it is only because some of the experiments did come off that we are interested in Archimedes at all.

So it is, I think, right to be interested in the poetry of Statement—the poetry in which the poet tell us, not about himself, but about something. Standing back from his poem, constructing it with infinite pains and pleasure, so that it may stand secure in its symmetry of balanced parts, he sets it before us as an abiding witness to the truth, which he has tested and found to be true. We ought, surely, to be able to enjoy poetry of all kinds, even the lucid kind, even the kind which comes to a conclusion, or issues in a momentous statement. Indeed, it would appear that some people are asking precisely for the poetry that does these things—though I do not feel it becomes them, either, to pour obloquy upon the poetry of Search. Each kind has its own beauties, and the beauty of integrated construction belongs in a very special manner to the poetry of Statement.

But I remain puzzled by the remark of a university student during a discussion which raised this question of the poets who write to find out what they feel, and those who write to tell what they know. "Perhaps", she said, "the poet ceases to be useful as soon as he reaches a conclusion." It was an oddly unexpected point of view: "the uses of poetry" is a phrase that seems to belong to the eighteenth century, rather than to our own, however little the Augustans would have approved the actual sentiment. The discussion swept past that point, and I never succeeded in getting it elucidated. We have been concerned here with the beauty, rather than the utility, of the poetry of Statement. But that remark has left me wondering.

(*All translations in the above essay are taken from* The Divine Comedy, *translated by J. D. Sinclair, published by the Bodley Head, revised edition, 1948.*)

CHAPTER III

THE BEATRICIAN VISION IN DANTE AND OTHER POETS

IT IS A favourite pastime of literary critics to debate the question: "Why did Wordsworth lose his inspiration?" The cognate question, "Why did Dante not lose his?" seldom appears among the quodlibets. Yet, given the one problem, the other is equally perplexing; for in both men the original wellspring of inspiration was a spiritual experience of exactly the same kind, and each after his own manner had to endure the drying-up of the well. If both of them had died at the age of forty-five, when Wordsworth had recently finished *The Excursion,* and Dante was failing to complete the *Convivio,* we should have said of both alike that here was a poet who, after a brilliant outburst of ecstatic song, had lost his first impetus and declined into an arid didacticism. We might even have added that Wordsworth, although he had written more positively bad verse than Dante, was the greater poet of the two. Yet, while Wordsworth was never able fully to recover the glory and the dream which had brooded over the first two books of *The Prelude,* and inspired their own magnificent obsequies in the *Immortality Ode* and *Tintern Abbey,* Dante went on to recover all and more than all that he had lost, dying at length triumphantly into silence with the raptures of the *Paradiso* upon his lips:.

> Quale alodetta che 'n aere si spazia
> prima cantando, e poi tace contenta
> dell'ultima dolcezza che la sazia.
> *Para.* xx. 73–75.

I have said that the experience of Dante and Wordsworth was identical; but this fact is not always recognized, even by those who have themselves shared the experience. Wordsworth is frequently classed as a "nature-worshipper", among a number of other people who took pleasure in flowers and skies and landscapes; Dante's love for Beatrice is often written off as an "erotic stimulus", although that kind of love is not necessarily erotic at all, except in the sense that it is an *eros* which strives upward to its object, rather than an *agape* which floods down charity from above. Other forms which the experience takes—for it is by no means a rare one—are similarly pigeonholed in separate compartments, with no apparent realization that they belong to the same type. It is generally felt that all such experiences are in some way "mystical"; but since they do not conform to the classical pattern of mysticism, they are sometimes denied even the shelter of that much-abused word, or allowed at most to rank as a "pseudo-mysticism". Let us begin by bringing together a few examples, drawn from the most diverse sources in fact and fiction; we shall then be in a position to identify the one invariable factor that persists throughout the series.

> Now Moses... came to the mountain of God, even to Horeb. And the angel of the Lord appeared unto him in a flame of fire out of the midst of a bush: and he looked, and, behold, the bush burned with fire, and the bush was not consumed. And Moses said, I will now turn aside, and see this great sight, why the bush is not burnt. And when the Lord saw that he turned aside to see, God called unto him out of the midst of the bush....
> *Exodus*, iii. 1–3.

> Vede perfettamente ogni salute
> Chi la mia donna tra le donne vede:
> Quelle, che van con lei, sono tenute
> Di bella grazia a Dio render mercede,...
> *Vita Nuova*, xxvii.

> "What," it will be Question'd, "when the Sun rises, do you not see a round disk of fire somewhat like a Guinea?" O no, no, I see an Innumerable company of the Heavenly host crying, "Holy, Holy, Holy is the Lord God Almighty."
> W. Blake, *A Vision of the Last Judgment*.

> And [he] was transfigured before them: and his face did shine as the sun, and his raiment was white as the light.... Then answered Peter, and said unto Jesus, Lord, it is good for us to be here....
> *Matthew*, xvii. 2–4.

> But she—
> The glory of life, the beauty of the world,
> The splendour of Heaven... well, Sirs, does no one move?

THE BEATRICIAN VISION

> Do I speak ambiguously? The glory, I say,
> And the beauty, I say, and splendour, still say I,
> Who, priest and trained to live my whole life long
> On beauty and splendour, solely at their source,
> God,—have thus recognized my food in her,
> You tell me, that's fast dying whilst we talk,
> Pompilia!
> > R. Browning, *The Ring and the Book*, vi. 117-125.

> [Plato] could never... have seen [as I was seeing] a bunch of flowers shining with their own inner light and all but quivering under the pressure of the significance with which they were charged; could never have perceived that what rose and iris and carnation so intensely signified was nothing more, and nothing less, than what they were—a transience that was yet eternal life, a perpetual perishing that was at the same time Being, a bundle of minute, unique particulars in which, by some unspeakable and yet self-evident paradox, was to be seen the divine source of all existence.... Words like Grace and Transfiguration came to my mind, and this of course was what, among other things, they stood for.
> > A. Huxley, *The Doors of Perception*, p. 12.

> Yet, looking back over the years... [what] I see most clearly... is a picture, precise in the sunshine, of Jones minor coming back up Keate's Lane from Lower Chapel on the morning of the Fourth of June. He is wearing a button-hole; he has just been singing "Now thank we all our God" with immense and genuine fervour; he is walking in a kind of intoxication. For everything that goes to the making of Eton, the mellow red bricks, the elms, the river and the playing-fields, the traditions, the community, the high privilege of belonging to it, had suddenly coalesced into a single flash of delight. It was a mystic moment for a Thomas Traherne, not for him, to describe. But it left a mark; and I cannot help thinking that a School which could visit with such a benediction a not very imaginative boy of thirteen must possess a singular grace.
> > L. E. Jones, *A Victorian Boyhood*, pp. 168-169.

> > And at the sacring of the mass I saw
> > The holy elements alone; but he,
> > "Saw ye no more? I, Galahad, saw the Grail,
> > The Holy Grail, descend upon the shrine;
> > I saw the fiery face as of a child
> > That smote itself into the bread, and went."
> > > Tennyson, *The Holy Grail*, 462-467.

The corn was orient and immortal wheat, which never should be reaped, nor was ever sown. I thought it had stood from everlasting to everlasting.... The green trees when I saw them first through one of the gates transported and ravished me, their sweetness and unusual beauty made my heart to leap, and almost mad with ecstasy, they were such strange and wonderful things. ... Boys and girls tumbling in the street, and playing, were moving jewels. I knew not that they were born or should die. But all things abided eternally as they were in their proper places. Eternity was manifest in the Light of the Day, and something infinite behind everything appeared: which talked with my expectation and moved my desire. The city seemed to stand in Eden, or to be built in Heaven.
T. Traherne, *Centuries of Meditations*, iii, 3,
(B. Dobell's modernised text).

> There was a time when meadow, grove, and stream,
> The earth, and every common sight,
> To me did seem
> Apparelled in celestial light,
> The glory and the freshness of a dream.
> Wordsworth, *Intimations of Immortality*, I, 1-5.

Now, all the experiences thus described, whether they belong to fact or fiction, are in the proper and technical sense mystical: what is experienced is the immediate and intuitive awareness of an eternal reality. The thing which they have in common, and which distinguishes them from mystical experiences of the classical type, is that every one has a basis in the world of physical phenomena. There is no imaginary vision, still less that total naughting of all forms and images which characterises the mysticism of the Negative Way. What is beheld is the transfiguration of something actually existing in the outer world of sense. There is an actual bush, which burns but is not consumed; Beatrice and Pompilia are women of flesh and blood; the human body of Christ is present upon Mount Tabor before, during, and after the vision of His divine glory; Blake's sun is the sun of astronomy, and Huxley's flowers stand in an ordinary vase upon the table; Wordsworth's meadow, grove and stream are geographically located at Cockermouth; Eton College is an earthly community, and so are the children who play in the streets and fields of Traherne's native town; the elements of Galahad's sacrament are common bread and wine. The physical bases are very diverse; but the quality of the experience is everywhere recognizably the same: we cannot separate it arbitrarily into "erotic", "religious", and "nature" mysticism. We could, indeed, say that it is all "nature mysticism"—if we mean by that that it has its basis in the natural order; but the phrase is not ordinarily used in that sense, and to use it so would, I think, be merely confusing. I have preferred to call it "The Beatrician Vision"—not because it is by any means always concerned with man's love for woman, but in honour of Dante, who was the first, and is perhaps still the only, writer to have systematically charted the mystical Way which leads from the Vision of Beatrice to the Beatific Vision. And it must be said that not all who have enjoyed that first vision go on to follow the Way, and that, of those who do, not all attain the end. Among those who have attained we may reckon Dante and Blake and Traherne, and probably Charles Williams and Coventry Patmore. Wordsworth went by the Way, yet his song failed and fell short of the ultimate ecstasy; and the same is true of Browning; Yeats saw the vision, but missed the Way—or perhaps deliberately refused it.

Although the end of the Way is the Vision of God, the first vision is not necessarily religious, much less necessarily Christian. The mystical gift, as such, is a natural, not a supernatural gift, and is far less rare than is usually supposed. Moments of Beatrician vision are experienced by a great many people when they first fall in love. Intimations of the eternal realities may occur at the psychological level, or may even (as in Aldous Huxley's experiment with mescalin) be artificially induced. In a morbid form, they sometimes appear as features of certain mental derangements. When, however, they occur spontaneously to healthy people, they tend to induce, if only temporarily, that condition which is theologically called "being in a state of grace" —"*sono tenute/Di bella grazia a Dio render mercede*"; "words like Grace and Transfiguration came to my mind"; "a school which could visit [a small boy] with such a benediction ... must possess a singular grace"—in describing the experience the word seems to spring naturally to the mind. Dante has left us the best of all accounts of this state of grace; he says that at the prospect of receiving Beatrice's *salute* (which means not only "salutation" but also "salvation") he was taken hold of by such a flame of charity that he forgave everyone who had ever offended him, and if he had been asked any question whatsoever could only have answered "Love", with a countenance clothed in humility. Meekness within, and an overflowing of charity to those without are thus the signs of this gracious state; and where they are present there is the assurance that the vision is a true one, and that we have not to do merely with aesthetic pleasure or with the lust of possession. The soul adores and loves. It prostrates itself before a fellow-creature whose bodily presence is somehow felt to be a vehicle of grace, and the image of a greater Reality that informs and indwells it and is the eternal truth of its being.

The outsider, of course, does not see this; he is persuaded that the lover is under an illusion: Beatrice is a good-looking girl with all the usual feminine faults; Eton is simply a school where education is scrambled into boys' heads among playing-fields and historic buildings rather above the average; mountain, wood and stream are the sort of scenery you get in Cumberland; and, as also to Peter Bell:

> A primrose by a river's brim
> A yellow primrose [is] to him,
> And it [is] nothing more.

But the lover insists that on the contrary it is *he* who is seeing the real person, the real Nature, the true community, as it really exists and is known to God. This is what Wordsworth means when he says:

> Let good men feel the soul of nature,
> And see things as they are.

The Beatrician mystic does not deny the reality of the phenomena: they are true so far as they go; they are the blessed means by which the truth is made known to us, but they are not in themselves the whole truth; "for", says Blake, "that call'd Body is a portion of Soul discern'd by the five Senses, the chief inlets of Soul in this age." And thus Etienne Gilson says, speaking of St. Francis:

> Hence the endlessly springing fountain of symbols or rather the permanent transfiguration of the universe in which he saw, not fragments of matter or beings deprived of knowledge, but precious images of God.
> *The Philosophy of St. Bonaventure*, p. 70.

Charles Williams, commenting on Dante's canzone, *Donne ch'avete intelletto d'amore*, sums up his experience:

What Dante sees is the glory of Beatrice as she is "in heaven"
—that is, as God chose her, unfallen, original; or (if better) redeemed; but at least, either way, celestial. What he sees is something real. It is not "realer" than the actual Beatrice who, no doubt, had many serious faults, but it is as real. Both Beatrices are aspects of one Beatrice. The revealed virtues are real; so is the celestial beauty.

The Figure of Beatrice, p. 27.

Now, this being the peculiar quality of the Beatrician vision, we have to acknowledge something else about it which sets it off sharply against certain other kinds of mystical experience; it is of its nature, and necessarily, extravert. The eyes of the soul are not turned inward to the true Self, but outward to a true Other. This of itself is enough to condemn it in the eyes of many contemporary psychologists, who are so deeply preoccupied with the problems of introversion that they are apt to dismiss the extravert as uninteresting and insensitive. It is also, I think, the reason why theologians are reluctant to allow that it is a mystical experience at all. From the fifteenth century on, Western mysticism has tended to conform itself to the Eastern pattern, which, rejecting all messages conveyed by the senses and all images derived from the outer world, contemplates in darkness, under the "cloud of unknowing", the dweller in the innermost—the immanent God who is the ground of the soul. The other pattern, which affirms all the images and contemplates the immanence of God in the visible things of the creation, is very generally assumed to be not mystical in any exact sense, but (merely) "poetical". I say "assumed", because in the majority of treatises upon mysticism, the Way of Affirmation is not discussed at all, but omitted as not being part of the subject. It is also true that the poet, whose whole insight into truth depends upon the creative handling of images, cannot possibly follow a purely negative way without denying his own vocation. In practice, the way of contemplation (as it was called in Dante's time) nearly always includes both affirmative and negative elements, and the opposition between "poetry" and "mysticism" may be more verbal than real. It is, however, well to note that where Christianity is concerned, a total retreat from the material world is not merely heretical but impossible; for the central Christian doctrine is precisely that of God incarnate in matter, its central act of worship the bodily receiving of God's substance in the sacrament of bread and wine, and its unique eschatological expectation the Resurrection of the Flesh. And in pondering the images used by Dante in the *Paradiso*, we may consider these words by an anonymous Catholic writer:

> The mystics heap up terms of negation—darkness, void, nothingness—in endeavouring to describe the Absolute which they have apprehended. It may be, of course, that their apprehension had such a fullness and richness of content that in human language it could only be described negatively. But one may, at least, point out that their method is the very opposite of the characteristically Christian one of affirmation; that where they say "darkness", St. John says "light", and that St. John says "fullness" where they say "void"; and St. Paul stresses, not ignorance but enhanced knowledge, as the result of religious experience.

So far, however, we have only defined a particular spiritual experience, not uncommon to lovers and poets, which we have agreed to call the "Beatrician Vision". It remains to be seen whether that experience develops into anything that can properly be called a way of ascent to God.

We may be inclined to say in our haste that normally it does not. If there is one thing about which the wiseacres of middle age are in desolating agreement, it is that youth's a stuff will not endure, and that the raptures of romantic love soon wear off. Nor do the exponents of the Affirmative Way deny this. With the greatest unanimity, they all record the loss, in one way or the other, of that first God-bearing Image which opened their eyes to the light invisible. To Dante, the shock came in the simplest, most inevitable way of all. The girl died; and it seemed to him that the light was extinguished, not only for him, but for the whole of Florence, among whose streets his blessed Lady had moved like a young miracle:

> Poichè la gentilissima donna fu partita da questo secolo, rimase tutta la sopradetta cittade quasi vedova e dispogliata di ogni dignitade, ond'io, ancora lagrimando in questa desolata cittade, scrissi a' principi della terra alquanto della sua condizione, pigliando quello cominciamento di Geremìa: *Quomodo sedet sola civitas!*
>
> *Vita Nuova,* xxxi.

In the *Vita Nuova*, he tells us how he went about weeping bitterly and refusing all comfort, until one day he saw a gentle lady looking compassionately upon him from a window. He was grateful for this lady's pity; he frequently went to see her; he wrote a sonnet to her; and presently, to his own extreme horror, he realized that his inconsolable grief was beginning to be consoled. He was as angry with himself as we all are under such circumstances. He reproached himself for his inconstancy, and worked himself up deliberately into fresh outbursts of weeping, with a good deal of success. Years later, when he is writing the Second Treatise of the *Convivio,* we find him still worrying about his state of mind—still excusing and justifying himself, and explaining that there was no real infidelity. By that time, he has identified the Lady of the Window with Philosophy, and has made of her another God-bearing Image, bringing a new revelation of the eternal beauty. He tells us that, after Beatrice's death, he read the *Consolations* of Boethius and Cicero's *De Amicitia,* and was thus led to attend the Schools and make a serious study of Philosophy, in which he found new and inexpressible delight. This is undoubtedly true. He had lost the First Image, but he had found a Second (the phrase is Charles Williams's), and his new rapture seemed to him in no way inferior to the first. But they were experienced at a different level. The vision of Beatrice had been an intuitive dedication of the whole person; the vision of the Lady Philosophy was the deliberate dedication of the awakened intellect.

Traherne also experienced the loss of that first intuitive vision, though in a quite different way. His own account of himself is very remarkable, for he claims that his conscious memories go back almost to the moment of his birth. I believe that many psychiatrists would agree that this was not impossible, but the content of his memory is, to say the least of it, very un-Freudian, for it includes no birth-trauma and no longing to retreat into the womb. He says that he remembers a state of pure paradisal happiness, like that of Adam before the Fall, going back to the time when he experienced only a simple awareness, without any clear distinction of the senses.

> My Body being Dead, my Lims unknown;
>   Before I skild to prize
>   Those living Stars mine Eys,
> Before my Tongue or Cheeks were to me shewn,
>   Before I knew my Hands were mine,
>   Or that my Sinews did my Members joyn,

>   When neither Nostril, Foot, nor Ear,
>   As yet was seen, or felt, or did appear;
>   I was within
>   A House I knew not, newly clothd with Skin.
>
>   Then was my Soul my only All to me,
>   A Living Endless Ey,
>   Just bounded with the Skie
>   Whose Power, whose Act, whose Essence was to see.
>   I was an Inward *Sphere of Light*,
>   Or an Interminable Orb of *Sight*,
>   An Endless and a Living Day,
>   *A vital Sun* that round about did *ray*
>   All Life, all Sence,
>   A Naked Simple Pure *Intelligence*...
>
>   For *Sight* inherits Beauty, *Hearing* Sounds,
>   The *Nostril* sweet Perfumes,
>   All *Tastes* have hidden Rooms
>   Within the *Tongue*; and *Feeling Feeling* Wounds
>   With Pleasure and Delight : but I
>   Forgot the rest, and was all Sight, or Ey.
>   Unbodied and Devoid of Care,
>   Just as in Heavn the Holy Angels are.
>   For Simple Sence
>   Is Lord of all Created Excellence.
>   *The Preparative*, stanzas i, ii and iv.

This remarkable synthesis of sense without and soul within reminds us of Wordsworth:

>   Those hallow'd and pure motions of the sense
>   Which seem in their simplicity to own
>   An intellectual charm, that calm delight
>   Which, if I err not, surely must belong
>   To those first-born affinities that fit
>   Our new existence to existing things,
>   And, in our dawn of being, constitute
>   The bond of union betwixt life and joy.
>   *The Prelude*, I. 551–558.

Or compare again Traherne:

>   This made me present evermore
>   With whatsoere I saw.
>   An Object, if it were before

THE BEATRICIAN VISION 55

> My Ey, was by Dame Natures Law,
>   Within my Soul. Her Store
> Was all at once within me; all her Treasures
> Were my Immediat and Internal Pleasures...
> *My Spirit*, 35-41.

and Wordsworth:

> Oh! then what soul was his when on the tops
> Of the high mountains he beheld the sun
> Rise up and bathe the world in light. He looked,
> The ocean and the earth beneath him lay
> In gladness and deep joy. The clouds were touched
> And in their silent faces did he read
> Unutterable love. Sound needed none
> Nor any voice of joy: his spirit drank
> The spectacle. Sensation, soul and form
> All melted into him. They swallowed up
> His animal being; in them did he live
> And by them did he live. They were his life.
> *The Excursion*, i, 198-210.

The boy of whom Wordsworth speaks (and that boy was himself) was then, he says, about nine years old, the age at which Dante first set eyes on the child Beatrice, and was so smitten, head, heart and reins, that from that day forward Love held lordship over his soul. Dante at least was to live to acknowledge with Traherne that—

> The first Impressions are Immortal all.
> *Dumnesse*, 85.

But like other immortal things they had to die and rise again. Traherne, always precocious, tells us in the Third Century of his *Meditations* that his "Apostasy" took place as soon as he was brought in contact with the worldly standards of his teachers and playfellows, whose hearts were fixed on tops and gew-gaws, on "ambitions, trades, luxuries, inordinate affections, casual and accidental riches invented since the Fall". It would have been easy, he says, to teach him otherwise; but nobody made any effort to bring his first innocent apprehensions into any kind of constructive relationship with the worship of "the God of Nature". So that before very long "my thoughts (as indeed what is more fleeting than a thought?) were blotted out; and at last all the celestial, great, and stable treasures to which I was born, as wholly forgotten as if they had never been". He is persuaded that—

> our misery proceedeth ten thousand times more from the outward bondage of opinion and custom, than from any inward corruption or depravation of Nature. And that it is not our parents' loins, so much as our parents' lives, that enthrals and blinds us. Yet is all our corruption derived from Adam : inasmuch as all the evil examples and inclinations of the world arise from his sin. But I speak it in the presence of God and of our Lord Jesus Christ, in my pure primitive virgin Light, while my apprehensions were natural and unmixed, I cannot remember but that I was ten thousand times more prone to good and excellent things than evil.
>
> *Centuries of Meditations*, iii. 8.

It may be that, like other people of his sunny and expansive temperament, he underrated that innate "will to destruction" which is the name psychologists give to what the theologian calls "original sin". What concerns us at the moment is his agreement with Wordsworth that "Heaven lies about us in our infancy". This was not, with either of them, the wishful thinking of the child-lover who has forgotten what his own childhood was like. Neither was it an adult sentimentality throwing a false glamour over their past : the quality of their writing guarantees their inspiration genuine. They spoke from experience, and we may believe them to have been accurate reporters. Perhaps they generalized a little too readily on behalf of the rest of us; but where they themselves were concerned they spoke of what they knew.

What happened to Wordsworth we all know only too well. His experience was the most distressing of the three. The beloved object was not taken from him, like Dante's Beatrice, by death or disaster; he could not, or at least he did not, like Traherne, lay any blame upon evil communications. The change took place in himself, and seemed to be a mere inevitable part of the process of growing older. He was like a man who, having married for love, wakes one day to the discovery that, although his wife is still as beautiful as she ever was, her presence now fails to stir him. Time and familiarity have destroyed romance and reduced the relationship to a daily humdrum which would be contentment if he did not so vividly remember the wonder and delight which he cannot now summon into experience :

> It is not now as it hath been of yore;—
>   Turn wheresoe'er I may,
>   By night or day,
> The things which I have seen I now can see no more.
>
>   The rainbow comes and goes,
>   And lovely is the Rose,
>   The Moon doth with delight
> Look round her when the heavens are bare,
>   Waters on a starry night
>   Are beautiful and fair;
>   The sunshine is a glorious birth;
>   But yet I know, where'er I go,
> That there hath past away a glory from the earth.
> *Intimations of Immortality*, I, 6—9, & II.

That is nothing unusual. It is what people always tell us will happen, and ninety-nine times out of a hundred it does happen. Something has come to an end in us, and it is in vain that we try to go back and relive it. It is not always marriage and daily contact that bring the change about—it may be simply age and time. After years of absence we return to look upon the face, or the place, that once meant everything to us, and whose memory has sustained us in our exile, and lo and behold! the magic has departed, and we stand like Wordsworth revisiting Tintern Abbey, while—

> ...with gleams of half-extinguished thought,
> With many recognitions dim and faint,
> And somewhat of a sad perplexity,
> The picture of the mind revives again.
> *Tintern Abbey*, 58–61.

It is, be it noted, not the primal glory itself but the memory of the glory, passionately relived, that inspires the verse of Wordsworth's "great decade".

>   I cannot paint
> What then I was. The sounding cataract
> Haunted me like a passion : the tall rock,
> The mountain, and the deep and gloomy wood,
> Their colours and their forms, were then to me
> An appetite; a feeling and a love,
> That had no need of a remoter charm,
> By thought supplied, nor any interest

58 THE POETRY OF SEARCH AND STATEMENT

>Unborrowed from the eye.—That time is past,
>And all its aching joys are now no more,
>And all its dizzy raptures.
>
>*ibid.*, 75–85.

He goes on:

>   Not for this
>Faint I, nor mourn nor murmur; other gifts
>Have followed; for such loss, I would believe,
>Abundant recompense. For I have learned
>To look on nature, not as in the hour
>Of thoughtless youth; but hearing oftentimes
>The still, sad music of humanity,
>Nor harsh nor grating, though of ample power
>To chasten and subdue. And I have felt
>A presence that disturbs me with the joy
>Of elevated thoughts; a sense sublime
>Of something far more deeply interfused,
>Whose dwelling is the light of setting suns,
>And the round ocean and the living air,
>And the blue sky, and in the mind of man :
>A motion and a spirit, that impels
>All thinking things, all objects of all thought,
>And rolls through all things. Therefore am I still
>A lover of the meadows and the woods,
>And mountains; and of all that we behold
>From this green earth; of all the mighty world
>Of eye, and ear,—both what they half create,
>And what perceive; well pleased to recognise
>In nature and the language of the sense
>The anchor of my purest thoughts, the nurse,
>The guide, the guardian of my heart, and soul
>Of all my moral being.
>
>*ibid.*, 85–111.

This was written in 1798; and with Dante's example before us we realize what is happening. We are listening to the poetry of the Second Image; *Tintern Abbey* is the counterpart of the Ode, *Voi che 'ntendendo,* and the Second Treatise of the *Convivio,* which deal with Dante's change of loves:

>Because love does not come to birth and grow and achieve perfection all in a moment, but needs time and the nourishment of thought (especially when it is hindered by other thoughts that run counter to it), this new love could not be made perfect with-

out much strife between the thought which nourished it and that which opposed it, and which still held the citadel of my mind on behalf of that glorious Beatrice.... And this was so strange (*mirabile*) and so hard to suffer that I addressed my voice to that quarter [the Heaven of Venus] whence came the victory of the new thought, which was greatly victorious, being a celestial virtue, and began to say:

> Voi che 'ntendendo il terzo ciel movete.
> *Conv.*, II. ii.

And a very magnificent ode it is: let nobody suppose that the appearance of the Second Image is not attended with its own raptures. Wordsworth is rather more honest than Dante in facing the nature of the change that has come over him; he frankly laments the loss of his first love, whereas Dante is so anxious to acquit himself of inconstancy that he involves himself in a good deal of rather disingenuous shuffling, which has an effect quite opposite to what he intended. But in the end they agree that the new love is the more adult, the more intellectual, and, in the end, the higher of the two.

> In a short time, [says Dante] I began to feel so much of her sweetness [that is, of the Lady Philosophy] that the love of her cast out and destroyed every other thought. Wherefore, feeling myself raised (*sentendomi levare*) from the thought of that first love to the excellence (*virtù*) of this... I opened my mouth in this Ode.

He has previously gone out of his way to inform us that, though he does not wish in any way to speak slightingly of the *Vita Nuova*, "it is only reasonable that it should have been fervid and impassioned, and [the *Convivio*] temperate and virile. For one way of speaking and acting is suitable at one age, and another way at another". In short, he has grown up, and now speaks "not as in the hour/Of thoughtless youth".

From Traherne we have nothing which (so far as we know) was actually written at the time of the change-over; we only know what he thought when he looked back upon it from a height which showed the whole of his past way clearly displayed beneath him. Four phrases sum up his mature judgement:

> To live the Life of God is to live all the Works of God, and to enjoy them in His Image.

These liquid, clear satisfactions were the emanations of the highest reason, but not achieved till a long time afterwards.

[As a child] I knew by intuition those things which since my Apostasy, I collected again by the highest reason.

With much ado I was corrupted, and made to learn the dirty devices of this world, which now I unlearn, and become, as it were, a little child again that I may enter into the Kingdom of God.

The First Image is the true image; when it is lost to intuition, the return must be made by means of the Second Image and the intellect; "the way forward is the way back." And the Last Image will be the First Image, but known differently: there is to be no denying of that immediate insight into the divine reality of the visible things. From the affirmation of the First Image, there follows the affirmation of all the images, until every created image is gathered up into that "express image of God's person" which is at the same time created and uncreate.

There is to be no denying—ultimately. But the immediate effect of substituting the analytical intellect for the simplicities of intuition is frequently to produce not merely an apparent denial of the First Image, but actually a painful awareness of the images in opposition. The tension may be so violent as to obscure the reason and almost to split the personality. Dante, looking back to the years when with an eager heart and high hopes he was pursuing his philosophical studies, says of himself:

> Nel mezzo del cammin di nostra vita
> mi ritrovai per una selva oscura,
> che la diritta via era smarrita.
> *Inferno* I, 1-3.

He was in the Dark Wood, and the Abyss was opening at his feet. His description is brief, but terrifying: a man bemused with sleep, wandering perplexed among thorns and clinging brambles; the far-off shining of the mountain he cannot reach because his own sins stand in the way like beasts, seen suddenly as forces exterior to himself, as it were powers of Nature uncontrollable, and hostile. Traherne uses a similar image:

> Thenceforth I lived among dreams and shadows, like a prodigal son feeding upon husks with swine. A comfortless wilderness full

of thorns and troubles the world was, or worse: a waste place covered with idleness. . . .

Another time in a lowering and sad evening, being alone in the field, when all things were dead and quiet, a certain want and horror fell upon me, beyond imagination. The unprofitableness and silence of the place dissatisfied me; its wideness terrified me; from the utmost ends of the earth fears surrounded me.
Centuries of Meditations, iii, 14 and 23.

It is in this mood that bewildered men deny and blaspheme the images. Thus even Blake, whose first and last cry is that "everything that lives is holy", and that the natural joys of the body, sexual and otherwise, are the very gates to full spiritual integration, goes through a period of dualism when, like any manichee, he sets flesh and spirit at enmity and seems to feel a Satanic power in Nature. This is the period between the *Songs of Experience* and *The Four Zoas*, when the soul, turned in upon itself and divided against itself by the logical reason, seems to be only a battleground in which the senses war against the spirit. Blake is so difficult a poet that to say anything about him usually involves one in saying far too much; it is perhaps enough to take note here and now that he, too, had to pass through the Dark Wood and the Vision of Hell, and come out by the Way of Affirmation: "I was a slave bound in a mill among beasts and devils. These beasts and these devils are now, together with myself, become children of light and liberty, and my feet and my wife's feet are free from fetters."

If Wordsworth never went down so deep into the Abyss as Blake or Dante, neither—perhaps for that very reason—did he ever ascend the hill of vision with so triumphant a song. I am speaking, of course, of Wordsworth the poet. Except in so far as it is expressed in their poetry, the spiritual experience of poets is no business of ours, and to make pronouncements about it is the height of critical presumption. But what the poet says, and the way he says it, are very much our business.

What Wordsworth says, then, is that when the mystical glory faded from what the eighteenth century called "Nature" (that is, the visible creation other than man), he began to find it again in the human soul. So far as one can tell, the process was a gradual one, and perhaps his philosophy of immanence was never very dogmatically defined. But we can trace three stages, which succeed one another logically, though perhaps not, in any rigid sense, chronologically. The first is the intuition of a "presence" exterior to himself, sustaining and (sometimes) judging him, as on the famous occasion when he stole the game from another boy's snare, and felt

> ... among the solitary hills
> Low breathings coming after [him], and sounds
> Of undistinguishable motion, steps
> Almost as silent as the earth they trod.

In the next stage, the "presence" is felt both without and within, and he feels himself to be in union with it. This stage is illustrated by the passage I quoted just now from *The Prelude,* or this, which is a cancelled passage from Book II—cancelled perhaps as being more pantheistic than he really meant to be; or because it did not accurately represent his mind at the time he speaks of:

> By such communion I was early taught
> That what we see of forms and images
> Which float along our minds, and what we feel
> Of active or recognizable thought,
> Prospectiveness, intelligence or will,
> Not only is not worthy to be deemed
> Our being, to be prized as what we are,
> But is the very littleness of life.
> Such consciousnesses seemed but accidents,
> Relapses from the one interior life
> Which is in all things, from that unity
> In which all beings live with God, are lost
> In God and Nature, in one mighty whole
> As indistinguishable as the cloudless east
> At noon is from the cloudless west, when all
> The Hemisphere is one cerulean blue.

This is transitional. The repudiation of "forms and images" shows a turning from the affirmative to the negative way, a redirection of the spiritual eye from the outward to the inward, from the true Other to the true Self; but at the same time "God and Nature" are bracketed together as one thing.

Finally, in the last book of *The Excursion,* the philosophy of age is exalted above the intuitions of youth (despite its tendency to look nostalgically back upon them), and the First Image is categorically denied:

THE BEATRICIAN VISION

> Rightly it is said
> That Man descends into the VALE of years;
> Yet have I thought that we might also speak,
> And not presumptuously, I trust, of Age,
> As of a final EMINENCE; though bare
> In aspect and forbidding, yet a point
> On which 'tis not impossible to sit
> In awful sovereignty.
>
> The Excursion, ix, 48–55.

From this eminence (which could scarcely be more "bare and forbidding" than the prosaic verse which celebrates it), the ancient sage surveys the summer landscape, and finds that

> .. the gross and visible frame of things
> Relinquishes its hold upon the sense,
> Yea, almost on the Mind herself, and seems
> All unsubstantialized....
>   For on that superior height
> Who sits, is disencumbered from the press
> Of near obstructions, and is privileged
> To breathe in solitude, above the host
> Of ever-humming insects, 'mid thin air
> That suits not them. The murmur of the leaves,
> Many and idle, visits not his ear:
> This he is freed from, and from thousand notes
> (Not less unceasing, not less vain than these),
> By which the finer passages of sense
> Are occupied; and the Soul, that would incline
> To listen, is prevented or deterred.
>
> ibid. ix. 63–66, 69–80.

Here is a change indeed! The creation with which the poet once enjoyed a mystical union has become "the gross and visible frame of things"; the sights and sounds of Nature have become vain and idle encumbrances, obstructions and deterrents, which are all the better for being "unsubstantialized". (What has become of the Wordsworth who wrote

> And beauty born of murmuring sound
> Did pass into her face?)

The sacred solitude which the "inward eye" once irradiated with bliss has become a privileged and superior isolation. And inspiration has been killed stone dead.

For this poetical disaster it is customary to blame Wordsworth's panic retreat from a broad-minded pantheism into a narrow and institutional Anglican orthodoxy. At this point it may be well to let the Anglican parson speak again:

> Your enjoyment of the world is never right, till every morning you awake in Heaven; see yourself in your Father's Palace; and look upon the skies, the earth, and the air as Celestial Joys.... You never enjoy the world aright, till the Sea itself floweth in your veins, till you are clothed with the heavens, and crowned with the stars: and perceive yourself to be the sole heir of the whole world, and more than so, because men are in it who are every one sole heirs as well as you.... Till your spirit filleth the whole world, and the stars are your jewels.
> Traherne, *Centuries of Meditations,* i. 28-30.

Contempt of material things as such is in fact no more orthodox than pantheism—it is the great dualist heresy which always lies in wait for an over-spiritualized Christianity. Let us notice in passing Traherne's use of the word "sole"; you are "sole heir of the whole world", and so is every one else: to be "sole" in this sense is not to be solitary; it is to enjoy, in community, the indivisible treasure.

And now let us hear Dante. He has completed his pilgrimage and purged his mind of distractions; he has re-entered the Garden of Innocence; and he has returned, like a penitent child, to his first love. Not, of course, in actual fact. He could not return to a material Beatrice as Wordsworth could return to a material Tintern. He returned to her in memory, as Wordsworth returned to the immortal intimations of his childhood. Wordsworth had said, recalling the past: "That was how I felt; I cannot feel it now—something better, perhaps, but not that." Dante says, reliving the past in the present: "I felt it then, I feel it now, better but still the same—yesterday, today, and for ever":

> d'antico amor sentì la gran potenza.
> *Purg.* xxx. 39.

The difference is a subtle one, not easy to put into words, but plain enough to the ear and mind of the reader. So that, whereas Wordsworth, at forty-three, is assuming old age and detaching himself from those sensible beauties which had been the inspiration of his boyhood and youth, Dante, at fifty-six, is writing the last cantos of the *Paradiso*. Standing on the threshold of the

Empyrean, and preparing to affirm in ringing tones all the great Images one after the other—time and space, form and substance, church and empire, city of earth and city of God, saint and angel, Mary and Christ—he turns to that image of First Love renewed, which has guided him on his journey:

> Se quanto infino a qui di lei si dice
>   fosse conchiuso tutto in una loda,
>   poco sarebbe a fornir questa vice.
> La bellezza ch'io vidi si trasmoda
>   non pur di là da noi, ma creto io credo
>   che solo il suo fattor tutta la goda.
> Da questo passo vinto mi concedo,
>   più che già mai da punto di suo tema
>   soprato fosse comico o tragedo;
> chè, come sole in viso che più trema,
>   così lo rimembrar de dolce riso
>   la mente mia di sè medesmo scema.
> Dal primo giorno ch'i' vidi il suo viso
>   in questa vita, infino a questa vista,
>   non m'è il seguire al mio cantar preciso;
> ma or convien che mio seguir desista
>   più dietro a sua bellezza, poetando,
>   come all'ultimo suo ciascuno artista.
>   *Para.* xxx. 16–33.

Wordsworth lived through his period of spiritual dryness and, like Blake, found in Incarnate Godhead the resolution of the dualism which had threatened to disintegrate both his personality and his genius. Their surrender is marked by that *umiltà* which is so conspicuously present in the Dante of the *Vita Nuova* and of the *Commedia,* and so conspicuously absent from the Dante of the *Convivio.* What Wordsworth never succeeded in regaining was the Beatrician vision. His gain and failure may be measured by the vision which he saw in the clouds at sunset, and records in the second book of *The Excursion*:

> Glory beyond all glory ever seen
> By waking sense or by the dreaming soul!
> The appearance, instantaneously disclosed,
> Was of a mighty city—boldly say
> A wilderness of building, sinking far
> And self-withdrawn into a boundless depth,
> Far sinking into splendour—without end!
>   *The Excursion,* ii. 832–838.

The description that follows is of great beauty and almost equal in power to the natural landscapes of the great decade. But it is not a landscape: it is a cloudscape; and he concludes:

> [The] little Vale, a dwelling-place of Man,
> Lay low beneath my feet; 'twas visible—
> I saw not, but I felt that it was there.
> That which I *saw* was the revealed abode
> Of Spirits in beatitude.
>
> *ibid*. ii. 870–874.

It is, as Mr. John Jones comments, remarkable that his vision should put on the image of the City—for in his earlier days he had cared little for cities, using them as a rule only as vague symbols of the artificial and the degenerate. There is already a movement from solitude towards community. But it is also noteworthy that the vision is not—and Wordsworth takes pains to tell us that it is not—the actual "dwelling-place of Man", transfigured and—in Dante's phrase—"transhumanised". It is not like the visionary London which broods over the bricks-and-mortar London in Charles Williams's *All Hallows Eve*, nor like Blake's holy city:

> The fields from Islington to Marybone,
> From Primrose Hill to St. John's Wood
> Were builded over with pillars of gold,
> And there Jerusalem's temple stood.

The inhabited vale is on earth: the imaginary vision of the City is built elsewhere and of other material. The spirit of Beatrice has been divorced from her body; the fire has consumed the bush.

It was perhaps fortunate for Dante the poet that his God-bearing Image was the image of a person, for it left him no option but to recognize from the start that devotion must be addressed to a real Other. The "presence" discerned in inanimate Nature may cease to be felt as otherness, and may come to seem only the projection of the mind of Man, or even of one's own mind. But there is no getting over the otherness of other people. The smiling face of Nature may indeed sometimes appear to mock one's inner mood, but she does not, as is recorded of the earthly Beatrice, cut one publicly in the street, or laugh at one with her girl friends. It was after this humiliation of public mockery that Dante reached his "point of total commitment", and gave himself over to the praise of his lady, regardless of her favours or his own feelings. He was fortunate also in that the fashion of his time understood and applauded a disinterested love—how fortunate we may see by the contrasting example of Yeats, in whom the Beatrician quality of his love for Maud Gonne was always embittered by a frustrate desire of possession, and by the knowledge that the society in which he lived had little reverence for a sublimated passion. Total commitment in devotion to a real Other involves total acceptance of the rights of that Other, who is loved, as God must be loved, for being what it divinely is, and for no other reason.

I have endeavoured to sketch a certain fundamental pattern in the spiritual experience of four poets who appear to have gone by the same way to the final goal of all vision. Dante, Blake and Traherne attained the goal, and carried their poetry with them; Wordsworth, as a man, did perhaps attain, but somehow lost much of his poetry by the way. I suggest that Wordsworth's comparative failure was due to a turning inward of the spiritual eye, which led to the loss of his authentic inspiration: the intuition of the divine in an Image extraneous to the self. Those who knew him in his old age said that he impressed them as a man "living as in the presence of God by habitual recollection". But, as Professor Lascelles Abercrombie has said, "to live self-conscious in a mystical experience of the Divine Being of the impersonal world, as transcendent as any mystic's experience of his personal God, is to live, as unspeakably *alone*; and that, for many years, was Wordsworth's experience". From this exalted and intolerable solitude, Wordsworth managed to withdraw—first into an effort to find community with his fellow-men, and finally, it would seem, into communion with a God more personal, and in that sense more orthodox, than the "God of Nature". But in finding this inner peace, he could not take his art with him. To quote Abercrombie again: "the crucial change in Wordsworth was a retreat from that mystical experience of the world which entailed a loneliness he could no longer support. *When he cut himself off from this, he cut off the native inspiration of his poetry*".

Dante's mysticism was of another kind. Not only was his God personal from the beginning; He manifested Himself throughout by means of persons. Nothing is more remarkable than the absence from his heavenly ascent of any feeling of the "flight of the alone to the Alone". From beginning to end the Images are always with him; his insight into the last mysteries is attained amid a very blaze of publicity, in the burning presence of all the courts of heaven. As Professor Lascelles Abercrombie has said, "it was a mysticism in which he was not alone, but unspeakably befriended".

The Way of Affirmation, if it is a mystical way at all, has received but little attention from the theologians. This is perhaps just as well, for it is pre-eminently the way of the poets, and few poets are as patient as Dante of theological analysis, or able to move so freely within a theological framework. Yet it is, as I have said, characteristically Christian in its outward look, directed upon that which is wholly other, and in its insistence upon the Divine Immanence within the *"santa e gloriosa carne"*. It is by its attention to the sacred significance of the material world that it enables the poet to affirm his proper inspiration: that is why Beatrice, in a passage rather shocking to our moral susceptibilities, stresses the fact that her paramount attraction for Dante lay in her bodily beauty. That is why the union of male and female supplied all Blake's symbols of spiritual integration; why Traherne repeats over and over again that to enjoy God and to enjoy the universe are one and the same thing; why the novels of Charles Williams continually emphasize the perils of a naked encounter of spiritual forces, not mediated through the flesh.

Yet the Way, though neglected and overgrown, has not been left wholly uncharted. Dante is its pioneer, Blake its prophet; Traherne has supplied it with a manual of devotion; Williams has outlined its theology. But it needs more scholars and historians—and this is perhaps as good a reason as any for commending it to the notice of the universities.

CHAPTER IV

CHARLES WILLIAMS: A POET'S CRITIC

WHEN EDWARD FITZGERALD scribbled to a friend: "Mrs. Browning is dead; we shall have no more *Aurora Leighs,* thank God!" he was only being flippant in a deplorably tasteless way. But when certain academic persons, "whom by ear and eye he never knew", expressed a similar relief at the passing of Charles Williams, they probably meant rather more by it, and expressed, unintentionally, a very much higher tribute to the dead. A chronic irritation had been removed from the intellectual atmosphere, and they breathed more freely.

Few things are more striking than the change which has taken place during my own lifetime in the attitude of the intelligentsia towards the spokesmen of Christian opinion. When I was a child, bishops expressed doubts about the Resurrection, and were called courageous. When I was a girl, G. K. Chesterton professed belief in the Resurrection, and was called whimsical. When I was at college, thoughtful people expressed belief in the Resurrection "in a spiritual sense", and were called advanced; (any other kind of belief was called obsolete, and its professors were held to be simpleminded). When I was middle-aged, a number of lay persons, including some poets and writers of popular fiction, put forward rational arguments for the Resurrection, and were called courageous. Today, any lay apologist for Christianity, who is not a clergyman and whose works are sold and read, is liable to be abused in no uncertain terms as a mountebank, a reactionary, a tool of the Inquisition, a spiritual snob, an intellectual bully, an escapist, an obstructionist, a psychopathic introvert, an insensitive extravert, and an enemy of society. The charges are not always mutually compatible, but the common animus behind them is unmistakable, and its name is fear. Writers who attack these domineering Christians are called courageous.

The wheel, it would appear, has come full circle. But in fact the situation is very different from what it was in my childhood. Then, the heretical bishops and the laymen whose lead they were in fact following were thought of as attacking a kind of Bastille of inert and outworn tyranny; the exponent of contemporary anti-Christian polemic is felt, on the contrary, to be standing in the breach against the threat of an invading, or at least of a revolutionary, army—possibly, as we shall see later, of a gang of jail-breakers. It is true that every effort is made to represent Christian affirmations as a mere attempt to reimpose the cold dead hand of the past. Phrases like "dogmatic", "scholastic", "mediaeval", "unscientific", "mystical obscurantism", "return to the Dark Ages", "conventional orthodoxy", "taboo", "authoritarian", and so on are bandied about freely in a pejorative sense, and often without any very clear notion of their meaning; but the tone of voice is a new one.

It is perhaps significant that, in this country, the peculiar acrimony of the "scientific humanists", as they like, I think, to call themselves, is seldom directed towards the Church of Rome. There, if anywhere, one would think, the grip of the mediaeval mortmain should be observable. But it is not so. Only Protestants trouble their heads about Rome : from the harrow of scientific humanism Mr. Evelyn Waugh and Mr. Graham Greene slip out almost untouched by the teeth. For so long as I remember, Romans have always received special treatment : they believe things because they have to; kindly people are careful not to offend their susceptibilities; anybody who "goes over" to Rome is philosophically written off, as though he had adopted an alien nationality; Romans do as Rome does, and nobody is surprised or aggrieved. The indignation is reserved for a small group of Anglicans, such as Charles Williams, C. S. Lewis (the special "Cambridge" number of *The Twentieth Century* was a monument to the irritant properties of Christian intellectualism in that university) and, of course, T. S. Eliot, whose so-called "retreat into Anglicanism" has exposed him to critical savagery which sometimes oversteps the limits not only of charity but of decency. In the critical attacks on these men there is, quite plainly discernible, a note of hysteria. The accents are not those of a man liberating a dog from a confined and unwholesome kennel; they are those of a child, who, picking up in the garden a dull and inoffensive-looking stone, sees it stretch forth a leg and wink a knowing eye : "Ugh ! it's *alive* !"

Now, it is precisely this power of evoking a very present and demanding life from that which might be supposed decently dead and sterilized, that characterizes all Charles Williams's literary criticism, and more especially his critical interpretation of Dante —to which, I promise you, I will eventually come. His genius moved him to make contact with the essential life in every work he handled; it was this which made him so inspiring a master to his students in London and Oxford, and this which explains the suspicion, and the occasional antagonism, which his whole method arouses in certain academic circles today. For he did in a measure run counter to the modern trend in criticism.

Perhaps the clearest way to put the matter briefly is to say that his judgements were as free as any modern man's judgements could be from what we call a "sense of period". It would not be altogether untrue to say that in this respect he was "mediaeval" —provided we add that "classical" or "Renaissance" would be an equally appropriate epithet. For "period-sense" is a thing of very recent origin—it scarcely begins to exist before the closing years of the eighteenth century. We may see this very vividly illustrated in the history of theatrical costume. Right down to Garrick's time, nobody thought it odd to play Coriolanus or Macbeth in a periwig, and all the classical heroines in panniers and powdered hair, any more than Shakespeare had boggled about making his Roman conspirators pull their hats about their brows, or giving Brutus a pocket in his gown. No doubt everybody knew that the costume worn in past ages was different from their own—they knew, but they did not feel that it mattered. They felt that the play was dealing with human beings in a human situation—not with historical personages conditioned by a historical environment. And this was a reflection of their whole attitude to the writers of the past—they judged them as though they were contemporaries, bringing their opinions to the bar of absolute, rather than of relative, truth.

The "period-sense", and the dynamic philosophy of history to which it belongs, is of course an admirable thing, quickening our understanding of the past and displaying all social and historical changes as movements in a great process of becoming. But if it is insisted upon too much it may defeat itself. It may end by actually destroying all contact, all sympathy between us and our forebears, and even that very awareness of continuity which it ought to foster. If we look upon Dante (for example) as a man *totally* explicable in terms of a vanished period, we may succeed in forgetting that he is a man like ourselves at all. If we account for everything that he said by the consideration that, being born when he was, there was nothing else he could very well say, we shall have provided ourselves with an excellent excuse for not applying what he said to ourselves: it performed a function in history, and there its interest ends. The "period-sense" may, that is, be used as a defence-mechanism against any categorical imperative which we may feel to be inconvenient. So long as we can look upon it as a mere incident in a historical pattern, our withers remain unwrung.

In this matter, as in so many others, Christianity displays its usual propensity for making everything as awkward as possible. It outrages the tidy-minded by occupying a paradoxical position. On the one hand, it made modern science and the modern views of history possible by insisting that the pattern of events was not (as the Greek philosophers thought) static or cyclic, but a progression in time from a beginning to an end. On the other, it tiresomely maintains that at every point in the developing temporal process, the conditioned truths are referable to an extra-temporal standard of absolute truth, before which all souls enjoy complete equality, no aristocratic privilege being attached to the accident of later birth.

To Williams, this spiritual equality of past and present was axiomatic: it was part of the co-inherence. For him, the solidarity of human society lay visibly extended, not only in space, but also in time. He was, of course, aware that periods had succeeded one another—a book like *The Descent of the Dove* bears witness to his strong awareness of historical process—but for him periods constituted no barriers. With precisely the same conviction that a modern Communist will assert the bond of fraternity between workers in China and workers in Whitechapel, Williams asserted (or, to speak more exactly, took for granted) the bond of fraternity between a poet in the twentieth century and a poet in the Middle Ages. He was thus never content with knowing under what pressure of social conditions a poet came to say what he did: he felt that this did not exhaust the subject or explain the poem away. He always went on to ask: "Did the poet speak truth? and if so, what ought we to do about it?" That is why I said that the life he evoked in his critical judgements was "present and demanding". He vivified the past; he did not "re-vivify" it, in the sense of conscientiously reconstructing it against its period décor. He was as ready as Sophocles or Shakespeare to see the whole drama of history performed in modern dress.

Thus he came to Dante prepared to hail him across the negligible gap of six centuries as a fellow-poet, a fellow-lover, and a fellow-Christian. In the first paragraph of *The Figure of Beatrice* he observes: "Dante is one of those poets who begin their work with what is declared to be an intense personal experience." In that seeming-casual phrase he sweeps Dante into the same trawl with all the other odd fish who swim in the "great sea of being"; —"one of those poets"—"intense personal experience". It is related of Charles Williams that on one occasion he was having his hair cut and at the same time lending a sympathetic ear to the history of the barber's love-affair. "When my girl's about" said the barber, "I'm that happy I don't feel as if I had an enemy in the world—I'd forgive anybody anything."—"My dear man", cried Charles, leaping up and wringing the barber's hand enthusiastically, "my dear man, that's exactly what Dante said." So it was; and no mediaeval theory of courtly love had to be invoked to account for it. In the Theology of Romantic Love the liturgy is all of one tradition.

It was not from Dante that Williams learned the Theology of Romantic Love; he learned it from his own experience. But when he encountered it in Dante, he recognized it immediately, and knew that Dante and he were living within the same tradition. I have seen a letter of his (written, I think, to the late J. D. Sinclair, but I have unfortunately lost the reference) in which he protests that what he is trying to impress upon all the learned commentators of Dante is that "the thing does happen". Whatever symbolism the interpreters, or Dante himself, may build upon it, the basis of the whole towering structure is the living experienced fact. His own first introduction to the *Commedia* took place, he told me, when he was hurriedly correcting the proofs of Cary's translation for the Oxford University Press, and his immediate reaction was: "But this is *true*." By this simple affirmation he opened up a road which had been closed for at least a century: or perhaps it was a road which had never before been driven through precisely that part of the forest. For Dante's position has always been curiously isolated. He has been treated as a theologian, as a moralist, as a political satirist, as a manufacturer of "wild Gothick fancies", as a repository of curious historical allusions, and, occasionally, as a mystic of a rather irregular kind, but very seldom as a poet among poets, creating after the manner of his kind "an accurate image of actual experience". Those are Williams's words,[1] and they define as nearly as possible what he looked for in all poets, and found in Dante as in any other poet. The Pre-Raphaelites had perhaps come nearest to thus including Dante in the free commonwealth of poets; but their attention was almost exclusively directed to the *Vita Nuova*—for the universalizing of the first human vision into the great divine vision of fulfilment their undisciplined minds could find no use. The great nineteenth-century Dantists had the merit of taking the substance of the poem seriously; but their approach tended to be rather too narrowly ethical, and suggestive of an intelligent but critical congregation listening to an instruction from the pulpit. The early twentieth century endeavoured, with no very striking success, to divorce the form from the content, and to save Dante's reputation as a poet by considering "the poetry" in abstraction from the religious experience—which they did not recognize as an experience, or at least not as a poetic experience. But Williams's approach, to Dante as to everybody else, was existential. He recognized in the *Comedy,* not merely the *doctrine* of Hell, Purgatory, and Heaven, but the *experience* of those states, expressed in the movements of the images—those creatures of true flesh and blood which, like the matter of a sacrament, *are* that which they symbolize. It is easy to see why, the poem being such as it is, this approach should be found disquieting. If the thing that happened to Dante in thirteenth-century Florence is identical with what happens today to a barber in Fleet Street, then the whole experience might happen to any of us at any time, and nobody can feel safe.

I do not propose to examine in detail the contents of *The Figure of Beatrice*. I should only be repeating much that I have said elsewhere, and in any case the book itself is its own best commentary, and should offer no very great difficulty to anybody who is at all familiar with the body of Williams's work as a whole. All his books illuminate one another, for the same master-themes govern them all, so that it is impossible to confine any one theme to a single book. For example, his most impressive commentary on Dante's dream of the Siren is to be

[1] *Love and Religion in Dante* (Dacre Press).

found, not in *The Figure of Beatrice*, but in those chapters of *Descent into Hell* which deal with Mrs. Sammile and the Succubus; and to read that novel along with the chapters on the *Inferno* is to enrich one's understanding of the whole conception of Hell, both in Williams and in Dante. The mystical theology of the Affirmative Way needs to be studied in *The Place of the Lion* and in the *Taliessin* poems, and its imaginative treatment there compared with its more formal exposition in the Dante volume. And so on. It will be enough to mention briefly some of the points at which the minds of the two poets touch each other most closely. To do more would be impossible, for they start up correspondences everywhere, so that it is possible to say that there is scarcely anything explicit in Williams which is not also explicit or implicit in Dante.

Mr. John Heath-Stubbs, in his admirable booklet on Charles Williams, tells us of a lecture delivered by Williams at Oxford, in which he enumerated the "five principal modes of the Romantic experience, or great images, which occur in poetry". They are: the religious experience itself; the Image of Woman; the Image of Nature; the Image of the City; and the experience of great art. Of these, four at least he found (whether in the sense of discovering or recognizing them) already manifest in Dante. The religious experience itself is the theme of Dante's work, from first to last, beginning with a conversion on the lower plane, followed by loss of faith, backsliding and the vision of Hell, and proceeding through a re-education on the intellectual level to a second conversion on the higher plane, and so to the Ascent of Vision. The pattern is a familiar one up to a point, its powerful individuality lying in the tenacity with which the validity of the Images is affirmed from first to last.

The Image of Woman is, of course, asserted in Beatrice, about whose person the Theology of Romantic Love is assembled and displayed. In calling it "the Image of Woman" I am not sure that Williams was doing full justice to himself or Dante. The Image is not of femaleness as such—the *ewig Weibliches* about which Goethe, and D. H. Lawrence and others, have made so much to-do. It is a *personal* relationship of adoration; and Williams himself was the first to insist that the adoration need not be (though in literature it most frequently is) that of a man for a woman. It might, in the exchange of hierarchies, be that of a woman for a man; if, he would say, Beatrice had written her version of the *Commedia,* Dante himself might have figured in it as the "God-bearing Image". Or the element of sex might not enter into it at all. But in one way or other, the Image is that of the God-bearing Person, whose earthly archetype is Mary, and whose heavenly archetype is Christ.

For Dante, the Image of the City is personified in Virgil and his Rome. But it exists also for Dante in Florence, as for Williams in London; and also in his dream of the just Empire, corresponding to Virgil's dream of that perfected Augustan Empire, of which the reality fell so far short. Finally, it is manifested directly in the Heavenly City of the Paradise, and also negatively in the perversions of the City of Dis.

The experience of Great Art is also there—in Virgil, in the great poets encountered at various stages on the way, in Dante's vivid consciousness of his own poetic calling. But its greatest Image is the poem itself, to which, as Dante says, "Heaven and earth have set hand". Immanent in him, but also transcending him, his own art is more than himself—like Beatrice, like City and Empire, it is a symbol subdued to the greater thing it symbolizes.

The Image of Nature, which Williams perceived most clearly and powerfully in Wordsworth, is not so distinctly present in Dante. Neither, for that matter, was it very observable in Charles Williams: "in his poetry", says Mr. Heath-Stubbs, "Nature as such has hardly any part to play. His poetry lacks particularity of observation." One might say the same of Dante, for though his treatment of animals and especially birds shows some "particularity of observation", it remains true of him as of Williams that his "landscapes are always emblematic of states of mind". We may, if we like, here refresh ourselves with a little "sense of period". Mediaeval poets are very seldom nature-worshippers, in the sense in which we moderns think of Nature. Bad roads, difficulties of transport, the uncertainties of a local and primitive agriculture, and relentless exposure at all times to the vagaries of the weather, made their relation to mists and mountains, crops and forests, heat, flood and tempest, a grim and practical one. The Image of the Forest, in particular, is always slightly uncanny—Williams was in tune with them when he took that image (Broceliande, the Dark Wood, the Forest of Arden) as a symbol of the subconscious. Mediaeval man preferred his Nature tamed and made orderly in gardens. Even here, his observation was seldom very particular: "red and yellow flowers", the rose, the lily, the violet, the daisy; the oak, the thorn, the beech, the poplar; "small fowls making melody", with an occasional nightingale, is about as far as most of his poets go. But there is one remarkable exception. If where we are particular they were vague and generalized, yet where we are usually most vague and generalized they were particular, and moreover felt all that numinous awe which we reserve for the terrestrial phenomena of Nature. Better than the earth at their feet they knew and loved the visible heavens. They knew the way of the Sun among the houses of the Zodiac as intimately and lovingly as we know the face of the landscape from our own windows; and they did not, like some modern novelists, carelessly indulge themselves with two full moons in a fortnight. When we talk of "Nature", we think of land and water, plants and animals; we have almost forgotten that the heavens too are "Nature". But the mediaevals did not; and when Dante is awestruck by Nature it is almost always in the face of the turning of the "Great Wheels"—the army of unalterable law. The visible heavens are, for him and his like, the Image of Mathematical Order. It is perhaps a little surprising that Williams did not list this image with the others; for mathematical order meant much to him, and supplied him with many of his most pregnant poetical images, particularly in the *Taliessin* poems.

The theme of the sanctity of the flesh is, of course, common to both poets, as it in reason ought to be to all those who acknowledge the Incarnation, and as it must necessarily be to all followers of the Affirmative Way. For that Way begins always with the intuitive perception of the Divine Image in the material creation—not displacing but informing it, as Moses beheld God in the burning bush, "and the bush was not consumed"; and, if pursued to the end, it leads to the illuminative vision of the Image of the Created Manhood in the uncreated "Image of the Glory". Dante, beholding in the flesh-and-blood Florentine girl the appearance of the in-godded Beatrice in her unfallen nature, and Pauline Anstruther, brought face to face with her own "body of glory" in the moment when she willingly takes to herself her ancestor's burden of fear, are variations upon this theme of the "holy and glorious flesh—*la santa e gloriosa carne*".

The doctrine of Substitution is not found very explicitly, I think, in Dante, except, of course, in so far as it is implied in the great passage on the Atonement in the Seventh canto of the *Paradiso*; and I will not therefore deal with it here. Characteristic of both poets is the great attention they give to the "knowledge of good and evil"—that is the knowledge of the good in its opposite identity of evil. Williams, in his chapter on the *Inferno*, speaks of the soul being "here drawn down the *perverted Way of Affirmation*"; and in *He Came Down from Heaven* he has brilliantly expounded the legend of the Fall in this sense: "The Adam ... knew good, they wished to know good and evil. Since there was not—since there was not and never has been and never will be—anything else than the good to know, they knew good as antagonism." Dante, in a series of carefully contrasted images, shows in Hell the perverted experience of those goodnesses which are seen exalted in Heaven. Paolo and Francesca, Ulysses and Diomede, Ugolino and Ruggiero are, at different levels, the perverted images of that mutuality which is the life of those Blessed who make up the body of the Eagle in the Heaven of Justice and "when they think We, say I", because they are members one of another. The angelic glory which, on the cornices of Purgatory, is light and song and courtesy, is known in Hell only as an appearance of terror and judgement. In *The Place of the Lion*, the Eagle which is here the principle of Knowledge, appears to Damaris Tighe as a horrible pterodactyl, stinking of decay, because she has perverted the good of knowledge to her own selfish uses. "They know evil; that is, they know the good of fact as repugnant to them." Even so, the Lady Julian of Norwich averred that she "saw no Hell but sin"; and St. Catherine of Genoa said that the eternal fires were no other than the light of God, seen by those who rejected it.

In pointing out parallels of this kind, I do not mean to suggest that Charles Williams "got his ideas out of Dante". That is a very crude and popular way of putting it. It is also a manner of speech far too common among the Damaris Tighes of scholarship, who tend to see everything in terms of "sources" and "influences". That poets derive from other poets in the same tradition is true, and they have never been ashamed to acknowledge their debts to one another; neither was such "borrowing" ever thought dishonourable until we decided to make a fetish out of the word "originality". But sources and influences and borrowings are not the whole story; the coinherence found among the practitioners of the Grand Art is not of this simple kind. We may say that, for example, the Theology of Romantic Love would not have existed in Williams, or not in that particular mode, if Dante had never written; but we may also say that it did not exist after that mode in Dante until Williams found it there. In the tradition—which means the "handing over"—of the symbols of art, time's arrow flies both ways. That which was always potentially in the earlier poet may be actualized in the later poet, and, once it has been actualized, it becomes and remains actual in the poet of its origin. In a letter which the late J. D. Sinclair was kind enough to show me, Williams wrote (à propos of the allegory of the Beatrician Pageant in *Purgatory*, xxix–xxx), "My chief point, though I should be cautious how I made it to the world in general, is that poets think of something which they then discover to have relevance all round. It is perhaps a little unfortunate that they so rarely bother to explain all the relevance. This has caused lesser poets than Dante to be called obscure." Since Williams was cautious of disclosing this fact about poets, it is perhaps a little treacherous of me to do so behind, as it were, his back; but I will hope that he does not regard you as "the world in general". What he says is exceedingly true, as I can myself bear witness. A poet creates a character, a situation, a phrase for a particular purpose and, *after* having done so, realizes that he has created a universal symbol, applicable in a far wider sense than that which he immediately intended. Thenceforth he uses it, with or without "bothering to explain all its relevance", in the wider context to which he has found it applicable. But it sometimes happens that it is not the poet himself, but another, who discovers the wider relevance. If so, he is justified in so interpreting it in the place where he finds it; for the relevance was always potentially there and, once seen and recognized, it is actually there for ever. This does not, of course, mean that we can "read into" poets anything that we jolly well like; any significance that contradicts the whole tenor of their work is obviously suspect. But it means that in a very real sense poets do sometimes write more greatly than they know; and it also means that every poet's work enriches not only those to whom he transmits the tradition, but also all those from whom he himself derived it.

It is here that we find ourselves returning, by a slightly different road, to that sense of poetic timelessness which enabled

Williams to break down Dante's isolation and treat him quite freely and naturally as a poet among other poets. I do not think that this had ever been done for Dante in quite the same way before. His "debts" to earlier poets have, indeed, been thoroughly investigated—verbal "borrowings" from Virgil and Ovid, Statius, Boethius and the Scriptures, "parallels" from Guido Guinicelli, Guido Cavalcanti, and other lyricists of the *dolce stil nuovo,* "allusions" to the *Song of Roland* and the Romance-writers of the Arthurian Cycle, "affinities" with the troubadours of Provence, and all the rest of it. His philosophy and theology have been tracked to their "sources" in Aristotle, Aquinas, St. Bernard, the Victorines, in the Gnostic pseudo-Scriptures of the second century, and in the Jewish Cabbala. All this is the daily bread of research-scholarship; and very exciting it can be, especially when it is carried out with sympathetic understanding of the workings of the poetic mind, as was done by John Livingston Lowes for Coleridge in that astonishing book *The Road to Xanadu.* Equally of course, the "influence" of Dante upon later poets has been duly noted—the quotations, the borrowings, the overt repudiations, denunciations, and eulogies. There have also been some sporadic attempts to compare—rather externally and superficially—Dante's Hell with Milton's, or his Satan with Goethe's Mephistopheles. But it is only Williams who, in discussing Dante's poetic theme and treatment, will readily and as it were casually bring in Shakespeare, Milton, Wordsworth, Coleridge, Bernard Shaw, Coventry Patmore, George Fox, Sir Thomas Browne, Spenser, Keats, Kierkegaard, Raymond Lully and Christopher Marlowe, to exchange ideas with him as though they were all democratic citizens of one and the same poetic Athens. I have taken these names from *The Figure of Beatrice,* in which they all appear; in conversation, Williams was equally ready to illuminate any passage in Dante from Browning, Tennyson or Gerard Manly Hopkins, and for aught I know he would have been prepared to illustrate him from Kafka, James Joyce or Dylan Thomas, or them from Dante, had the occasion arisen. We are accustomed to deal thus with our own poets—Shakespeare is not too great for such treatment, nor Chaucer too remote; but, believe me, it is rare to find any critic of Dante using this pleasant familiarity with him. "It might not be unwise", says Charles Williams, speaking of the perils of the Beatrician Way, "to point a few extracts from Mr. Shaw's *Arms and the Man . . .*

in every edition of the *Commedia*." Others have solemnly warned us of those perils, but who except Williams would ever have proposed such a prophylactic? The death of Beatrice is the figure of a spiritual disillusionment: "this state", he adds, "has been put to us most clearly in two places in English verse; the first is in Shakespeare's *Troilus and Cressida*; the second in Wordsworth's *Prelude*". Or again: "The forest itself has different names in different tongues—Westermain, Arden, Birnam, Broceliande". Meredith, too, drops in to the poetic party, adds a word to the discussion, and drops out again. Across the centuries, the poets hold communication.

In the same way, and quite apart from formal "criticism", we find Dante discoursing with his fellows in the body of Williams's tales and poems. Here, for example, is a short passage from *The Calling of Taliessin*. Merlin and his sister Brisen, the figures of time and space, are beginning the magical operation which is to call in the spiritual powers to the founding of the kingdom of Logres in Britain.

> The cone's shadow of earth fell into space,
> and into (other than space) the third heaven.
> In the third heaven are the living unriven truths,
> climax tranquil in Venus. Merlin and Brisen
> heard, as in faint bee-like humming
> round the cone's point, the feeling intellect hasten
> to fasten on the earth's image; in the third heaven
> the stones of the waste glimmered like summer stars.
> Between wood and waste the yoked children of Nimue
> opened the rite; they invoked the third heaven,
> heard in the far humming of the spiritual intellect,
> to the building of Logres and the coming of the Land of the
>   Trinity
> which is called Sarras in maps of the soul.

For the full elucidation of this beautiful and complex image I must refer you to C. S. Lewis in *Arthurian Torso*. Briefly, as he says, "we are in fact watching the impregnation of Nimue by her Pattern"—that is, of the earthly ectype by its heavenly Principle. We know the heavenly Principles—the Platonic Ideas; we have met them in *The Place of the Lion*, there called down wrongly for selfish ends and in their own naked power; here invoked to a right end and in the right way, that is, through the earthly ectype. The earth's shadow—"as we all know", says Lewis, though perhaps he flatters us—is a cone of darkness, extending through outer space and touching with its apex the Third Heaven, the sphere of Venus. We have met that shadowy cone in the *Paradiso*, though it there fulfils a different symbolic function. The Third Heaven in the *Paradiso* is the heaven of love and poetry, and therefore a very suitable source for this poetic image of the impregnation of matter by form—"matter yearns towards form as a woman yearns towards a man", according to the saying of the Schoolmen. Lewis adds that "Williams is here (perhaps unconsciously) reproducing the doctrine of the Renaissance Platonists that Venus—celestial love and beauty—was the pattern or model after which God created the material universe". But "what resides in the third heaven... is called by [Williams] 'the feeling intellect' or *mens sensitiva*. The expression 'feeling intellect' is borrowed from Wordsworth's *Prelude* (xiv. 226) and the whole passage in which it occurs is a comment on the later poet's meaning". (I am still quoting from Lewis.) Plato, Dante, the Renaissance Platonists, and Wordsworth have thus all contributed to the passage, while Merlin, Taliessin himself, and the phrase "the summer stars" belong to the ancient poems of the Arthurian cycle. And we might add two further points. First, about the "feeling intellect", which a few lines later is called the "spiritual intellect", Lewis notes that "the important difference between the two poets is that where Wordsworth is thinking of a subjective state in human minds, Williams is thinking of an objective celestial fact". And here we can scarcely help remembering—as Williams can scarcely have helped remembering —how Dante speaks of the Tenth Heaven, the Empyrean or Heaven of God's presence, from which all the other heavens derive their being, as "pure Intellectual light fulfilled with love" —"*luce intellettual piena d'amore*". This "intellectual love" or "loving intellect" is the ultimate "objective celestial fact"—a greater thing than Wordsworth's "feeling intellect" and incomparably greater than the *mens sensitiva*. Secondly, we shall recall the combination of intellect with love in the opening line of Dante's great ode addressed to "the celestial Intelligences" : "You that *by understanding* move the Third Heaven—*Voi che 'ntendendo il terzo ciel movete*"; and perhaps also that of the still more famous sonnet "*Donne ch'avete intelletto d'amore*—Ladies that have *intelligence* in love". The words "source" and "borrowing" are inadequate for this close fusion of poetic images, gathered over twenty-one centuries from Greece and Italy, Wales and England. It is nothing in itself unusual; it is the way in which the poet's mind habitually deals with images, and the process is partly conscious and partly subconscious. The point that I am trying to make is that Williams's critical approach to Dante is of precisely the same kind as his poetic approach—and the same, no doubt, holds good of all the books listed in his biography as "literary criticism". It is not a scholarly approach at all, and it is not the kind of thing that has any real place in a "history of literature". It is a poet's approach: creative, vital, existential, seminal, timeless—and therefore, in a sense, without perspective. For this reason it is always, quite understandably, a little suspect by purely academic standards, and received with some reserve by those whose view is powerfully influenced by that awareness of historic perspective to which we have grown accustomed. And where Dante is concerned, it is (very naturally) vigorously repudiated by those who are only too anxious to have Dante's experience thrust firmly back into those remote Middle Ages to which they feel it should belong.

Williams's approach to Dante was able to be thus peculiarly intimate, because he shared with him certain kinds of experience —a poetic experience, an experience of romantic love, and (so far as one can tell with either man) a mystical experience of the Affirmative Way—in addition to sharing with him a common religious faith. That combination of shared experience is rare among Dante's interpreters—in fact, I will venture to call it unique. He also shared with him something else, namely, a temperament capable of the experience of Heaven and Hell. It is well to say a few words about this, because it is a matter very liable to misconception. The capacity for joy and the capacity for something like despair tend to be found together; sometimes, as in Williams or Blake, joy appears to predominate and to communicate itself the more readily to the outside world; in others, as in Hopkins or T. S. Eliot, we receive on the whole a stronger impression of the suffering than of the joy. In a few men, as Traherne on the one hand, and James Thomson of *The City of the Dreadful Night*, either the hellish or the heavenly element seems to be almost entirely absent. In Dante's writing, the balance inclines to the side of joy (all the rubbish about the grimness and cruelty and "the poet of Hell" is a piece of Gothic fancy inherited from the eighteenth century); though in his private life one gathers that he was rather reserved and severe except among his intimate friends. Or perhaps he was merely absent-minded, like a good many other people given to very close mental concentration. In general it remains true that a very strong awareness of horror attends upon any very strong awareness of joy. Note that I say "joy", and not "happiness"—they are by no means the same thing. Indeed it would scarcely be untrue to say that people of a happy temperament are seldom capable of joy; they are insufficiently sensitive. The word "joy" is a favourite word with Williams, as is the word "*gioia*" with Dante; beneath the coruscations of that joy, the blackness and squalor of the Pit open, and run down to the centre.

This tension between joy and the opposite of joy is, once again, something that is viewed with a certain distrust by an age committed to the pursuit of happiness. It can be readily pigeonholed as lack of adjustment or, in severe cases, as a psychosis. In very severe cases it may indeed be a psychosis. But we must not disguise from ourselves that happiness is a gift of the heathen gods, whereas joy is a Christian duty. It was, I think, L. P. Jacks who pointed out that the word "happiness" does not occur in the Gospels; the word "joy", on the other hand, occurs frequently —and so does the name and image of Hell. The command is to rejoice: not to display a placid contentment or a stoic fortitude. "Call no man happy until he is dead", said the Greek philosopher; and happiness, whether applied to a man's fortunes or his disposition, is the assessment of something extended in time along his whole career. But joy (except for those saints who live continually in the presence of God) is of its nature brief and almost instantaneous—it is an apprehension of the eternal moment. And, as such, it is the great invading adversary that can break open the gates of Hell. In *Descent into Hell* there are two moments when Wentworth might have saved his soul by accepting what one might call a Dantean vision. The first is a Beatrician moment, the vision of joy.

> There was presented to him at once and clearly an opportunity for joy—casual, accidental joy, but joy. If he could not manage joy, at least he might have managed the intention of joy, or (if that were also too much) an effort towards the intention of joy. The infinity of grace could have been contented and invoked by a mere mental refusal of anything but such an effort.... He

could enjoy; at least he could refuse not to enjoy. He could refuse and reject damnation.

With a perfectly clear, if instantaneous, knowledge of what he did, he rejected joy instead. He instantaneously preferred anger, and at once it came; he invoked envy, and it obliged him.

The second moment is when Wentworth is almost arrested at a much later and lower stage of his descent into the Hell of self-absorption by a simple appeal to his professional integrity. This is the vision of Virgil.

All this may be read, and was perhaps intended by Williams himself, as an imaginative gloss upon two incidents in the *Commedia*. The first is Beatrice's mission to Virgil described in the second canto of the *Inferno*, where she says, "Dante has sunk so far in sin that he can no longer hear my voice—do *you* go and recall him". Later on she says in Dante's own presence:

> "With inspirations, prayer-wrung for his sake,
> Vainly in dreams and other ways as well,
> I called him home; so little did he reck"—

and therefore, she says, she was obliged to send Virgil. These correspond to the two offers of possible salvation, by the way of spiritual joy, and by the way of natural duty. The other incident is the Dream of the Siren, in which Dante's fascinated gaze upon "that ancient witch" who is Lilith and the Succubus, is broken by the Discreet Lady, calling upon Virgil to unmask the Siren and show her for the Hell-born obscenity that she is.

And along with the two passages of the *Commedia*, and the two passages from *Descent into Hell*, we may set the critical comment on the Siren in *The Figure of Beatrice*, in which Williams speaks of the Siren as the false image of Beatrice—Beatrice known in her "opposite identity" of Hell: "If Sloth overtakes Love, Beatrice is lost in the Siren, the romantic Image in the pseudo-romantic mirage." He goes on:

> She [the Siren] has been called the image of Sensual Pleasure, but this (it would seem) need not be the whole significance. She is as much—let us say—Ideal Gratification; all the sighs that lament the imperfection of a man's actual mistress, the verses that sweetly moan over *her* failure to live up to *his* dreams (or the other way round), the self-condolences, the "disillusions"—all these are the Siren's song. She takes flesh and colour and music

within the night-reveries of laziness; she is then—what? what we want; and that is? we do not rightly know, but certainly a Siren and a song.

The Siren is, therefore, the image of the false Joy, and it is significant that in *Descent into Hell* the Succubus appears to Wentworth immediately after his deliberate rejection of the true joy.

We may be inclined to ask: "But is that really what Dante meant? One sees what Williams meant, and one can see how he contrived to extract it from Dante's words. But is not this merely a reading into the text of subtleties which a mediaeval poet could never have thought of?" The only answer we can well make is something which Williams himself saw and pointed out: the appearance of the Siren and the opening words of her song are a deliberate echo, and almost a parody, of the subsequent appearance and words of Beatrice. In the dream, Dante *gazes* upon the Siren until she becomes beautiful and "puts on the hues of love", and then she sings: "*Io son . . . io son dolce serena*—I am, I am the sweet siren." Beatrice, appearing, veiled, to Dante in the Sacred Forest, addresses him: "*Guardaci ben! ben sem, ben sem Beatrice*—Look on us well, we are, we are Beatrice." Once again we have Dante's trick of the corresponding and contrasting images. We must be prepared, I think, to believe that supreme artists do not produce these elaborate symmetries by accident.

Thus we return to the point from which we set out—the peculiar quality of Williams's interpretation of Dante, and the reason why it offends some people as much as it delights others. To say that it offends by being Christian is a great part of the truth, but it is not the whole truth.

You will perhaps have noticed that criticism today tends to divide itself into two schools, which (as usually happens in such cases) diverge as they develop. One, of which we have already spoken, may be called the historical school; and its attitude may be roughly but not altogether unfairly summed up by saying that it considers a poet's meaning to have been important in his own day, but to be of no importance to us except as a part of the historical perspective. This is the more academic and scholarly kind of criticism; and its great virtue is that it does oblige us to consider what the poet's language actually meant to himself and his contemporaries.

There is, however, another school, which may be called the school of interpretative criticism. This pays very little attention to what the poet himself, or his contemporary readers, may have thought he meant; it is almost exclusively concerned with the psychological symbolisms and overtones which we can contrive to extract from it. The great virtue of this school is that it does demand some kind of contemporary relevance and so keeps the work of the past present to us as a living force; its weakness is that its interpretations become purely arbitrary—they cease, as C. S. Lewis has said, to be "right" or "wrong" and become more or less brilliant executive "performances": variations, so to speak, upon a theme suggested by the poet's words. This kind of interpretation is by no means new: it is in fact almost exactly the way in which the allegorists used to treat biblical texts. What Isaiah or Daniel intended to say about contemporary Israel was discarded or ignored in favour of the mystical or moral significations which might be put upon it for the purpose of Christian devotion.

Now, both these methods of criticism are perfectly legitimate, and indeed indispensable, so far as they go. But you will have noticed that they have one thing in common: Both alike, although for quite opposite reasons, dispense us from any obligation to take the poet's meaning seriously. If his language is sufficiently ambiguous to mean almost anything, we can give it our own meaning, and this does not matter. If his language, like Dante's, makes his meaning as unambiguous as it is unwelcome, we can shut him up firmly in the prison of the past and, because it is of the past, his meaning does not matter.

Now, to my mind—and I am not alone—any critical method which altogether nullifies the poet's belief and intention is bad for criticism and bad for poetry. A writer in the *Sunday Times*, in reviewing Stephen Spender's *The Making of a Poem*, has observed: "Despite the blandishments of Dr. I. A. Richards, poets can neither regard the beliefs of dead poets as pseudo-statements, nor themselves exist on psychologically valuable delusions." Poets themselves desire and need a different kind of criticism, which shall allow them not only, in Middleton Murry's words, "to mean what they say", but to go on meaning it.

Charles Williams's criticism is of this kind. He is, a poet in criticism—a poet's critic. Of this kind of critic Dante has hitherto had too few; and that is why *The Figure of Beatrice* and the other books seem to me to usher in a new era of Dante-criticism. But, since this kind of criticism undermines the assumptions of both the fashionable schools of criticism, we can scarcely be surprised if it is received in some quarters with hostility and contempt. And all the more so because the meaning which it thus drags out to confront us from the cage of the past and the decent mufflings of psychologically valuable delusion is a Christian meaning. For Christianity also rests upon the assumption that the Word uttered in the past meant something then and means the same thing now. There is an unseemliness about the Easter appearances of something that has no business to be alive. We cannot really be surprised if some people find it more comfortable to sit down to a quiet, objective, laboratory examination of the grave clothes.

APPENDIX

Stephen Spender: *The Making of a Poem*

If you have not as yet read this book of Spender's, I most strongly urge you to do so. The first two essays in particular throw a most revealing light upon the situation of the poet in the contemporary world, and are curiously tinged with resentment against the "advanced" type of critic, hailing (this is Spender's identification, not mine) from "Cambridge, Eng. and Mass."

I can only quote now a few short passages which bear more or less directly upon our subject. His thesis is summed up in this reaction to I. A. Richards's statement that modern poetry must learn to exist "in a complete severance from all beliefs":

> When the poet abandons the belief which connects visible with invisible worlds, he is left with nothing but a problem of adjustment through poetry to the situation of man in the surroundings of alien nature. He is in a cage with bars that are mirrors reflecting only himself, and there is no possibility of entering through the imagination into the factual realities outside.

In other words, Spender sees the poet shut up with the Siren— the projection of his own desires. And here we may remember

Virgil's dry little scholastic statement, in the Discourse on Love in *Purg.* xviii, that love is excited "by the apprehension of some *real fact*"—it is directed, that is, to something actually existing outside the self—to a *real other*. In the absence of the real other, there is only the projected image, the mirror-bars of the cage.

Spender notes "the attempts of the poets, in the cage, to find—even within the cage—an *unconditioned centre*". He adds:

> After the collapse of the attempts to put poetry back into the symbolism of creeds or politics, and even make it an alternative religion or way of life, we now find poets accepting the idea that the imagination has no autonomy, is completely conditioned by circumstances. Writing and criticism have become closed systems, and it is considered bad taste to relate the work that is written back to the view of life from which the writer's attitude derives. Yet unless the questions and answers on which the present attitude is based are reopened, poetry will not find a way out of its cage.

He goes on to speak of poets like Blake, Wordsworth and Yeats, "who expressed in their poetry mystical experiences which they believed to be true and to which they bore witness":

> Now (he says) to accept or interpret all such statements as being only "psychologically true", is to understand them in a sense the opposite that in which they were intended. The effect of this kind of acceptance of the past on terms which those who lived then would regard as their rejection, may be justified by science, but to the poetic mind, which has its own kind of literalness, it is an extremely dubious proceeding. There is always the danger of turning the present into a kind of prison of our own science and ideologies and analyses where every idea that enters from outside is doctored and treated with our modern medicine that renders it—in its own, historic terms—meaningless....
>
> Thus the situation envisaged by I. A. Richards is one in which the poet finds himself shut out from God and the past, and inside the cage of contemporary attitudes.

In another paragraph, Spender is in almost exact agreement with C. S. Lewis in his Cambridge Inaugural: "The really important distinction today is not between different creeds but believing and not believing."

This testimony seems to me extremely important, and especially because nobody can dismiss it as Christian propaganda.

Spender is not a Christian, though he observes, sympathetically, that many of his leading poetic contemporaries are—he instances Eliot, Auden, and Dylan Thomas. It is as a poet, not as a Christian, that he experiences the desperate situation of the contemporary poet, caged up *incommunicado*, and he is specific in laying a good part of the responsibility at the door of the modern academic schools of criticism.

CHAPTER V

ON TRANSLATING THE *DIVINA COMMEDIA*

ANY TRANSLATOR OF Dante is nowadays in an awkward position. Hundreds of translations have already appeared—in prose, in blank verse, in *terza rima*, in blank *terza rima*, in octosyllabic *terza rima*, in heroic couplets, in Spenserian stanzas, in Marvellian quatrains, and I know not what besides. If he supposes that he is going to surpass all his predecessors, he is in danger of appearing a presumptuous ass. If he modestly admits that he cannot surpass them, then he *is* a presumptuous ass— since what reason, except an overweening personal vanity, can he possibly have for demanding that the world should buy and read an inferior version which has no recommendation except that it is his?

There is, however, one consideration which a little reduces the apparent presumption of every new attempt at translating the *Commedia*. No translation of any great classic can ever in the nature of things be definitive; for each one necessarily takes some colour from the age in which it is written, and to that extent falsifies its original. As time goes on, it becomes dated and alien; we cannot now read Pope's *Iliad* without feeling the English eighteenth century descend like a thick curtain between us and Homer's Greece; that which was transparent to Pope's contemporaries is opaque to us. For this reason, all great works should be retranslated from time to time, lest we should have to wrestle with two strange frames of discourse instead of one.

But this is not all. It is in the nature of things impossible that any translation should give us the *whole* of the original work, especially if that work is a poem. Something, somewhere, is always lost, modified, to some extent travestied in passing from one language to the other. A prose-translation, however literally exact, loses, precisely, the rhythmic enchantment of the verse; a verse-translation not only is bound to be less verbally exact but also alters the original rhythms. No translation can be identical with its original; it takes colour from the age, the language and the personality of the translator. There is, therefore, always room for a new one, for there is always the chance that some value previously sacrificed may, this time, be salvaged, some emphasis readjusted, some unintentional distortion straightened out.

I do not propose to lead you, yet again, over the trampled battle-field of *a priori* argument about what the aims of a good translation should be: whether to be verbally exact and no more; or to write the kind of poem the writer would have written in his own age if he had happened to live in our country, or (on the other hand) what he would have written if he were writing in our country today; whether to try to reproduce the effect produced by the original on the original readers, or the effect produced on our own contemporaries by reading the original now; whether to preserve a foreign flavour in idiom and metre, or to aim simply at writing a readable work in our native idiom and native rhythm. Life is short; and, to tell you the truth, any translator is lucky if he can live up to a quarter of his own theory. What he usually does is to grapple with his task as best he can; then read up the rival theories; and finally construct a theory of his own to explain and defend his practice. In this spirit I will deal with these and other problems only as one encounters them, in practice, when trying to translate the *Divine Comedy*.

Now, the translation on which I am at present engaged is aimed, very particularly, at reaching the "common reader". That is its chief excuse for existing. I must begin by admitting that this country is not, nowadays, very conscious (as we say) of Dante. Things have changed a great deal since the last century, when England was the nursing-mother of a very great tradition of Dante scholarship. At that time also, Italian was the "second language" which nearly all well-educated young women studied at home or in their finishing schools in addition to French; while their brothers, well grounded in Latin, found little difficulty in learning to speak and read Italian when the time came for them to travel abroad, as most of them did, in vacation or on leaving the university, to see the sights and the picture-galleries and obtain a little knowledge of the world. For those who could not afford such expensive educational luxuries, but who realized that some acquaintance with Dante was fashionable, there were various translations, of which incomparably the best-known was that of H. F. Cary. He was the first great English "vulgariser" of Dante, who translated him into the Miltonic blank verse which was, in his time, the recognized medium for any long and important English narrative poem. You may say that right up to the last few decades of the century, when the Brownings and Rossettis were writing, and every one was following with great excitement the fortunes of the Italian *risorgimento*, all decently educated persons of the upper and middle classes could be counted on to take an intelligent interest in Dante, or at least not to look perfectly blank at the mention of his name. And in most of their houses you would find the volumes of the *Commedia*, either in Italian or in English, very often handsomely illustrated with Flaxman's refined copper-plates or with the more modern, moving and theatrical steel-engravings of the ever-popular Doré.

As for the lower-middle class and the workers, they did not count in this connection. They were wrestling with education at a more primitive level; and it was sufficiently laudable in them to be able to read English, and to throng the galleries of the Lyceum and the Old Vic to see the plays of Shakespeare.

But already by the middle of the century the cultural swing-over from Italian to German had begun; and by the date of my own schooldays it was complete. We had all heard of Dante; but we read Goethe and Schiller. Already the two great movements to which Dante had been a living inspiration—the Romantic movement in literature and the Tractarian movement in the Church of England—were losing their original impetus and developing into new forms and other activities. Already the new interest in the sciences was beginning to oust the Humanities from school and university. And already the improvement of the general level of education among the working classes was releasing into the literary world a vast mass of book-hungry readers whose appetites were not ruled by any of the traditional canons of civilized taste. Fifty years of social development and two catastrophic wars have increased and accelerated these changes. The gulf between 1854 and 1954 is perhaps as wide a gulf as was ever spanned by a single century.

We are, in fact, faced in England today with an enormous new reading public—literate, but not (in the old sense of the word) educated; eagerly and indeed anxiously interested in religious questions, but for the most part very incompletely instructed in the Christian faith; internationally minded, but mostly ignorant of any language but their own; haunted by social problems, but with little historical sense, and cut off by the bias of their education from that heritage of Mediterranean culture which, as late even as my own youth, every middle-class child sucked in instinctively with its mother's milk; and moreover—let us face it —perennially short of time, leisure and money. It is to people like these, ranging from boys and girls in the upper forms, through university students of all types, to the intelligent suburban housewife and office-worker who snatch their culture at odd moments—at lunch, in the train, or on such evenings at home as are not taken up with television—that it is the translator's task to present the most profound, the most subtle, the most civilized, the most Catholic, the most intellectual and the most exalted of all Christian poets—perhaps of all poets without qualification : a poet whose living voice is made inaudible to them by an alien language, an alien cosmology, and six intervening centuries of religious and political confusion.

The Penguin *Dante* is, I think, the first attempt ever made to introduce the *Commedia*, in English verse and with a full critical apparatus, to a vast multitude of "ordinary readers", having only a few shillings to spend, and having for the most part *no* knowledge whatever of Catholic theology, scholastic philosophy, Classical mythology, Italian mediaeval history, Ptolemaic astronomy, the theory of courtly love, or any of the thousand-and-one things that go to make up Dante's "cultural background"— readers to whom the mere skill of reading and interpreting allegory is almost a lost art. The forerunner which comes nearest to it in respect of cheapness is the Temple Classics edition : but this is actually an Italian text with an English prose crib, and its notes, which are brief and condensed almost to crabbedness, presuppose a reader to whom the background is reasonably familiar. Other, more modern, versions, such as Laurence Binyon's *terza rima* version (which offers practically no critical help at all), or J. D. Sinclair's admirably annotated prose translation, also print the Italian along with the English and in consequence of this, and of their dignified but expensive format, work out at about a guinea a cantica—and three guineas is far more than the average student or casual reader is able or willing to pay.

Such, then, is our task. Somehow we have to capture this elusive and ill-prepared "common reader", and persuade him or her to embark on a 14,000 line poem by a writer six hundred years dead, of whom all that is generally known is that he has a great reputation for obscurity, believed that the sun went round the earth, and took a vindictive delight in describing the torments of a physical Hell in which no enlightened person now believes.

Two things, obviously, we have to do. We must write readable English. It does not matter how accurate we are, or how copious and helpful our commentary, if the first few pages of the text are so hopelessly cumbersome and dull as to extinguish all desire to go farther. And we must contrive that something—it cannot be all—but *something* of Dante's quality shall come over; something of his spare and sinewy strength, his astonishing speed and drive, his salty and astringent humour, his curious mixture of extreme simplicity and intellectual subtlety, and even something perhaps (Heaven help us) of his lyrical sweetness and his towering ecstasy of song.

Our translation, if it is to do anything for the present generation in England, must be made, not *merely* to please the translator (though it must spring spontaneously from his joy in the work), nor *merely* to content Italian scholars (though it must submit itself to their criticism and hope to win their approval). Like Dante's own writings it must address itself to those who, *per malvagia disusanza del mondo,* are only literate in the modern sense, and not in Dante's sense *litterati*; and of whom he rightly says that there are many noble souls, *non solamente maschi ma femmine, che sono molti e molte in questa lingua, volgari e non litterati.*[1] And we must hope that by now charity has enabled him to set aside his notorious dislike of translators; for even in his lifetime he learned condescension; and he that had once boasted that there would be few to understand his great odes, humbled himself to write of the sublimities in the tongue that cries *babbo* and *mamma,* and to ask the reader's forgiveness if he was sometimes unintentionally obscure.

So now we come to our task; and the first question is: Shall

[1] *Convivio* I, ix, 5, Buonelli and Vandelli, 1934, p. 58.

we use prose or verse? If our translation were intended to assist people to read Dante in Italian, my vote would be for prose every time: as verbally exact as is consistent with writing intelligible English. With the help of a sound crib, any intelligent person who is able to decline *mensa* could learn to read Dante's Italian in a month. But since our educators, in their wisdom, have thought it well to make life ten times more difficult for scientist and humanist alike by driving the Latin grammar out of the schools, there are, as we have seen, a very great many people who will never tackle Dante at all except in an English version. And for these, although prose is the soft option, yet in my opinion it sacrifices too much to a superficial simplicity. Too much of the characteristic quality is lost. To give these readers even the faintest idea of what Dante is like, I think we must use verse and, if verse, then Dante's own *terza rima*. Dante uses his verse-form so brilliantly to drive home his meaning, carries his narrative along so swiftly on the flowing rhyme-linked stanza, makes such epigrammatic play with rhyme-scheme and ternary structure to isolate and emphasize his points as he goes along, that his form and matter are as indissolubly three-in-one as the Trinitarian Persons and Substance in whose honour he is thought to have invented the *terza rima* itself. The articulation of the original anatomy shows awkwardly through any prose version, and prevents it from reading naturally; blank verse, or, *a fortiori*, any stanza that does not naturally divide the sense where the *terza rima* divides it, dislocates the rhythmical structure.

Neither is there, I maintain, any good reason for avoiding *terza rima* in English. The usual argument about the scarcity of rhymes will not do—it would apply even more forcibly to the Spenserian stanza and to *ottava rima*, both of which have always been perfectly at home in English. And the *terza rima* itself has been successfully handled by many English poets, from Shelley and Morris to Browning and Bridges, though usually with a freer over-running of line and stanza than Dante is accustomed to use. And fortunately there is no difficulty about the metre. There are certain metres, such as the classical hexameter and the French alexandrine, whose effect remains stubbornly recalcitrant to any attempt to reproduce it in English verse. But the English heroic line of five stresses corresponds, in its main structure, almost exactly to the Italian hendecasyllable—as is not altogether surprising, since it derives mainly from Italian models.

Terza rima, then, is our choice, and handled as far as possible as Dante handles it.

So far as Dante is concerned, we may dismiss the idea of writing the poem he would have written had he been a contemporary Englishman. This would involve using an idiom and vocabulary about fifty years older than Chaucer: a task which I, for one, am not qualified to perform, even if my readers were inclined to take the trouble of reading it. We may also dismiss the idea of writing the poem that Dante would have written if he had been a twentieth-century Englishman, and, along with it, the attempt to produce on twentieth-century English readers the same effect that Dante produced on fourteenth-century Italians. We do not know precisely what that effect was, but we can guess. For if Dante had been writing here and now, he would not be writing about Jacopo Rusticucci, Forese Donati, Arnaut Daniel and Pope Boniface VIII, but about Queen Victoria, Hitler, James Joyce, Lord Northcliffe, William Temple and Little Tich; and our sensations on finding such personages as these either roasting in Hell, toiling round the cornices of Purgatory or glowing like living flames in the company of St. Peter, St. Thomas Aquinas and Judas Maccabaeus—all according to the unpredictable taste and fancy of the poet—would have a peculiar poignancy about them which no straight translator of the mediaeval text can very well hope to recapture. Exciting Dante is—perhaps the most exciting narrative poet who ever drove a quill—but to write as he would have written today would involve a drastic reconstruction of the whole edifice of the *Comedy* from top to bottom. It would be fun to do—though rather dangerous fun. I have myself sometimes dallied with the notion of an *Inferno Revisited,* in which the Lake of Ordure in which the Flatterers are plunged should be found undergoing repairs and extensions on a large scale in order to accommodate the hordes of propagandists, journalists and advertisers who have been tumbling into it at so rapid a rate since Dante first surveyed it. But one could scarcely call that kind of thing translation.

The argument about idiom and rhythm is more delicate. There is the question of period and the question of locality. A consistent archaism is, I believe, not only irritating to the reader, but also false in a material respect to the original; for it is almost bound to impart an atmosphere of quaintness and Wardour Street—an atmosphere about as foreign to Dante as anything well could be. A thoroughgoing up-to-the-minute modernism, on the other hand, is going to clash most horribly with the content of the poem: you cannot suitably expound Ptolemaic astronomy, or conduct long scholastic arguments, whose mere presentation and structure are period-stamped in every line, in the idiom of Hollywood, or even of a *Times* leader; there will be a continual and disastrous fight between form and substance. In my own practice, I have given myself a pretty free hand, excluding at one end the wholly obsolete and at the other the merely slangy and ephemeral; and indeed it will be found that not only the exigencies of rhyme and metre, but also the variations in Dante's own style, demand that one should not restrict too severely the choice of available words. The rule I have followed—in so far as I have a rule—is to keep the more modern forms for the colloquial passages and the more noble, ancient and poetic forms for passages in the "grand manner", and hope that, in Dante's rapid transitions from the one to the other, the mixture may not slop over too incongruously. It is comforting to realize that in this one is only following Dante's own example. He, too, uses provincial words, nonsense words, nursery words, and phrases which the pundits of the eighteenth century stigmatized as "barbarous", alongside with elaborate Latinisms of vocabulary and syntax which, it must be remembered, were for him (since Latin is simply ancient Italian) the equivalent of what, for us, is archaism and Elizabethan English.

Finally, the question of locality—of *foreignness*: should we try to imitate the Italian rhythm in English, or should we try to reproduce by means native to English verse the emotional effect which the Italian verse makes by its own native means? This is a very fascinating technical problem. Indeed, if one studies it too much one may become too deeply fascinated, and end by writing something that is not so much a readable English poem as a metrical exercise which only technicians can enjoy. Professor Bickersteth has argued eloquently in defence of the "Italianizing" manner adopted by Laurence Binyon in his translation of the *Commedia*. He says:

> Now it would seem clear that if, by aiming at the highest level of translation, the English translator wishes to make the move-

ment of his verses no less Dantesque than their tone, he should go to all extremes that his ear allows and his metre does not absolutely forbid in admitting frequently into his rendering of the Italian any of those rhythms which, common there, are less common, or even unusual, in English. And this is precisely what Mr. Binyon has done. His translation of the *Inferno* will from time to time seem to play daring tricks with the metre, his rhythms to pile up their accents, pause, hesitate and then run on in a fashion strange and at first perhaps puzzling to the English ear; but read each sentence with the precise phrasing the translator intends, place the emphasis where the meaning of the original intends it to fall, and comparison with the Italian will show you that the translator is moving with Dante's movement and yet nowhere disobeying the laws of English prosody.[1]

He chooses for his example a very fine terzain from Binyon's translation of the fifth canto of the *Inferno*:

> I came into a place of all light dumb
> That bellows like a storm in the sea-deep
> When the thwart winds that strike it roar and hum—

and points out how faithfully it follows the accent and rhythm of the original:

> Io venni in luogo d'ogni luce muto,
> che mugghia come fa mar per tempesta,
> se da contrari venti è combattuto.
> > *Inf.* v. 28–30.

The critical test of the Italianate method comes, of course, as Professor Bickersteth well recognizes, over those rhythms which are, as he says, "common in Italian, and less common or even unusual, in English"—in particular the line which has a caesura after the fourth or fifth syllable, and ends either with a strong dactylic rhythm, or with an accent on the seventh syllable. Famous examples of these in Milton are, of the first:

> Burned after them/down to the bottomless pit.

and of the second:

> Light from above/from the fountain of light.

Now, the point is that these rhythms are, precisely, so common in

[1] "On Translating Dante," the third Herford Memorial Lecture delivered by Professor G. L. Bickersteth before the Manchester Dante Society, publ. by Sherratt & Hughes, Manchester, 1934, of which see p. 35.

Italian that you could pick a handful of them from any canto of the *Comedy* chosen at random; but in English so rare that our poets use them only for special effects. There is no doubt at all that the translator is perfectly justified in using them, if he thinks fit, *for* special effects—that is, after the English manner. Indeed, one great fault of the average nineteenth-century translator of Dante (usually a conscientious scholar but an uninspired poet) is the deadly monotony of his impeccably regular rhythm. Take, for example, the passage quoted above as it appears in the version of the Rev. Ichabod Wright. (He is using, not *terza rima*, but a stanza rhymed a b a, c b c—but that does not affect the matter in hand):

> Throughout the place speaks not the light of heaven;
> And the vast region bellows loud and deep,
> As when o'er ocean warring winds are driven.

The tempest roars like any sucking-dove.

But it is perhaps questionable whether, if we try to make a rhythm which is, admittedly, rare in English, as common in the English version as it is in the Italian, we shall not end by disintegrating the verse completely, and producing an effect of strain and oddity which is quite absent from the original. If the greatest English poets have been cautious of introducing the dactylic close and the accented seventh into their verse, it is perhaps because they were good judges of what their own language would stand.

Italians have made kindly fun of the enthusiastic English Dantist, crying in his barbarous accent:

"Dolchy collar d'óriental záffiro! What melody! what beauty!"

And I must admit that when I find Binyon rendering this exquisite, lingering and (as I freely confess) untranslatable line in the very rhythm of that, let us hope, apocryphal Englishman:

> "Tender colour of orient sapphire",

I have my doubts whether Dante's effect is being even approximately got over—not to say whether such a line can really pass itself off as an English five-foot line; especially as it is necessary for its unstressed final syllable to rhyme with "choir". And when we find, only one terzain away, a passage containing yet another dactylic close, with *two* unstressed rhymes, I am fairly sure that the constitution of English verse does not take kindly to frequent doses of this rather drastic stimulant:

> The planet that promoteth Love was there,
>   Making all the East to laugh and be joyful,
>   And veiled the Fishes that escorted her.
>
> I turned to the right and contemplated all
>   The other pole; and four stars o'er me came,
>   Never yet seen save by the first people.
>   *Purg.* i. 19–24.

Let me say at once that I am all for the translator's availing himself of the widest possible liberty in the way of rhyme: half-rhyme, eye-rhyme, cockney rhyme, feminine rhyme, unaccented rhyme, and so on, that he likes to give himself. The frigid perfection of Augustan rhyme, end-stopping every line with a heavy thump on the last syllable, and necessitating a continual reiteration of trees and breeze, mountain and fountain, love and dove, was threatening to bind up English verse in chains and iron when Tennyson and the Romantics mercifully came to unshackle it and restore it to the liberty of tradition. And I would rather a thousand times have approximate rhymes than approximate meaning—and in translating Dante into *terza rima* one must continually choose between the one and the other. If you are going to rhyme the last syllable of "joyful" or "people" with anything, it may as well be with "all" as with "wool" or "bull". It is not the rhyme I am objecting to, but the cramming of so many metrical oddities into so short a passage, so that the lines limp. (I may say that, in this case, there is no particular justification for eccentricity in the Italian, whose rhythm is here iambic and perfectly straightforward.) Clarity, serenity, and repose are demanded in this passage by the general tone of the verse, which here describes Dante's first sight of the tranquil skies of Purgatory as he emerges from the squalid gloom and stink of Hell; and an evenness and lucidity of metrical structure are surely appropriate here, just as metrical irregularity was appropriate to the whirling blast of the infernal circle of the Lustful.

It is perhaps only fair that, having criticized Binyon and disagreed with Bickersteth, I should now present my own version of the passages under discussion. Of the first I am not particularly proud; it is not better than Binyon's, and may be worse.

The point is that it goes about getting the uproar of the wind in a different way—not by Italianizing but by Anglicizing the metre—using, that is, a metrical trick which is quite common in English but impossible in Italian, and which is best summed up in the limerick about—was it the Young Man of Japan?—who said it was his principle "always to get as many words into the last line as I possibly can":

> A place made dumb of every glimmer of light,
> Which bellows like tempestuous ocean birling
> In the batter of a two-way wind's buffet and fight.

The *Purgatorio* passage has more merit:

> Colour unclouded, orient-sapphirine,
> Softly suffusing from meridian height
> Down the still sky to the horizon-line,
>
> Brought to my eyes renewal of delight
> So soon as I came forth from that dead air
> Which had oppressed my bosom and my sight.
>
> The lovely planet, love's own quickener,
> Now lit to laughter all the eastern sky,
> Veiling the Fishes that attended her.
>
> Right-hand I turned, and, setting me to spy
> That alien pole, beheld four stars, the same
> The first men saw, and since, no living eye;
>
> Meseemed the heavens exulted in their flame—
> O widowed world beneath the northern Plough,
> For ever famished of the sight of them!

I have carried on the quotation to the following terzain for the pleasure of pointing out one of those small niceties which are at once the translator's despair and his delight. The Italian has:

> Oh settentrional vedovo sito,

which every translator renders quite simply: "O widowed Northern clime." But *settentrional*, the ordinary Italian word for Northern, means by etymology "under the septentrion"—the constellation which we call the Plough, or the Wain; and in the very next stanza, Dante goes on to say that he now turns and looks towards "the other pole"—that is, the northern part of the sky, from which, since they are now at the Antipodes, the familiar Wain has vanished. This imparts a quite special significance to the word "*settentrional*", which in English one can only bring out by mentioning the constellation, and so dragging to the surface the astronomical meaning which, though obscured by daily use, is still alive beneath the merely cartographical surface-meaning of the Italian word. I do not, of course, suggest that Dante need *consciously* have thought about this hidden derivational meaning—though it may have been vaguely present to his mind, since later in the poem he speaks of the "Septentrion of the First Heaven" and deliberately compares it to the Wain. But it is more probable that here the language itself did for him, unconsciously, what English can do only by a conscious paraphrase. We may compare the effect of the English title of Spengler's book, *The Decline of the West*—a flat statement devoid of overtones—with the rich emotive suggestiveness of the original—again the common German words for "decline" and "West"—*Der Untergang des Abendlandes*: The Going-Down of the Evening-land.

This is a digression, which, however, serves to illustrate one of the most fascinating things about Dante. He has been called a "miser of words", because he never wastes a word, nor uses a word idly. This means that to bring out the full implication of what he says, we often need to use a periphrasis, or an amplification—a fact which has considerable bearing upon the vexed question of "padding", to which I hope to come later on. But I should like first to add something to what we have been saying about Italian verse-rhythm.

There is one modification of the normal verse-stress which Dante uses from time to time for special effects, and which is very startling indeed to the English ear—so startling that neither Binyon, nor Bickersteth, nor so far as I know any English translator has so far ventured to reproduce it. This is the sudden intrusion of a line or passage running to the lilt of

Diddle-diddle-dumpling, my son John.

It occurs, for instance, in the first line of *Purgatorio* vi— "*Quando si parte il gioco della zara*", and (again as an isolated line) in the notorious opening of *Inferno* xxii—"*quando con trombe, e quando con campane*"; and in *Purgatorio* iv it occurs again, running over two lines and leading to a whole line of anapaests:

> Vassi in Sanleo e discendesi in Noli,
>   montasi su Bismantova in cacume
>   con esso i piè; ma qui convien ch'om voli.
> *Purg.* iv. 25–27.

These are all comic, or semi-comic passages. In *Inferno* xxv we get a whole terzain and more of it—used here to suggest the flickering speed of a running lizard.

> Come 'l ramarro sotto la gran fersa
>   dei dì canicular, cangiando sepe,
>   folgore par se la via attraversa.
> *Inf.* xxv. 79–81.

Here, I must admit that I have been tempted to experiment. The metrical pull of the English verse-stress is so powerful that it is almost impossible to get into this rhythm and out again to normal in the course of three lines, without inflicting an intolerable shock on the reader. I have therefore not attempted to use it in the *Inferno* xxii passage; but in *Purgatorio* vi, where it begins the canto, I have made a shot at it, easing it back to normal by way of a neutral kind of line which might scan either way:

> The loser at the hazard, when the game breaks up,
>   Sadder and sorrier lingers on alone,
>   Re-plays each throw, and drinks of wisdom's cup.

In the *Purgatorio* iv passage, I have used it again, resolving it into anapaests as in the original, and here I have eased it in at the beginning with a line of indeterminate scansion in the preceding terzain. I will give the whole context, so as to show the final resolution of the anapaests also into the norm. It will be noticed that the rhythm swings continually between iamb and anapaest for several stanzas—as indeed it does also in the Italian —before it settles down.

> Often the labourer fills a gap more wide
>   With a little forkful of thorns, when the purple dye
>   Darkens upon the grape toward vintage-tide,

> A wider gap than the cleft my guide and I,
>   He first, I after him, had to climb alone
>   When that flock left us, bidding us good-bye.
>
> You can mount up to San Leo, or to Noli scramble down,
>   You can tackle tall Bismantova and clamber to the top
>   On your two flat feet; but this way has to be flown;
>
> You must fly with the plumes, I mean, and be lifted up
>   On the wings of desire, still following at the back
>   Of that great leader who gave to me light and hope.
>
> So in we went and up through the stony crack,
>   Wedged either side between the rock-walls sheer,
>   Needing both hands and feet to grip the track.
>
> And when we had scaled the cranny and got out clear
>   At the high cliff's top on the slope of the open hill:
>   "Master," said I, "where do we go from here?"
>
> And he: "Let not one foot fall back, but still
>   Follow on up the mountain...."

The rhythm of:

> "Master," said I, "where do we go from here?"

is almost identical with that of:

> "Maestro mio," diss' io, "che via faremo?"

except that, in the Italian, this last lingering skip of the anapaest is emphasized by an interior rhyme.

The passage from the *Inferno*, on the other hand, is intended by Dante to supply a violent contrast between the slow, dazed movement of the thief who has been changed into a kind of half-human, half-reptilian monstrosity and the swift darting of the lizard. Accordingly, I have here not softened the shock, but let the metre rip:

> All former forms wholly extinct in it,
>   The perverse image—both at once and neither—
>   Reeled slowly out of sight on languid feet.
>
> And just as a lizard, with a quick, slick slither,
>   Flicks across the highway from hedge to hedge,
>   Fleeter than a flash, in the battering dog-day weather,

> A fiery little monster, livid, in a rage,
> Black as any peppercorn...

The excitement diddle-diddle-dumples over two normal Italian lines, picks up the Italian rhythm again in the last line of this terzain:

> livido e nero come gran di pepe

and subsides, suitably, at the moment when the "little monster", having stung its victim, drops from him to the ground.

This revolutionary experiment, then, I have tried, as also the resolution into anapaests which is as common in English as it is in Italian. But I am not certain whether Italianization is wise in every case. Here, for example, is an instance in whch I have not yet made up my mind—a famous pitfall in which innumerable translators have come to grief—the account in *Paradiso* xi of the calling of the first Franciscans. Here is the plain English prose of it:

> So that the venerable Bernard first cast off his
> shoes (*si scalzò*) and ran to follow so great peace,
> and, running, thought he was all too slow.
>
> O wealth untold, O fertile good! Egidius casts
> off his shoes, so too Sylvester, following the
> bridegroom, so doth the bride delight them.
>   *Par.* xi. 79–84.

Longfellow, in his blank terzains (to take an example at random) translates:

> So much so that the venerable Bernard
>   First bared his feet, and after so great peace
>   Ran, and, in running, thought himself too slow.
>
> O wealth unknown! O veritable[1] good!
>   Giles bares his feet, and bares his feet Sylvester
>   Behind the bridegroom, so doth please the bride!

The difficulty here is the verb *scalzare*, to throw off one's shoes, for which the only one-word English equivalent would be "to discalce one's self"—a rare and awkward word, recalcitrant to verse. As Miss Alice Curtayne remarks, in the course of a ferocious attack on all verse-translations of Dante, "this 'baring of

[1] Reading *verace*, where others read *ferace*.

the feet'... is altogether too leisurely a process. It suggests the action of a man preparing for a bath, and not all the tumultuous haste of the men who ran along the streets of Assisi after Francis".[1] The really crucial line is the fifth. Here Cary has:

> Egidius bares him next, and next Sylvester,

Binyon:

> Barefoot goes Giles, barefoot Sylvester, toward
> The bridegroom, following him: so charms the bride.

Bickersteth has:

> Giles bares his feet, his feet Sylvester bares.

Nor must we forget the calamity of the unfortunate Anderson, usually a very sound and sometimes an excellent translator, who disastrously allowed himself to write:

> Giles bares his feet, Sylvester his behind
> The bridegroom,...

"Let it stand", says Miss Curtayne, venomously, "as a warning against English *terza rima* renderings of Dante." I do not know why she says that. It is the kind of accident that might happen to anybody, even in prose.

But now listen to the Italian:

> tanto che 'l venerabile Bernardo
> si scalzò prima, e dietro a tanta pace
> corse e, correndo, li parve esser tardo.
>
> O ignota richezza! o ben ferace!
> Scalzasi Egidio, scalzasi Silvestro
> dietro allo sposo, sì la sposa piace.

"Scalzasi Egidio, scalzasi Silvestro"—it is our old friend the diddle-diddle-dumpling, heavily reinforced with sibilants; a sound as of people madly shuffling off their shoes in the changing-room before rushing out on to the running-track.

Now, there is nothing whatever in the English language to prevent one from reproducing this effect exactly, both as to metre and alliteration, if one likes, and is not deterred by

[1] *A Recall to Dante*, 1932, p. 144.

108   THE POETRY OF SEARCH AND STATEMENT

convention and a misplaced hankering for the "grand manner". One can, for example, say this:

> The venerable Bernard first threw off
> His shoes and ran, and thought himself too slow
> Running to so great peace with so great love.
>
> O wealth untold! O fertile gold! for lo,
> Sylvester, Egidius, cast aside their shoes now,
> Following the groom, the bride delights them so!
>
> Father and master, he his way pursues now,
> With him his lady and his family
> Girt with the humble cord that each endues now.

(I have run on into the next terzain, lest anybody should object that there are no conceivable rhymes to "shoes now".)

But it would be equally possible, instead of directly imitating the Italianate scansion, to get a similar effect of speed and excitement by means more native to the English five-foot line, thus:

> O wealth untold! O fertile gold! For lo,
> Sylvester, Giles, they fling off their shoes, they fly
> To follow the groom, the bride delights them so.
>
> This father and this master, see him hie
> On with his lady and his household too,
> Corded already with humility.

I have dwelt rather long on this question of metre and rhythm, because it is important, and because it leads me up to the point where I can catalogue a few of the qualities which, to me, seem indispensable in any rendering of Dante. Binyon says: "A melodious smoothness is not the characteristic of Dante's verse so much as an extraordinary fullness and volume."[1] That is doubtless true; but what strikes *me* most forcibly about it is neither of these things but its speed and versatility. The first thing that his translator must at all costs avoid is slowness, stiffness or dullness; and the second is monotony. The sheer pace of Dante's narrative is astonishing; and he can run in a few consecutive lines the full gamut of the grandiose, the lyrical, the staggeringly simple, the colloquial, the high-comedy and the coarse. It is far better to err on the side of exaggerating the

[1] *Dante's Inferno*, 1933, p. viii.

variety of his style than to allow a misplaced reverence for a sublime poet or a religious subject to strap him up in a straitjacket of unmitigated decorum. The great majority of his translators, especially in the last century, suffered from hypertrophy of the bump of veneration. Cary, for example, confronted at the end of *Inferno* xxi with the vulgar behaviour of Malacoda, who, after taking the salute of the poets' demon escorts,

> ... avea del cul fatto trombetta—
> He promptly made a bugle of his breech—

turns pale, renders it

> a signal...,
> Which he with sound obscene triumphant gave,

hastily scrapes a Greek footnote over the indelicacy, and proceeds in his stately Miltonics:

> It hath been heretofore my chance to see
> Horsemen with martial order shifting camp,
> To onset sallying, or in muster ranged,
> Or in retreat sometimes outstretch'd for flight:
> Light-armèd squadrons and fleet foragers
> Scouring thy plains, Arezzo! have I seen,
> And clashing tournaments, and tilting jousts,
> Now with the sound of trumpets, now of bells,
> Tabors, or signals made from castled heights,
> And with inventions multiform, our own,
> Or introduced from foreign land; but ne'er
> To such a strange recorder I beheld
> In evolution moving, horse nor foot,
> Nor ship, that tack'd by sign from land or star.
>   With the ten demons on our way we went;
> Ah, fearful company! but in the church
> With saints, with gluttons at the tavern's mess.
> *Inf.* xxii. 1–15.

One would scarcely think that the passage was intended to be funny. Yet the vocabulary—"*nè già con sì diversa cennamella*" —and the diddle-dumpling jolt and jangle of the metre:

> quando con trombe, e quando con campane,
> con tamburi e con cenni di castella—

should have warned him that Dante was up to mischief. But no doubt he would have said, like the Emperor Trajan: "*Pietà mi ritiene."* Piety held him back, and his firm hand compelled his master to decorum.

Nevertheless, all honour is for ever due to Cary, the first English translator of Dante to handle the text with loving accuracy. The modern trend in translation is all towards accuracy; we do not now expect translators to correct the sentiments as they go along, add embellishments which were not in the original, spin out one line into six with meditations of their own, or skim over difficulties with a handful of vague poetic clichés. That was the early method—one "imitated" rather than translated; and it is odd to find Fowler Wright, as late as 1928, starting off his *Inferno* with a stanza which actually suppresses all mention of the Dark Wood:

> One night, when half my life behind me lay,
>   I wandered from the straight lost path afar.
>   Through the great dark was no releasing way:
>
> Above that dark was no relieving star.

A reasonable fidelity to the text is, then, the third requirement for the translator. I do not mean a lumbering literalism. He need not produce contortions like William Rossetti's:

> Then took I hold upon him by the scalp,
>   And said: " 'Twill have to be thou name thyself
>   Or that no hair remain to thee hereon."

Or Longfellow's:

> Already with sight of this one I am not unfed.

Or Binyon's:

> For here can those there much our weal advance
>   (Chè qui per quei di là molto s'avanza)

But he *must* get the theology right, and he *must* get the astronomy right, and he *must* get the shades of meaning as right as possible. It is a useful and often a humbling discipline to be obliged to write analytical notes to accompany one's version. Nothing is more mortifying than to elucidate a difficult passage elaborately in a footnote and then discover that the important point has not survived in one's translation to receive one's comment. A nodding acquaintance with scholastic theology is needful, lest, in choosing some word that scans and rhymes conveniently, one should inadvertently land Dante and one's self in heresy or nonsense. And I need not dwell upon the discomfort of the conscientious translator when he sees this kind of thing looming up in the distance:

> "Indeed, Master", said I, "I never saw so clearly what I now discern, there where my wit seemed to be at fault, that the median circle of the celestial motion, which in one of the sciences is called the Equator, and which always remains between the sun and winter, departs here (for the reason you give) as far towards the North as the Hebrews used to see it towards the hot climes."

I regret to say that, whatever care one uses in the translation, modern readers always burst out laughing at this point, and say that, however clear it may have been to Dante, you have not succeeded in making it clear to *them*.

The next requirement is, as I firmly maintain, a quick sense of comedy. I cannot understand why so many people say that Dante had no humour. He abounds in comedy—mostly of a sly, dry, delicate sort—and for appreciation of a comic social situation is only rivalled by Jane Austen. His own portrait in the *Comedy* is full of self-mockery, and his conversations, especially with Virgil, are shot through with amusement at his own absurdity. This high-comedy style is so inherent in the whole situation and so dependent on little, unemphatic touches here and there that it hardly lends itself to illustration in brief snippets, and is apt to vanish like the scales of a moth's wings under the heavy touch of commentary. I can only repeat that it is abundantly there, and that the translator will miss it at his peril.

The fifth requirement in the translator is a resolute determination not to be afraid of the rhyme, but to make it do the work for him, as it does it for Dante, who is the one and only original Humpty-Dumpty in the slave-driving energy with which he whips the last ounce of usefulness out of a word. Weak, lazy, fill-up rhymes on unimportant words will produce a texture as unlike Dante as anything could well be. Professor Bickersteth, in his Introduction has dealt with this point so well that I will venture to quote him at some length:

> In the Italian hendecasyllable the mètre itself involves that the end of the line should be specially emphatic. For the tenth syllable is the only one which must invariably bear the stress. The

fourth or sixth comes next in importance. Dante makes the rhyme reinforce the final stress, with the result that in nine cases out of ten the rhyme-word—and, of the three in the *terzina*, often one in particular—is the outstanding or key-word of the argument. So true is this that in whole passages together you may follow the drift of the thought by a mere glance at the rhymes. It would be foolish to suggest that the translator must always so manipulate his thought as to emphasize by rhyme the very same idea that Dante does. For translation is art, not mechanism.[1]

I will here interrupt the quotation to observe that a mechanical accuracy of this sort is in any case impossible, because it frequently happens that two ideas which readily rhyme in Italian will not rhyme in English. But in every pair of rhymes one may, nearly always, by thinking with one's ears, distinguish a hammer-rhyme and an anvil-rhyme—one which beats out the principal idea, and the other which provides a surface for it to beat upon. In any terzain, you may find one hammer-rhyme and two anvil-rhymes, or two hammer-rhymes and one anvil-rhyme; but, if the verse is to be effective, one hammer-rhyme at least there must be. When, in translating, the line-endings fall awkwardly for the rhyme, the trick is to look for the hammer-rhyme—or, if there are two, the more important of them—get *that* of a good weight and ring, and then provide it with as good a pair of anvils as you can. You will do better that way than by removing all the important words to the middle of the line and rhyming on three nonentities. But, let us return to Professor Bickersteth, who proceeds to drive one's heart into one's boots by observing that "the translator, like any other good craftsman, must conceal his art and make his rhymes seem to occur as easily and inevitably as they do in the original". Indeed, indeed, that is the counsel of perfection; but I will add here the comment that, oddly enough, the translators into blank verse tend to indulge in even more awkward contortions and inversions than the translators into rhymed verse. This is mysterious; and I do not pretend to understand it. After emphasizing that the translator must reserve to himself a certain freedom with his material, Professor Bickersteth goes on:

> Yet there are countless passages, where unless he can contrive

[1] *The Paradiso of Dante Alighieri*, 1932, pp. xxiv-xxv.

to place at the end of the line the same word as Dante does, he will not in the strict sense be translating him.

And he gives this illustration:

> In St. Peter's famous denunciation of Boniface VIII (*Para.* xxvii. 22) the saint refers to the pope as follows:
>
>> Quelli ch'usurpa in terra il luogo mio,
>> il luogo mio, il luogo mio, che vaca
>> nella presenza del Figliuol di Dio....
>
> The "*luogo mio*", thrice repeated for the sake of emphasis, must obviously be retained by the translator, who (since, rendered literally, the words fall naturally into English verse) might be inclined to translate it—
>
>> He that usurps on earth my place, my place,
>> My place, etc.
>
> But this is precisely what he must not do. For the rhythm, the grammatical inversion, but chiefly the rhyme, all show that the emphasis falls on the possessive, not the noun. What St. Peter says is "the place that is *mine*". He is not concerned with the papal see as such, but to underline the contrast between himself and Boniface as occupants of it. Nor is "my place" a mistranslation of the meaning only. It also fails to render the feeling of indignation which is expressed not merely by the repetition of the words, but by the *sound* of the rhyme-word. The deep, open "o" of the "*luogo*" passing into the long-drawn-out, close, high-pitched "i" of "*mio*" (and dropping back to short "o" again) conveys the very inflection of the apostle's voice, rising on the rhyme-word to a shriek (*grido*) of fury, which trembles indeed on the verge of the comic. Boniface represents not God but Satan, "*il perverso*" (another rhyme-word) "*che cadde di qua su*", whereas St. Peter was truly the vicar of God, as the triple rhyme, "*io—mio—Dio*", subconsciously impresses through the ear on the mind by association of ideas. If the translator cannot, throughout the poem, be constantly using the rhyme for this sort of effect, he had better not attempt *terza rima* at all.[1]

Now, constructive criticism of this kind is taking the art of translation on a very high level indeed; and nothing would better show how far we have come from the pedestrian, hit-or-miss methods of some of the earlier Dante-translators, who care nothing

---

[1] *The Paradiso of Dante Alighieri*, 1932, xxv-xxvi.

for such niceties, provided their lines more or less convey the gist of the passage and scan by rule of thumb. "Progress" is not a term we can very often use, with any real meaning, in the sphere of the Humanities; but where, as in translation, it is a question, not only of good writing but of intelligent scholarship, I believe that time and experience can bring definite improvements, and that our own century can claim to have learned by the example, and failures, of the past.

I hope nobody will accuse me of cattiness or crabbing if I say that when I turn to see what Professor Bickersteth has himself made of this passage I am a little disappointed. Here it is, first in the Italian, then in the English—and I give the terzain before and after, so that it may be seen how the rhymes run. (Dante sees the "living flame" which is the soul of St. Peter glow angrily, changing from white to red; then St. Peter speaks, and the other spirits of the Redeemed glow red in sympathy):

> quand'io udi': "Se io mi trascoloro,
>   non ti maravigliar; chè, dicend'io,
>   vedrai trascolorar tutti costoro.
>
> Quelli ch'usurpa in terra il luogo mio,
>   il luogo mio, il luogo mio, che vaca
>   nella presenza del Figliuol di Dio,
>
> fatt' ha del cimiterio mio cloaca
>   del sangue e della puzza; onde 'l perverso
>   che cadde di qua su là giù si placa."

> ... when thus I heard: "Marvel not, if my hue
>   Be changed; for while I'm speaking, thou wilt see
>   All my companions changing colour too.
>
> He who usurps the place bestowed on me,
>   On me, on me, that place on earth, which now
>   The Son of God regards as vacant—he
>
> Hath made my cemetery, like sewer, flow
>   With blood and filth; whereby the renegade
>   Who fell from hence, comforts himself below."

It is, I think, evident that though the translator has got his emphasis on "me", he has paid a rather heavy price for it. The rhyme-sequence *"io—mio—Dio"* has gone—and that, we may say at once, cannot be helped, since no power on earth will make the word "I" rhyme with "God". Instead, we have a strongish sequence—"see—me—he", which, instead of emphasizing the *parallel* between God and St. Peter, emphasizes the *contrast* between him and Satan ("*il perverso*"). That is quite a good substitute. But the other rhyme-sequence, with its snarling emphasis on "*vaca—cloaca—placa*" has also gone, to give place to a mild-mannered and rather weak sequence, "now—flow—below", which has practically no hammer-rhyme at all. Still more serious, the two extremely important words, "*vaca*" and "*cloaca*", have been pushed into the weakest place in the line—the fourth stress; and moreover, instead of the vigorous phrase, "has made my cemetery a sewer", we have a subordinate simile "like sewer", which is made still weaker by the omission of the indefinite article. Similarly, instead of "which now stands vacant in the presence of God's Son", we have "which now the Son of God *regards* as vacant". Theologically, no doubt, it comes to the same thing; since if God regards a thing as being so, clearly it is so. But poetically the force is much weakened, and the word "regards" leaves us with a subconscious feeling that there might be two opinions on the subject. Further, the enjambing of the two terzains—though this is not by any means unknown in Dante's verse—has here the unfortunate effect of giving pride of emphatic place, not to the Son of God but to Pope Boniface VIII. And finally we may say that, although the possessive of "*il luogo mio*" is duly stressed, the thrice-reiterated "on me, on me, on me" is less effective than the repetition of the longer phrase "*il luogo mio*".

Let us now, just for amusement and instruction, see if we can do yet better than this.

The first thing to occur to us is that the only rendering of "*il luogo mio*" to have the length and weight of the original is "that place of mine"; and the obvious temptation is to start off simply and forcibly:

He who on earth usurps that place of mine.

A moment's forethought, however, warns us that when we get to the "*Figliuol di Dio*", the rhyme is going to land us with "the Son Divine"—one of those phrases that absolutely stink of translation. Regretfully, therefore, we refuse the soft option and think again. Then it occurs to us that, provided "of mine" comes on the rhyme, it does not really matter in which line it comes. Thus encouraged, we start off again, doing this time exactly what we have been told not to, and rhyming the first line on "place".

> He who upon the earth usurps that place
> Of mine, that place of mine, that place of mine—

This emphasizes the "mine" by the slight pause at the enjambment, and gives it the first, third and fifth stresses in the second line, and the rhyme-sound. But we have now left ourselves only one line in which to dispose of the presence of the Son of God and also the important word "*vaca*". Lack of rhymes forbids us even to think about putting "vacant" or "empty" at the end of a line, so the best we can do, in any case, is to transfer the word to the middle of the line and give it a heavy stress. And now the peculiar genius of the English language comes to our rescue. We have no room for the rolling polysyllables of "*nella presenza del Figliuol di Dio*"—but in English, if you really want to be impressive, it is not polysyllables you use, but a bunch of heavy monosyllabic thumps, and if you can isolate them by a preceding weak stress, all the better. This gives us:

> Which now stands vacant before God's Son's face.

We are now left to find two rhymes in "-ine", one for the sewer, and one for Satan's consolation at the end of the terzain. By a singular piece of good fortune, there is an excellent old West-country word, "rhine", meaning an open ditch. This has the disadvantage of not being familiar to everybody; but a suitable adjective will make the meaning clear in the context: "an open rhine"—no, much better give it a nasty, rasping alliteration: "a running rhine". And while we are about it, we will get rid of the cemetery (a word always faintly suggestive of the London Necropolis) in favour of a "burial-ground", which gives us two more "r's" instead of one; and we will invert the order of "blood and filth", so as to bring the thudding sound of "blood" to the caesura. The third -ine rhyme was a teaser, and I will admit that I was at my wit's end, until, in desperation, I opened (of all things) a Rhyming Dictionary; and to my amazement, it flew out and hit me in the eye—a word I might not have thought of in a twelve-month, but exactly right. But in the meanwhile, there is a rhyme in -ace still missing from the terzain before. And here is where we pay for our fun, because, so far, I have been able to think of nothing better than "apace", which sounds rather feeble and unmeaning in the context. Still, everything has its price, and if we must have a weakness, it had better be in the least important stanza of the three. The opening of our original first line is also a little weak: "He that *upon the earth*" is padding, and flabby padding at that. Better, perhaps, to pad boldly and say:

> He that on earth *has dared* usurp...

We now fill in the rest of the preceding terzain, taking the opportunity to render "*trascolorar*" each time by "change colour", instead of having one "change colour" and one "change hue", a variation which is less Dantesque. Now we can put the bits and pieces together and see what we have got:

> I heard: "If I change colour, as I do,
> Marvel not thou; for I will speak apace,
> And thou shalt see all these change colour too.
>
> He that on earth has dared usurp that place
> Of mine, that place of mine, that place of mine
> Which now stands vacant before God's Son's face,
>
> Has made my burial-ground a running rhine
> Of filth and blood; which to the Renegade
> Down there, who fell from here, is anodyne."

I was going to say something about padding; but I find I have already said it. Padding there has to be sometimes, simply because Italian words are usually longer than their English equivalents. "*Fecemi la divina potestate*"—"God's power made me"; "*per che tremavano amendue le sponde*"—"which made both banks shake"; "*e 'n la sua voluntade è nostra pace*"—"His will is our peace." What one does in crises of this kind must depend on the context; but it is safe to say that a good, strong, vigorous piece of unabashed padding, which contributes to the sense, is always better than a lot of little words which mean nothing in particular. This excess of elbow-room which one finds one has in translating from Italian into English has induced one translator at least (Auchtermuchty) to use octosyllabic instead of decasyllabic *terza rima,* with rather unexpectedly good effect.

But the jig of the short line is tiring to the ear, and imparts a disastrous jauntiness to the elegiac passages:

> Who go in mind, in body stay

cannot render the lingering nostalgia of

> che va col cuore e col corpo dimora;

we *must* have

> Whose bodies linger, though the heart hies on—

or something along those lines. Besides, we are frequently faced with a difficulty of the opposite kind. It is extremely tiresome that the word "*già*", which occurs so often, requires the three cumbersome syllables "already"; and that the Italian reflexives can only be rendered either by the lumbering "myself, himself" and so on, which clog up the line and refuse to rhyme with anything, or by such convenient but archaic forms as "I moved me", "I turned me"; while the impersonal "*per me si va*", and the like, demand an awkward periphrasis. One must have a line which allows a little margin for these things.

There are a thousand other things one could and should discuss: Dante's use of alliteration, internal rhyme, jingles and word-play, not to say downright puns, and his exploitation of words derived from the same root, as in the famous:

> che'l suo *fattore*
> non disdegnò di *farsi* sua *fattura*.

What to do with Dante's odds and ends of Latin quotations, which are so characteristic that one does not like to translate them, but which often involve one in the most appalling Ingoldsby-Legend acrobatics to provide them with a rhyme. How to provide a suitable equivalent for the three terzains of Provençal which burst so unexpectedly and gaily into the sonority of the Italian on the last triumphant ledge of Purgatory. What line one is to take about the ingenious acrostic[1] in *Purgatory* xi; whether one is justified in substituting a plain "said he" for the continued repetition of "And he to me", and so on; how to wrestle with names like Jacopo Rusticucci, Guglielmo Aldobrandesco, the Monaldi and Filippeschi, and so forth, which appear, recalcitrant to English scansion, sometimes as many as four or five crammed into a single terzain. And, above all—the

---

[1] If it is indeed an acrostic and not an accident.

ON TRANSLATING THE *DIVINA COMMEDIA* 119

outstanding difficulty of difficulties—the passages where Dante's Italian is so simple, lucid, and colloquial, falling so limpidly and easily into rhyme with all the words in the natural order, that the smallest artificiality is an outrage.

But I have been asked to submit to you my practice as well as my theory; and it is, as I freely admit, by his practice that the translator stands or falls. I will therefore ask your indulgence for a little longer while I give to you, first my less reverent version of that opening of *Inferno* xxii, which in the Rev. Mr. Cary's version was made to "bear itself more seeming". Technically, I have tried to get the high-spirited effect by a jog-trot metre, an irresponsible vocabulary, comic rhyme, and an abundance of feminine endings:

> I have seen horsemen moving camp, and beating
>   The muster and assault, seen troops advancing,
>   And sometimes with uncommon haste retreating,
>
> Seen forays in your land, and coursers prancing,
>   O Aretines! and I've beheld some grandish
>   Tilts run and tourneys fought, with banners dancing,
>
> And fife and drum, and signal-flares a-brandish
>   From towers, and cars with tintinnabulation
>   Of bells, and things both native and outlandish;
>
> But to so strange a trumpet's proclamation
>   I ne'er saw move or infantry or cavalry,
>   Or ship by sea-mark or by constellation.
>
> Well, off we started with that bunch of devilry;
>   Queer company—but there! "with saints at church,
>   And at the inn with roisterers and revelry."

Secondly, I think I will choose the great denunciation of Italy and the Emperor from the sixth canto of *Purgatory*. This is the ironic and epigrammatic Dante; and everything has to yield to getting an almost savage directness, with the rhyme driven smack home on the nail every time. Notice the rhetorical use of the terzain-structure, particularly in the four successive stanzas which begin with "Come". (We begin where Dante and Virgil meet Sordello on the lower slopes of the mountain):

We came to him. O lofty Lombard soul,
  How stately didst thou bear thyself, avouching
  Scorn in thine eyes' slow glance majestical!

He said no word to us, but, gravely watching,
  Let us come on, and sat and eyed us there,
  After the fashion of a lion couching.

Yet Virgil still drew nigh him, with a prayer
  That he would show the ascent; the shadowy man
  Ignored all this, demanding who we were,

And whence. Straightway my courteous guide began :
  "Mantua...." And, starting from his sullen smother,
  All self-absorbed, the shade leapt up and ran

From where he was to meet him, crying : "Brother!
  O brother-Mantuan! Sordello am I
  Of thine own city!" And they embraced each other.

O house of grief! O bond-slave Italy!
  Ship without pilot in a raging gale!
  No mistress-province, but a stews and sty!

That noble soul was swift; he did not fail,
  For the sweet name, his city's name—no more—
  To bid his fellow-countryman all-hail.

But in thy borders is no rest from war
  For living men; those whom one moat doth bound,
  One wall, destroy each other and devour.

Search, wretched! search thy seas and coasts around;
  Then search thy bosom; see if thou canst hit
  On any nook where pleasant peace is found.

What though Justinian fettled up thy bit
  If still the saddle's empty? That can do
  Nought but make worse the bitter shame of it.

You reverend gentlemen, who should pursue
  Your calling, and let Caesar mount and ride,
  Could you but read what God set down for you,

See how this brute turns vicious in her pride,
  Missing the spurred heel, since you snatched at her,
  Fumbling the rein with hands not fit to guide.

Thou, German Albert, who hast left this mare
  To run wild and ungoverned, thou indeed
  Shouldst now bestride her back—what dost thou care?

Let judgement fall, judgement on all thy breed
  From the just stars! be it strange and manifest,
  So that thine heir shall tremble and give heed;

Because thy father and thou, by greed possessed,
  Lingering up there, have suffered this abuse
  To lay the garden of the Empire waste.

Come, see the Capulets and Montagues;
  See, heedless man, Monaldi's house made poor,
  The Filippeschi shaking in their shoes.

Come, see thy nobles, persecuted sore,
  And bind their bleeding wounds; come, heart of stone,
  And see how safe life is in Santafior.

Come, see thy city, weeping there alone,
  That cries by night and day, poor widowed Rome,
  "Caesar and husband, whither art thou gone?"

Come, see how all thy people here at home
  Love one another. If no ruth can move,
  Then for fame's sake, for very shame's sake, come!

Nay (be the thought permitted) most high Jove,
  Once for our sins slain here upon the rood,
  Are Thy just eyes turned elsewhere and aloof?

Or dost Thou thus prepare, as seemeth good
  To Thine abysmal wisdom, some great plan,
  Dark to our eyes, not to be understood?

For every town in Italy is a den
  Swarming with tyrants; any churl's Marcellus,
  Who comes along to play the partisan.

Florence, my Florence, laugh! enjoy this jealous
  Little digression, for it galls thee not,
  Thanks to thy citizens, so wise, so zealous!

Some people's justice is heart-deep, slow-shot,
  Stopping to think ere loosing from the bow;
  Thy folk have justice at tongue's tip, I wot.

Some shun the cares of office: thy folk? No!
  "I'll sacrifice myself!" they gaily shout
  Long before anybody asks them to.

Be glad, with so much to be glad about,
  Thou rich, thou peaceable, thou well-advised!
  Do I speak truth? the facts will bear me out.

Athens and Lacedaemon, that devised
  Old laws and arts urbane in years bygone,
  Had scarcely started to be civilized

Compared with thee, whose planning's so well-done,
  Thou hast ere now run through by mid-November
  The store of thread that thy October spun.

How often, in the days thou canst remember,
  Have customs, coinage, codes been redesigned,
  Each office changed, and changed thy every member!

Bethink thee then, and if thou art not blind
  Thou'lt see thyself a woman sick with pain,
  Who on the softest down no rest can find,

Tossing and turning weary limbs in vain.
                Purg. vi. 61–151.

Lastly, for a complete contrast, there is the famous "Last Voyage of Ulysses"—the most astonishing synthesis of the classical and romantic in all literature. The difficulty here is to achieve anything like the sheer, unornamented, limpid simplicity of the original. Notice how the *terza rima* is locked into six-line or nine-line stanzas for such special effects as Virgil's conjuration of the spirits and the "little speech" of Ulysses; and elsewhere carried forward in continuous narrative by the over-running of the lines and by the conjunctions which link the stanzas. (The flame which conceals the spirits of Diomed and Ulysses is advancing towards the poets along the bottom of the Bolgia) :

> So, when by time and place the twin-fire peak,
>   As to my guide seemed fitting, had come on,
>   With this form conjuring it, I heard him speak:
>
> "You that within one flame go two as one,
>   By whatsoever I merited once of you,
>   By whatsoever I merited under the sun
>
> When I sang the high songs, whether little or great my due,
>   Stand; and let one of you say what distant bourne,
>   When he voyaged to loss and death, he voyaged unto."
>
> Then of that age-old fire the loftier horn
>   Began to mutter and move, as a wavering flame
>   Wrestles against the wind and is over-worn;
>
> And, like a speaking tongue vibrant to frame
>   Language, the tip of it flickering to and fro
>   Threw out a voice and answered: "When I came
>
> From Circe at last, who would not let me go,
>   But twelve months near Caieta hindered me
>   Before Aeneas ever named it so,
>
> No tenderness for my son, nor piety
>   To my old father, nor the wedded love
>   That should have comforted Penelope
>
> Could conquer in me the restless itch to rove
>   And rummage through the world exploring it,
>   All human worth and wickedness to prove.
>
> So on the deep and open sea I set
>   Forth, with a single ship and that small band
>   Of comrades that had never left me yet.
>
> Far as Morocco, far as Spain I scanned
>   Both shores; I saw the island of the Sardi,
>   And all that sea, and every wave-girt land.
>
> I and my fellows were grown old and tardy
>   Or ere we made the straits where Hercules
>   Set up his marks, that none should prove so hardy

To venture the uncharted distances;
   Ceuta I'd left to larboard, sailing by,
   Seville I now left in the starboard seas.

'Brothers', said I, 'that have come valiantly
   Through hundred thousand jeopardies undergone
   To reach the West, you will not now deny

To this last little vigil left to run
   Of feeling life, the new experience
   Of the uninhabited world behind the sun.

Think of your breed; for brutish ignorance
   Your mettle was not made; you were made men,
   To follow after knowledge and excellence.'

My little speech made every one so keen
   To forge ahead, that even if I'd tried
   I hardly think I could have held them in.

So, with our poop shouldering the dawn, we plied,
   Making our oars wings to the witless flight,
   And steadily gaining on the larboard side.

Already the other pole was up by night
   With all its stars, and ours had sunk so low,
   It rose no more from the ocean-floor to sight;

Five times we had seen the light kindle and grow
   Beneath the moon, and five times wane away,
   Since to the deep we had set course to go,

When at long last hove up a mountain, grey
   With distance, and so lofty and so steep,
   I never had seen the like on any day.

Then we rejoiced; but soon we had to weep,
   For out of the unknown land there blew foul weather,
   And a whirlwind struck the forepart of the ship;

And three times round she went in a roaring smother
   With all the waters; at the fourth, the poop
   Rose, and the prow went down, as pleased Another,

And over our heads the hollow seas closed up."
Inf. xxvi. 76–142.

[Passages, included in this essay, from Dr. Sayers's translations of the *Inferno* and the *Purgatorio*, published in the Penguin Classics series, are reprinted here by kind permission of the General Editor of that series, Dr. E. V. Rieu.]

CHAPTER VI

THE TRANSLATION OF VERSE

THE PASSION FOR verse-translation is a kind of congenital disease. I have suffered from it all my life—that is, I began to suffer from it as soon as I was able to think in any language but my own. At school, I wasted my prep time producing metrical translation of French and German set passages, when all that I was asked for was a simple construe. When I took my scholarship exam at Somerville, the French Unseen paper presented me with a sonnet—by whom? I have forgotten—which I succeeded in rendering, *tant bien que mal,* in its strict Petrarchan form, though I am haunted to this day by the recollection that pressure of time compelled me to conclude one line with the revolting cliché: "a (something) great and grand"—ruining the effect of the following line, which was quite a good one. Dear Mr. Herbert May, who in those days lived in Wellington Square and gallantly thrust whole battalions of imperfectly trained recruits through the Hot Gates of Responsions, smiled tolerantly on receiving a chorus from the *Hecuba* rendered into fluent and undistinguished iambics. The Schools examiners obliged with another sonnet, of which I remember only that I was tackled at the viva about a miserable sprig of rue that had crept into the rhyme in place of heliotrope, and was obliged to confess with blushes that it was the only plant that fitted the rhyme. They shook their heads, but forgave me. Shortly after going down, I embarked on a translation of the *Song of Roland,* in the original metre, but in rhyme instead of assonance. I still have it. It is very bad. I completed the task much later—in assonance this time, and I hope with better results. It was nice to get something finished that had been lying about for forty years or so. The *Tristan* of Thomas, begun not very much later, took a less unconscionable time in being born. It was actually done and published in 1929. It brought no great financial reward, and is now hopelessly out of print.

At this point, it seemed necessary to abandon verse translation, and produce something that would earn its keep and mine. But I am still bothered at leaving behind me so many castles that I assaulted in those days and was obliged to abandon unreduced. For the notoriously untranslatable "mon panache" of *Cyrano de Bergerac*, I have never been able to find anything remotely satisfactory, and it is little consolation to me to know that nobody else has ever done so either. The first stanza of Alfred de Vigny's *Le Cor*, with its dying fall; the inimitable tripping rhythm of Leconte de Lisle's refrain:

> Couronnés de thym et de marjolaine,
> Les Elfes joyeux dansent sur la plaine;

I still have the book with tentative phrases scribbled down the margins. Nothing ever came of it and nothing, I suppose, ever will. But these things still trouble me from time to time—in bed, or in the bath, or on a railway journey.

I have said that this itch to translate is a kind of disease, and indeed if one is not careful it may become a very real nuisance. It may mean that one cannot read a foreign poet with concentrated attention, because one is all the time nagged and distracted by lines and phrases which offer a challenge to the translator. One must either turn a severely deaf ear to these enticements, or else accept the challenge and set about seriously tackling the whole poem. It was in this way that I found myself obliged to lay siege to the *Divine Comedy*. It is perhaps rather late in the day to begin doing a job one has wanted to do all one's life; but the melancholy fact remains that the translation of verse does not pay one very well or very quickly, and one cannot devote one's self to it until one can afford to be content with small and slow returns. However, the prospects for the translator are better than they were. At the beginning of the century, translation, whether of verse or prose, was the job either of miserably paid literary hacks, or of disinterested scholars who could treat themselves to a private hobby. The translator is now getting back some of the rewards and some of the esteem which he enjoyed in the days when the names of Chaucer and Chapman and Pope and Dryden could be as famous for their translations as for their original work, and when other names, like those of Urquhart and Malory, Fairfax and Le Motteux, were made and preserved by their translations alone.

I hope you will not expect me to produce an infallible recipe for the successful translation of verse. I believe that the born translator, who has the bug in his blood, very seldom works by a rule. He tackles the job in whatsoever manner seems good to him, and formulates a theory afterwards, if at all, with the twin hope of forestalling criticism, and telling the world exactly what he thinks of his rival translators.

If you want fun, procure and read the little book called *On Translating Homer*, which contains Matthew Arnold's attack on F. W. Newman's version of the *Iliad*, Newman's reply to his criticism, and Arnold's final rejoinder. You need not know any Greek to find it highly entertaining. Each man has an elaborate theory, which he supports with admirable and convincing arguments. You find yourself nodding hearty agreement, first with one and then with the other, grinning at the same time over Arnold's intolerable smooth insolence, and Newman's pained protests from the vantage-point of a more generous nature and a far superior scholarship. Unhappily, when it comes to the test of practice, it is seen that theory by itself is no guarantee of excellence. We are given specimens both of what Newman did and of what Arnold would have done in his place. Both are bad, in the sense of being bad English verse—Newman's with a clumsy and conscientious badness, Arnold's with a slick and facile badness that is still more displeasing.

I will not recapitulate all the arguments, but I will pick out two points which are of general interest to those who are trying to translate any classical or "period" poet. The first is: what should be the translator's aim? Should he try to write the kind of poem the poet *would* have written, had he been an Englishman living today? Or should he try to produce on the general reader today the same effect which the original poem had on the poet's contemporaries? Arnold maintains (truly, I think) that both aims are impossible, because we cannot know what the poet would have done had he lived in another age and country, nor can we know exactly how his contemporaries reacted—and if we could, we cannot put ourselves in their shoes. Arnold's suggestion is that the translator should aim at producing upon the best scholars the same effect which the original produces upon them. I believe that this is impossible also. On the scholar steeped in the original language, no translation can possibly produce the same effect. He is inoculated against it, because he knows too much. We must, of course, endeavour to satisfy the scholar by a reasonable accuracy, and consult him whenever we are in doubt as to the meaning of a line, but we cannot hope to move and delight him as Homer moves the Grecian, Virgil the Latinist, or Dante the Italian expert. Translations are not intended for those who can read the original. What is more, too heavy a burden of scholarship may even hamper the translator by making him too self-conscious, and too painfully aware of minutiae of interpretation, so that he cannot see the wood for the trees. The translator must bear in mind that he is writing for the general reader, who does *not* know the language, but wants to get some idea of the effect made by the poet on those general readers who do.

I believe that the only thing a translator can hope to produce, or should aim at reproducing, is the effect of the original upon *himself*. In that way (if he is a competent writer of his own language, and if he knows his period—two indispensable requirements) his translation will at any rate be honest and individual, because he will not be attempting to make himself into anything other than he is. His translation will not please everybody—no translation does; it will never be the definitive translation—no translation is. But it may succeed in conveying something of the force and freshness with which the original poem struck him when he first encountered it; and it may even prompt some of his readers to learn the language and tackle the original for themselves. Greater rewards than these no translator can expect —nor should he.

The other point is this: that just as no translator can escape from his own personality neither can he escape from the habit of mind of his own contemporaries. Though a hundred generations may agree that a poet is great, each one will feel his greatness differently, and each will praise him for beauties that their predecessors or followers have not seen, or have seen differently, or have even blamed as blemishes. It is indeed a mark of greatness that it speaks in different tones to men in every age. Thus, to Arnold, one of Homer's chief characteristics is the consistent and civilized nobility of his style; he denies strenuously that any passages in him are odd, or primitive, or flat, or homely, or should be translated in anything but the "grand manner". In this he agrees with Pope and Cowper (though he detests both their versions), who each in his own manner rendered Homer into the "noble" style of his own day—Pope into the rhymed heroic couplet, and Cowper into sub-Miltonic blank verse. Newman, on the other hand, sees Homer (though he does not use that word) as a splendid barbarian, writing a language that was antiquated to Sophocles, with a style rising in the lofty parts of the narrative and sinking in the more prosaic parts, and more closely akin to the ballad-writers or the makers of folk-epic than to conscious literary artists like Virgil or Milton. Consequently, he chooses a modified ballad-metre (the double-ended fourteener), and uses a great number of archaisms in his translation; whereas Arnold is all for an accentual hexameter, and a style purged of anything that might savour of "lowness" or eccentricity. Of the two, we should say now that Newman is nearer to the modern outlook, whereas Arnold—for all he lived in the "Romantic" period—was harking back to the age of the Augustans. But we cannot be sure that the outlook of the times may not change again. We can only take warning that every translation bears upon itself the stamp of its own age. And on the whole, it is well that it should do so. To have presented the eighteenth century with a Homer written in the style of *Beowulf* or the *Song of Roland* would not have opened men's eyes to the splendours of primitive epic; it would merely have prevented them from reading the poem at all. Pope gave them what they could assimilate; and if "you must not call it Homer", yet it is perhaps as much of Homer as Pope's age could take. So was Chapman's Homer to the Jacobeans, Cowper's Homer to the Romantic age, so is Dr. Rieu's prose rendering to the age in which we live. In the literature of a past age, we recognize and admire chiefly that which it has in common, not necessarily with our own experience, but with our own sympathies, and it is those sympathies which our translation is bound to reflect. If we idealise any age as a Golden Age, we shall find all its poets uniformly "noble"; Dante is just emerging from the aura of "nobility" shed upon him by the ideal glamour which the nineteenth century saw enveloping the Middle Ages. Since our present tendency is to think no past age Golden, it is not surprising that editors, readers, and translators of today alike are nervous in the presence of the Grand Style. The fashionable translation of today will as a rule lack nobility, and seek after an easy colloquial and familiar manner. This is probably a wholesome change, taken by and large; though it may easily decline into the flat, the humdrum, or (worse) the knowing, buttonholing familiarity which nudges the reader in the ribs.

There is another aspect of the translator's task which is quite surprisingly subject to the fluctuating dictates of fashion, and that is: what, exactly, is meant by fidelity to the text. This is not merely a question of tone and diction, to which we shall presently return, but of actual content. Setting aside, of course, the verbal crib or construe, which is not meant for reading but only for getting people through examinations, what liberties is a translator justified in taking with his author? The old tradition, which lasted well on into the eighteenth century, was a very liberal one. You were not only expected to do justice to the beauties which you found in the original, but if any extra beauties suggested themselves to you as you went along, you were fully at liberty to insert them into the text. This, so far from being an insult to the author, was felt to do him honour. Besides, it was only a just compensation. There must always be many felicities lost in translation, owing to the difference between the two tongues; it seemed therefore only fair, when a suitable moment came, to make up for this by brightening a dull passage, or by bestowing upon your author a flourish, a fancy, or a conceit in the taste of your own time, which would adorn him and commend him to the judicious mind. The baroque ornaments which Chapman imposed upon the classical pediment of Homer were not, in Chapman's own view, an impertinence; they were a tribute paid by one poet to another. The compact terseness of the Latin language as compared to our own was felt to give, when too-faithfully rendered, an effect of baldness and bareness which amounted to an essential misinterpretation. Hence it was not unusual, and was not felt to be criminal, to expand a condensed phrase into a whole stanza, by making explicit all the implied associations, and working up every suggestion into a whole descriptive picture. This was all very well up to a point; but sometimes we may well feel that it went too far. What, for instance, can we say to the following, which purports to be Congreve's version of a winter landscape from one of Horace's *Odes*? Here are the two-and-a-half original lines:

> Vides, ut altâ stet nive candidum
> Soracte : nec jam sustineant onus
> Sylvae laborantes.
>
> *I.* 9.

("See, how Soracte stands white with lofty snows, and the overladen woods can scarcely sustain their burden.")

Here is Congreve:

> Bless me, 'tis cold! how chill the air!
> How naked does the world appear!
> Behold the mountain tops around,
>   As if with fur of ermine crown'd:
>   And lo! how by degrees,
> The universal mantle hides the trees,
>   In hoary flakes which downward fly,
> As if it were the autumn of the sky,
>   Whose fall of leaf would theirs supply:
> Trembling the groves sustain the weight and bow,
>   Like aged limbs which feebly go,
> Beneath a venerable head of snow.

This can hardly be called translation: it is rather a meditation upon Horace, or variations played upon his theme. To our present-day notions it is quite shocking; and we do not feel that the various conceits by which the mountain's crown of snow is embellished with an ermine-furred cap of maintenance and supplemented with a mantle of the same material; the falling snow is likened to a fall of autumn leaves, supplying the deficiency which winter creates; and the overladen groves are compared to aged limbs tottering beneath a hoary head—however ingenious in themselves—faithfully represent Horace, or compensate for the total disappearance of Soracte from the scene. If this is the impression which Horace produces on Congreve, then Congreve is altogether too impressionable; he would have done better to bind himself within the limits of Horace's stanza.

If Congreve's period was too ready to allow the translator a free hand, our own tends now to err in the opposite direction. It has a rooted, and indeed an unreasonable, horror of "padding". It demands that the verse-translator should render, not merely line for line, but almost word for word, and leaps indignantly upon an extra adjective or on an additional word brought in for the sake of the rhyme, as though it were a felony. The critic, and especially the newspaper reviewer, has fallen into a habit of counting words, and if he finds anything at all "extra to establishment" will triumphantly conclude, not only that the translation is bad, but that verse-translation as such is bad, because it sometimes demands these slight verbal redundancies. He will sometimes forget that an extra word or syllable may be needed to bring, not the sense, but the metre of the line into a musical conformity with the original. I do not defend padding for padding's sake; but I do say that this method of judging verse-translation is far too easy and mechanical. It is, however, a morbid growth upon what is in itself a welcome reversion towards a greater sobriety in the translator, and a demand that he should submit himself more humbly to his author and not be so eager to display his own versatility in elegant attitudes. As for "beauties", I know only too well to how many of them one must necessarily fail to do justice, and I see no reason why one should not occasionally repay the debt if an opportunity occurs. When one is rendering stanza for stanza and as far as possible line for line, the strictness of the form will prevent one from indulging in Congreve's kind of extravagance. I have myself made Dante a present of two or three felicitous puns, which were possible in my language though not in his, to make up for several others which were incapable of translation from Italian into English. To this I plead guilty, but not to having added to, altered, or omitted any part of his thought in the process. One cannot, indeed, make drastic structural alterations when one is working within the author's original metrical scheme.

Curiously enough, the present-day demand for verbal exactness, in this sense, does not extend from verse to prose translation. There, not only is it considered permissible, and indeed laudable, so to modify, modernize, and re-paragraph that the poet's style is in as much danger of becoming lost as it ever was in the time of Chapman or Pope, but quite considerable additions to the text are also favourably received by the critics. These do not take the form of gratuitous "beauties", or of extemporizations upon the theme. They are merely informative, and consist in what has been called "incorporating the footnotes in the text". There is a reason for this, which is not altogether complimentary to the common reader. When translating any ancient author, it is now no longer possible, as it was at one time, to rely upon the reader's ability to recognize at sight an allusion to classical myth, Bible history, Arthurian legend, the astronomy of the visible heavens, and other standard sources of the poet's inspiration. The passing away of compulsory Latin and Greek, of regular church-going and religious instruction, the shift of interest from folk-lore and natural history to sociology and the abstract and mechanical sciences, have made the understanding of literature much more difficult, even for those who have received a liberal education. Moreover, the translator has to consider a whole class of new readers who have received nothing but a technical training, and need to have the path into the literary past made smooth for them. Hence the necessity for footnotes in some form or the other. But many editors have made up their minds that the average reader is so lazy, or so prejudiced against any form of "instructive" reading, that if he sees any kind of critical apparatus attached to a book, he will instantly refuse to purchase it. I have always firmly refused to entertain so poor an opinion of the reader. But the editorial prejudice exists, and translators must do what they can to make the text intelligible without footnotes. Thus we find Mr. Day Lewis writing in the preface to his translation of the *Georgics*: "I have avoided footnotes, and attempted wherever I could to make these allusions explicit in the text (e.g. by translating 'Pales' as 'goddess of sheepfolds')." This is modest enough, and little exception can be taken to it, especially as Mr. Lewis is translating in verse and line for line, so that his explanatory interpretations are of necessity limited. But here is a more dubious case, from Mr. Robert Graves's prose version of Lucan's *Pharsalia*:

> The fire on Vesta's altar was mysteriously extinguished, and the blaze of the bonfire which always concludes the Latin festival, divided—a portent recalling a similar occurence at Thebes long ago, when the inveterate animosity of the brothers Eteocles and Polyneices, who had killed each other, prevented the flames of their common funeral pyre from uniting.
> *I.* 549–552.

Now what Lucan wrote was that the blaze of the bonfire divided, "*Thebanos imitata rogos*"—three words—like the Theban pyres". Mr. Graves, who has no tenderness whatever for his author's style, says in *his* preface, of this and similar passages: "Since this is what [they] mean, surely they should be so rendered? I see no point in letting them remain obscure, just because a few Latinists can nod appreciatively at the concealed references." This contempt for the Latinists is, of course, a telling bid for the approval of the lowbrow and the popular reviewer. But one asks one's self a little uneasily what idea the reader is going to get of a poet's style if this method of translation spreads very much further. Suppose a foreign translator were to apply it to Shakespeare:

> For valour, is not love a Hercules
> Still climbing trees in the Hesperides?

This would presumably become:

> Does not love make a man so valiant as to be always undertaking risky and difficult adventures, like Hercules the strong man, who, as one of the Twelve Labours which he was compelled to perform for King Eurystheus, went to fetch the golden apples from the dragon-guarded tree growing in the fabulous Island of the Hesperides, by some authorities identified with the Canaries?

One would feel some sympathy for the Berowne who had to get *that* across the footlights, especially as the speech contains further allusions to Bacchus, the Sphinx, Apollo's lute and the Promethean fire, all standing in need of similar elucidation.

Personally, unless the explanation can be given in a couple of words, I am all for an honest footnote, in an easily get-at-able position—not at the back of the book, so that you need to be an octopus to keep your place while you read it, but so discreetly arranged that if you do happen to recognize the allusion you may enjoy the simple pleasure of nodding your head at it, and if by any chance you don't, you can look up the reference with the minimum of trouble and delay.

All this brings us to the vexed and difficult question whether the translation of a poem should be made in verse or in prose.

I do not think this question admits of any dogmatic pronouncement applicable to all cases. It is true that the present fashion rather favours a plain straightforward prose, with no "nobility" and no hank. But that is a matter of style rather than of measure—it is quite as easy to be bald and brutal in verse as in prose. Neither is it true that a prose translation is necessarily more faithful than a verse translation, even in the matter of mere verbal accuracy. Rhymed verse translations are frequently accused of sacrificing accuracy to the requirements of the rhyme; and this may, of course, very frequently be true. But in some ways, the rhyme may be an aid to accuracy, since it obliges the translator to think closely and carefully about the *sense* of the passage, in order that he may render it into a quite different set of words. Translation into prose, or into the more prosaic kind of blank verse, offers a perpetual temptation to be too free, but it may also, oddly enough, offer the opposite temptation to be too literal—i.e. to transcribe the original words without regard to the original sense. Take for example Dante's famous simile of the damned souls leaping into Charon's boat:

>come d'autunno si levan le foglie
>l'una appresso dell'altra, fin che 'l ramo
>vede alla terra tutte le sue spoglie.

Even so careful a translator as J. D. Sinclair renders it:

>"As in autumn the leaves drop off one after the other
>till the branch sees all its spoils on the ground."

"*Spoglie*"—"spoils": the word slips off the pen without a thought. But in what sense can the leaves of a tree be called its "spoils" in modern English? The tree has robbed nobody. True, autumn may be said to "despoil" it—but then the spoils belong to autumn, and not to the tree. The fact is that in Italian the word "*spoglie*" has acquired the secondary sense of "cast-off clothing", and should be so rendered: the verse-translators, having been forced to think, do so render it, using phrases like "bravery", "rich array", or other words to do with clothing. Similarly, the word "*peregrin*" brings up "pilgrim" by a natural association; and too often the prose-translator leaves it at that, where the versifier renders more exactly "pilgrim", "stranger", "traveller", "sojourner", "exile", "foreigner", as the context demands.

These, however, are only temptations which the translator can resist if he chooses; and I think there is a case today for the translation of certain long narrative works into a medium that the present-day reader is ready to accept—always provided that the story is of a kind that will stand up to straightforward narration without the aid of verse. Dr. Rieu's version of the *Odyssey* has introduced Homer to thousands of readers who would never have tackled him in any other form, and is, I think, very agreeable to read in that form. But then, the *Odyssey* is a folk-tale full of charm and romantic incident which lends itself to an easygoing and colloquial manner of story-telling. His *Iliad* seems to me less successful, because the stark brutality of character and event becomes depressing without the metre to carry it, and reminds us a little too forcibly of Goethe's remark: "From Homer and Polygnotus I learn every day more clearly that in our life here above ground we have, properly speaking, to enact Hell." Though we might indeed learn that equally well from some modern novels and films. And here we come up against the true objection to the use of prose in epic: that to render the particular kind of brutality we encounter there, its pace is too slow. We shall see this even more clearly if we look at the *Song of Roland*, which is, in its way, much more primitive than the *Iliad*. Without the aid of the rocking clash of the verse, its long succession of single combats would be pure tedium. Or, to take a long poem of a very different type, what *The Rape of the Lock* would sound like in prose, I do not know.

But I will leave this question; because, for the verse-translator with the bug in his veins, prose-translation lacks all the fun of the game. It is a kind of cheating at Patience. The pleasure lies in rendering, as best he can, the whole form and content of the original: sense for sense, sound for sound, accent for accent, rhyme for rhyme, and, where this is impossible (as it nearly always is), delicately weighing up which of the various features of the verse is, *in that place*, the most important—the one thing that must at all costs be preserved and to which every other consideration has to be sacrificed.

For the happy playing of this according to the best sporting rules, it is essential (a) that if the translator's language possesses a metre exactly or nearly equivalent to that of the original, he should use that metre and no other; (b) that if the original is in stanza-form, that stanza should be used and no other; (c) that tonic stresses and the rhymes (if any), though they cannot always fall upon the same words as in the original, should perform their task of distributing the emphasis in a manner corresponding to the original.

The reason for this is plain: the metre, the stanza and the rhyme are what paragraph the poem. Take, for example, Dante's *terza rima*. This, although the interlaced rhymes link a whole canto together in a continuous flow, which carries the ear on from terzain to terzain, nevertheless tends to fall into regular stanza-paragraphs, consisting of three, six, nine or occasionally twelve lines apiece. These are used to give to some passages a gnomic or epigrammatic quality, as in the sharp interjection which breaks suddenly through the description of the souls burning upon the Abominable Sands:

> Fearful indeed art thou, vengeance of God!
> He that now reads what mine own eyes with awe
> Plainly beheld, well may he dread thy rod!
> *Inf.* xiv. 16–18.

or to mark off a set speech from the narrative, like Ulysses' speech to his shipmates; or to space out a catalogue, like the catalogue of the pavement-sculptures on the Cornice of Pride; or to produce the effect of an inserted lyric, like the dream of Leah and Rachel, or the Song of the Siren. If the poem is translated—as has been done before now—into heroic couplets, or into Spenserian stanzas, or into any rhymed stanza other than the original, these effects will be lost even more surely than if the medium were blank verse or prose; for the breaks in the rhythm will come in the wrong places, binding that which should be loosed, and loosing that which should be bound. For the same reason, it would be undesirable to use for the *Comedy* the modern form of *terza rima* which Mr. Louis MacNeice has revived for his *Autumn Journal*. In this, the end-stopping of lines and paragraphs is studiously avoided, and the verse made to run on continuously, like blanks. It is a good prosodical form for its purpose (incidentally giving the lie to the superstition that *terza rima* cannot be written in English because of the dearth of rhyme); but it is so unlike Dante's use of the metre that it cannot translate him.

Indeed, it will not do to be misled by Dante's own statement that he owed his style to Virgil. That may be perfectly true, but his *versification* derives, as any experienced ear can tell in a moment, directly from the mediaeval fixed forms—the Canzone, the Sonnet, the Ballata—with their intricate rhyme-scheme and close association with the actual sung lyric. And these fixed forms are the very ones which it would scarcely occur to anybody to translate into a metrical arrangement other than their own. Nor is there any better way of learning every stroke in this translation-game than by serving an apprenticeship to the fixed form. It is in fact from the corpus of Romance literature, to which the set forms belong, that all post-Chaucerian English metres and stanzes derive, so that, with one outstanding exception, we can produce equivalent prosodic forms for almost every classical Italian or French form, as also for the German forms which share the same cultural origin. I say "equivalent" and not "identical", since a certain adjustment of metrical values has always to be made. French and Italian verse is predominantly syllabic; English and German verse, predominantly accentual. But English and Italian metre have more in common than English and French, because the continual elision in the Italian gives an effect of fullness and sometimes of an almost dactylic rhythm, which can be matched by the English tolerance of extra unaccented syllables and triple feet within the norm of the iambic line. German, on the other hand, being heavily inflected, can reproduce exactly the overwhelming preponderance of feminine endings in the Italian line, as may be seen by Stefan George's translation of selected passages from Dante's *Commedia*. To write 14,000 lines of English verse, all with feminine endings, would not be impossible—as we have seen, F. W. Newman accomplished a version of the whole *Iliad* in feminine-ended fourteeners —but it would not be very desirable, because in English the feminine ending needs very careful handling if it is not to produce a jaunty and rollicking effect; and in particular, a spate of feminine *rhymes* is liable to suggest Gilbertian Opera, or the *Ingoldsby Legends*, rather than any kind of epic nobility or "grand style". Even in German, where the feminine rhyme is quite natural, I think the heavy fall of the tonic-stress tends to impart to the line a slightly monotonous rigidity which the Italian hendecasyllable escapes by the great fluidity of its internal accentual structure. (I dare not give examples to illustrate this, for the effect is cumulative over long passages, and is scarcely perceptible in the short extracts which are all that we should have time for). In translating into English from German, we encounter a rather different set of difficulties, the chief of which is the preponderance in German of short lines starting regularly with a trochee; these in English are apt to degenerate into an

THE TRANSLATION OF VERSE 141

unpleasant jingle, reminiscent of *Hiawatha*—particularly when combined, as they often are, with feminine endings. It is interesting to compare two versions of the same chorus from Goethe's *Faust* (Part I)—the chorus beginning: *Schwindet, ihr dunkeln Wölbungen droben*, which consists of fifty-eight lines each of two stresses only, and all but two of them with feminine endings. The older version is by Bayard Taylor, and follows the German rhyme-pattern exactly. The more recent is by Philip Wayne, who has interspersed a number of masculine endings, in the hope of pulling up the runaway gallop. A short passage will be enough. Here is Bayard Taylor; you will notice that here and there the opening trochee has defeated him:

>   Bower on bower!
>   Tendrils unblighted!
>   Lo! in a shower
>   Grapes that o'ercluster
>   Gush into must, or
>   Flow into rivers
>   Of foaming and flashing
>   Wine, that is dashing
>   Gems, as it boundeth
>   Down the high places,
>   And spreading, surroundeth
>   With crystalline spaces,
>   In happy embraces,
>   Blossoming forelands,
>   Emerald shorelands!

Here is Philip Wayne:

>   Then from the vine
>   Tendrils will twine,
>   Grapes in their masses
>   Burden the presses,
>   Pour purple lustres
>   Crushed from their clusters.
>   Gushing in streams
>   Runs the rich wine,
>   Flowing where gleams
>   Amethyst shine,
>   Flowing by hills
>   Wooded, benign,
>   Leaving the rills
>   Incarnadine.

His trochees are impeccable, except "Incarnadine", which is, I think, rather infelicitous. But I am not sure whether the masculine rhymes do not aggravate rather than subdue the bounce.

It is again the combination of the short line, the trochaic rhythm and the feminine endings that renders almost untranslatable Goethe's tiny masterpiece:

> Ueber allen Gipfeln
> Ist Ruh';
> In allen Wipfeln
> Spürest du
> Kaum einen Hauch;
> Die Vöglein schweigen im Walde.
> Warte nur, balde
> Ruhest du auch.

Nevertheless, with sufficient dexterity and a sensitive ear, the translator can master these metres, which are all of one kindred. The real difficulty arises when he is faced with metres which can by no means be adapted to the English speech. In the Romance language, the outstanding exception which I mentioned earlier is, of course, the classical French alexandrine, with its six feet, end-stopped couplet, and heavy caesura. In general tone, its nearest equivalent is the Heroic couplet which, however, drives the translator nearly demented by obliging him to pack into ten syllables the content of the original twelve. This is not easy. It would be easy in Italian, where the average length of a word is greater than the equivalent English, so that the translator is apt to find himself with too much space left on his hands: *fecemi la divina potestate,* for instance, has a nasty way of boiling down into "God's power made me", and leaving one wondering what to do with the remaining six syllables. But French is, if anything, more compact than English. The English alexandrine —"which like a wounded snake drags its slow length along"— has never really approved itself to the English ear. Blank verse, which is the standard verse for English drama of the golden age, is too loose and free; it favours over-running and an informal construction of sentence and syntax. It might, perhaps, be just possible for Racine: but what can we do with Corneille, whose every couplet is as epigrammatic and as antithetically balanced as a couplet of Pope, and produces its rhetorical effect precisely by this? It is not, of course, impossible to have a balanced antithesis in blank verse, but its pattern tends to be of two lines rather than one; for every line of the type:

> I come to bury Caesar, not to praise him:

there will be many of the type:

> The evil that men do lives after them;
> The good is oft interred with their bones;

or:

> If it were so, it was a grievous fault;
> And grievously hath Caesar answered it;

whereas in Corneille, the single-line antithesis is predominant:

> Mais il n'est pas moins vrai que cet ordre des Cieux
> Change selon les temps, comme selon les lieux.
> Rome a receu des Rois ses murs et sa naissance,
> Elle tient des Consuls sa gloire et sa puissance

> Puissé-je de mes yeux y voir tomber ce foudre,
> Voir ses maisons en cendre, et tes lauriers en poudre,
> Voir le dernier Romain à son dernier soupir
> Moi seule en être cause, et mourir de plaisir!

Or, to put it another way: the rhetorical unit in this kind of verse is not the line, but the hemistich; and it is built up, not into periods, but into couplets.

But the difficulty of domesticating the alexandrine is as nothing to the difficulty of domesticating the classical hexameter, and, indeed, all the classical quantitative metres. On this vexed question, I do not propose to dwell; the ground has been gone over too often. I will only say that any attempt to write English quantitative verse is a mere obstination of theory over practice. The English ear doggedly refuses to assimilate it—and quite rightly; since English syllables seldom possess any fixed quantity, owing to the persistent and increasing English habit of swallowing unaccented vowels and approximating them all to the undifferentiated "ǝ". Consider "Tottenham Court Road". One may assert with some confidence that "Court Road" is a spondee. By every classical rule, "Tottenham" followed by "Court" should consist of three long syllables; but in practice it is a dactyl: though what a classical metrist would say to a dactyl ending in "'n'm" I do not know. I do know, however, what any English reader would say if he were required to pronounce those two syllables "enham", and reckon them as a spondee:

> Ergo omnis longo solvit se Teucria luctu

From Tottenham Court Road walking slowly to Earls Court. And even at that, what exactly is the quantity of "to", with its long vowel which nobody ever pronounces? No; the rejection is categorical; and I am sometimes heretic enough to wish that the Roman ear had resisted as stoutly as the English the literary fashion which forced upon the naturally accentual Latin speech a scansion which was as foreign to it as it is to our own. But I will leave this—only staying to direct your attention to Mr. Day Lewis's interesting experiment in rendering the *Georgics* in a loosely knit line, predominantly iambic (or "duple-rising") metre, which is neither the alexandrine, nor the hideous accentual hexameter—

> Trundling along the high-road, clip-clop clopetty-wallop—

which (despite *Evangeline*, and other efforts less naïve, and for that very reason less popular), has never recommended itself to any person of sensitive taste.

Here is a short passage from Mr. Day Lewis's *Georgics*:

> Wherefore the golden sun commands an orbit measured
> In fixed divisions through the twelvefold signs of the universe.
> Five zones make up the heavens: one of them in the flaming
> Sun glows red for ever, for ever seared by his fire:
> Round it to right and left the furthermost zones extend,
> Blue with cold, ice-bound, frozen with black blizzards:
> Between these and the middle one, weak mortals are given
> Two zones by the grace of God, and a path was cut through both
> Where the slanting signs might march and countermarch. The world,
> Rising steeply to Scythia and the Riphaean plateaux,
> Slopes down in the south to Libya.
> This North pole's always above us: the South appears beneath
> The feet of darkling Styx, of the deep-down Shadow People.
> Here the great Snake glides out with weaving, elastic body
> Writhing-riverwise around and between the two Bears—
> The Bears that are afraid to get wet in the water of Ocean.
> At the South pole, men say, either it's dead of night,
> Dead still, the shadows shrouded in night, blacked out for ever;

Or dawn returns from us thither, bringing the daylight back,
And when sunrise salutes us with the breath of his panting horses,
Down there eve's crimson star is lighting his lamp at last.

This flexible, unemphatic but dignified line seems to me to offer great possibilities for the translation, not only of the classical hexameter, but also of the French alexandrine of the Romantic period; though it could of course never carry the hard ring and glitter of the Cornelian couplet. I have chosen one of the statelier passages to illustrate it; but it is also capable of an easy colloquialism. It would adapt itself very well to narrative, and I can imagine an *Odyssey* in it. A modern verse rendering of the *Iliad* might call for a rougher and more sharply stressed line—something perhaps akin to the Old English alliterative measure. So too for the lyric and choric metres: English will not reproduce them exactly: it is a question of finding something that will supply an equivalent texture.

We must not linger too long over the fascinating problem of metre. But it is important, because it is that first choice of a metre that determines the medium in which all subsequent choices have to be made. And I cannot emphasize too strongly that every line, every word, every syllable of a translation is a delicate balance of choice. No version can *be* the original: at every point we have to decide which, of all the factors that go to make the passage what it is, are the ones which must be retained at all costs, and to which the others must needs be sacrificed.

One cannot precisely enumerate all the factors, but we may mention just a few.

The first is *Accuracy*. I do not mean simply that we must be careful not to mistranslate, though this is naturally important. And perhaps I should say here, in view of at least one popular translation that has recently appeared, that if at any point your author appears to you to be talking nonsense, it is better not to assume that he is, but to call in the assistance of scholars and experts, and—if they give you no satisfaction—then to confine yourself to translating as faithfully as possible what is in the text, without any additions of your own, since these are only too likely to make confusion worse confounded. And if you feel compelled to add a footnote, do not bluntly inform your readers that the author is an ignorant fool, but say modestly—like Pietro di

Dante, when commenting his distinguished father's poem: "As for the rest of this, work it out for yourselves, for I do not see it and can make nothing of it." But, leaving aside passages of genuine obscurity, we have sometimes to ask whether, in a particular passage, strict verbal accuracy is necessary, or whether a paraphrase will do. Obviously, if there is any question of theological or scientific vocabulary involved, nothing but strict verbal accuracy *will* do: whatever happens to rhyme, metre or elegance, one must not saddle one's author with heresies or absurdities which he did not commit. Where technicalities are concerned, all loose language is perilous:

> There's a great text in Galatians,
>   Once you trip on it, entails
> Twenty-nine distinct damnations,
>   One sure if another fails—

and this remains true whether you are dealing with philosophy, atomic physics, chemistry, astronomy, or the working parts of sailing-ships. If you are slapdash about these, the experts will be down on you like a shot.

But there is another kind of inaccuracy which is even more damaging because it is much more likely to escape the notice of the critic or the readers, and that is the failure to render precisely the point of an image or simile. Here is one outstanding instance from Binyon's version of Dante's *Commedia*. It is from the scene in the Bolgia of the Thieves, where one of the sinners is changing his shape from that of a man to that of a lizard. Dante, who had a wonderful eye for living creatures, says

> e li orecchi ritira per la testa
>   come face le corna la lumaccia—

"he pulled his ears inside his head, as a snail pulls its horns". It is impossible to see a thing more vividly than that. But Binyon —as though he had never in his life looked a snail in the face— placidly renders it:

> And quite into his head drew back the ears
>   As a snail draws its horn *into its shell*—

The whole point of that exquisite and accurate simile—that perfect piece of observation, dead right on the precise likeness of the two actions—goes straight down the drain with that deadly phrase "into its shell". It is no excuse to say that Binyon did it for the rhyme's sake—this is one of the moments where the worst rhyme in the world would be preferable to the sacrifice of accuracy. And I have a horrible suspicion that the rhyme (which is not particularly helpful in the other parts of the stanza) was deliberately chosen for that line, merely because the word "snail" automatically calls up the word "shell", and because the translator neither visualized the image nor realized how important the precision of that image was.

The second important factor is *Readability*. This should be fairly obvious, since (cribs and construes apart) what is the use of translating any poem, however accurately and learnedly, if the result is so repellent to the reader that he cannot force himself to plough through it? If your intention is to introduce a foreign poet to a native public, then you had far better err by being too smooth than by being too crabbed. Some great poets *are* crabbed—but you will not help them by adding a crabbedness of your own devising. The best defence of prose translations, or of translations into a verse-style that is fashionable, is that these things make for easy reading, even at the sacrifice of some of the characteristics of the original language and style. Greek, like German, is a language in which compound epithets abound; but it is not advisable to make one's translation so characteristically Greek as, for instance, this from Browning's *Agamemnon*:

              so prevails audacious
The man's-way-planning hoping heart of woman.
But when I, driven from night-rest, dew-drenched hold to
This couch of mine—not looked upon by visions,
Since fear instead of sleep still stands beside me,
So as that fast in sleep I fix no eyelids.

The translator may insist that the movement of the verse is Greek; the reader will only feel quite sure that out of half a dozen lines only two can be called English. The *Agamemnon*, moreover, is a play and, when translating a play, we have to remember that the lines must be not only readable but *speakable*. They must not have clusters of awkward sibilants, and each sentence must be properly balanced about its own centre of gravity, not trailing off into qualifying clauses, but leading up to the cue-word which is the springboard for the following sentence of speech. No other virtues will save unspeakable dialogue. So also when translating words written for music—they must be *singable*. They must fit the original tune, note for note and accent for accent: not only the original lyric but the composer has to be translated; neither must one ever call on the singer to execute a closed vowel on a high note. The extreme difficulty of these conditions is what accounts for the notorious awfulness of almost all translated libretti. But the writing of words for music is an art entirely by itself; nor can it well be illustrated without the assistance of a choir.

Tone and style are another factor. Disagreement about this lies at the root of all the most violent quarrels about the translation of classical works. Most people would agree that the verse of Milton is solemn in tone and elaborate in style, and that the verse of Ariosto is light in tone and witty in style. But no two people, and no two generations, agree about the tone and style of Homer or of Dante or St. Paul; and the diction used in translating them tends to fluctuate dangerously between Wardour Street and Main Street. As to this, the translator must make up his own mind and, if he possibly can, stick to it. But he will continually be faced with the difficulty of deciding whether he is at all costs to maintain a unity of tone, or whether he is called upon to choose at every point the rendering which most closely represents the sense of the original, and effect as best he can the transition from the ancient to the modern, and the noble to the colloquial. Whatever he does, he is certain to get into trouble. The translation of Sacred Writ in particular is full of springes and man-traps, and the fact that the greater part of the New Testament is written in very unclassical and sometimes undistinguished or slangy Greek will be found no defence against accusations of blasphemy. Prose, from this point of view, has its peculiar pitfalls; a transition from one style and tone to the other is more easily managed in verse, where a quiet, unemphatic line of no very marked period or quality will often act as a bridge between two lines which would clash horribly in juxtaposition. Only tact and a trained ear will tell the translator when and where he can venture the archaism, the banging of the big drum, the flat phrase, or the startling modernism menaced on the one side by the established public who have pigeonholed a great poet as noble and dignified, and on the other by the new literates and the journalists, who clamour for the human touch and the new look in everything. On this point it is perhaps well to utter one warning: namely, that the more resolutely up-to-date your translation is, the more swiftly and certainly will it become dated. A poetic diction that is old-fashioned and even a little archaic will seem fresher in twenty years' time than the up-to-the-minute nonce-phrase. We are a little unenthusiastic at present about a "fair maiden"; nevertheless, such beauty as she has she is likely to retain. Whereas, if you are rash enough to bid for present popularity by calling her a "smashing blonde", she will soon be as prematurely aged as the "regular stunner" of the nineties, and as irresistibly ridiculous as her slightly elder sister, the "blooming girl".

The last factor that we shall have time to discuss is *Emphasis* —by which I mean deciding which aspect of any passage is the important one, and which words have, consequently, to be brought to the rhyme and/or stress-point in order to get this emphasis right. One of the chief secrets of good verse-translation is to make rhyme and rhythm pull their weight in the translation as they did in the original: a good many competent and accurate renderings of couplets or stanzaic verse fall down through using insignificant rhyme. Indeed, one of the marks which distinguish the professional poet from the amateur translator is the authoritarian handling of rhyme and metre.

And here, I think, despite the horrible cautionary example of Newman and Arnold, I had better stick my neck out by taking one or two passages from Dante which illustrate the importance of this factor, and showing how, to the best of my skill and judgement, I have dealt with the problems involved.

I will begin with the last line of the Ulysses story in *Inf.* xxvi. The Italian has:

    Infin che 'l mar fu sopra noi richiuso.

"Until the sea had closed over us." There is nothing very recondite about this, and it is easy to render it almost word for word. Longfellow has: "Until the sea above us closed again"; Anderson: "Till at last/The ocean had above us closed again"; Bickersteth says that the whirling water "... downed/The prow, until the sea closed over us"; Binyon (mistakenly to my mind) brings in the *sound* of the sea: "Till over us we heard the waters close" —I doubt whether the drowning men would really have heard precisely that; though Binyon's line is less unfortunate than Cary's "And over us the booming billow closed"—"booming" is a word that needs careful handling if it is not to be ridiculous. I wanted the line to end with the phrase "closed up"; and it would have been quite easy to write: "Until the sea above us had closed up", or "Till over us the ocean had closed up". But none of these lines has the swaying rhythm of the Italian; which falls into three parts—a surge, and a smaller surge, and a silence —the first surge having a faintly triple rhythm:

> Infin che 'l mar/fu sopra noi/richiuso.

and here it seemed to me better to defy the word-counters and the condemners of "padding", and to introduce an epithet unwarranted by the text, simply for the sake of reproducing that rhythm. So, not liking "booming billows" and other sound-effects, I used a traditional and slightly archaic adjective which is almost a "Homeric epithet"—so habitually associated with the word "seas" as to add scarcely anything to it—though what it does add fits into the picture:

> Infin che 'l mar/fu sopra noi/richiuso.
> Till over our heads/the hollow seas/closed up.

Apart from the feminine ending, which did not seem practicable, the original rhythm is repeated exactly. I did not, of course, escape censure on the score of "padding"; and it may well be that I made the wrong choice between verbal accuracy and rhythmic equivalence. The point is that here is the *kind* of choice that the translator is continually faced with; and he alone can say which of the two values seems to him to reproduce most nearly the intention of the poet in writing.

Here is something a little more intricate, because meaning as well as rhyme and metre are involved. Dante has notoriously set his English translators a hard nut to crack by ending each book of his *Comedy* with the word "*stelle*". It was evidently important to him to do so, since in the *Paradiso* it involved him in rhyming on the Latin word "*velle*" rather than on the Italian word "*volier*", which would have been more consistent. He frequently uses "*talento*" and "*volier*" for the opposition or "desire" and "will"; but here, for the rhyme's sake, he uses "*desir*" and "*velle*". The ending on "*stelle*" is, therefore, a major consideration for which he himself was prepared to sacrifice something;

and the translator is bound to respect his judgement. Unhappily, the word "stars" is provided with a singularly unhelpful set of rhymes—cars, bars, jars, mars, spars, parse, nenuphars, jolly Jack Tars—nothing very appropriate to any of the contexts. One can but do one's best. The terzain I propose to discuss now is the one that ends the *Purgatorio*. Dante, having drunk of the waters of Eunoë, announces that:

> Io ritornai dalla santissima onda
> rifatto sì come piante novelle
> rinovellate di novella fronda,
> puro e disposto a salire alle stelle.

This J. D. Sinclair renders in prose:

> From the most holy waters I came forth again remade, even as new plants renewed with new leaves, pure and ready to mount to the stars.

Now it is evident that the other thing which is important here besides the rhyme is the reiteration of the words: "*novelle, rinovellate, novella*"—"new plants renewed with new leaves". The prose translator transcribes this so automatically that this is one of the occasions on which he scarcely pauses to think what the words mean. But what in fact does Dante mean by "new plants renewed"? If they are new, why do they need renewing? And in any case, how can Dante—the sinner now purged—be likened to a *new* plant? If you say, "Come and see my new apple trees", you mean literally *new* ones, that have never borne fruit; but Dante is an old tree that has borne the fruits of sin: he is no tender sapling, but one that is "made new"—and that is the whole point. What is a "new" tree, when it is not a young tree?

A line of Chaucer throws light on this riddle. He says of Alisoun, in *The Miller's Tale*:

> She was ful morë blisful on to see
> Than is the newë pere-jonettë tree—

which John Livingston Lowes paraphrases without hesitation: "the fairness of the pear-tree in the spring". As for Chaucer, so for Dante: the "new" tree is the tree in spring-time, "renewed with new leaves". Now that we know the meaning, our only problem is to find a phrase meaning "in spring-time", which will also provide a rhyme for "stars". Here fortune, so grudging in the matters of these rhymes, suddenly presents us with a pure gift:

> ———born anew
> I came, like trees *by change of calendars*
> Renewed with new-sprung foliage—

And let nobody raise the bright objection that trees do not get their new leaves on New Year's Day; those who have had to cope with the dates in the Italian chroniclers know only too well that in Dante's time the calendar changed at the end of March.

You may call this kind of thing a *tour de force*, a lucky accident, or an unwarrantable tampering with the text. The point is that a choice had to be made between such tampering and the usual "new trees which nothing mars", or something equally inexact and inoffensive. It is this incessant burden of choice that weighs upon the translator, and sets him muttering in his dreams. I have by me some twelve or fifteen different renderings of the opening two terzains of *Paradiso* xxvii, each dealing in its own way with the key-problems of the passage—the rise and lift of the verse which throws the "*gloria*" across the enjambement, the bringing to the rhyme of such awkward words as "Holy Ghost" and "smile", the placing of the bold technical term of the mystics, "*inebriava*", in such a way that it is not offensive and without abstracting it into some generality like "ecstatic", and the antithetical play with "heard and saw", "eye and ear". All the renderings are adequate: none is perfect; for in the translator's work there is no perfection short of identity, and identity is, in the nature of things, always unattainable.

There is one thing I ought to emphasize in conclusion. I have said that the best aim the translator can set before him is to reproduce upon others the effect which the original poem had on him. I ought to add to that, that if the effect is one with which he does not feel himself in sympathy, he had far better leave the whole thing alone, for where there is any kind of antagonism or any inability to enter humbly into the poet's mind and intention, there will be essential falsification. Nobody should undertake to translate a poet whose whole manner of thought and feeling is alien to him. Between poet and translator there needs to be that kind of relation that exists between a tiger and a cat. The cat is very much smaller than the tiger, but there are things she instinctively knows about tigers which the elephant cannot know, because the tiger is her kind of animal. If the poet is not your tiger, leave him alone, for you will never know how his mind works, nor distinguish his pounce from his playfulness. But if he *is* your tiger, go ahead; you may make a few wrong guesses, you are almost bound to diminish his stature, but you will never fall into grievous and essential error, because it is, after all, only a matter of knowing which way the cat jumps.

CHAPTER VII

THE LOST TOOLS OF LEARNING

THAT I, WHOSE EXPERIENCE of teaching is extremely limited, and whose life of recent years has been almost wholly out of touch with educational circles, should presume to discuss education is a matter, surely, that calls for no apology. It is a kind of behaviour to which the present climate of opinion is wholly favourable. Bishops air their opinions about economics; biologists, about metaphysics; celibates, about matrimony; inorganic chemists, about theology; the most irrelevant people are appointed to highly technical ministries; and plain, blunt men write to the papers to say that Epstein and Picasso do not know how to draw. Up to a certain point, and provided that the criticisms are made with a reasonable modesty, these activities are commendable. Too much specialization is not a good thing. There is also one excellent reason why the veriest amateur may feel entitled to have an opinion about education. For if we are not all professional teachers, we have all, at some time or other, been taught. Even if we learnt nothing—perhaps in particular if we learnt nothing—our contribution to the discussion may have a potential value.

Without apology, then, I will begin. But since much that I have to say is highly controversial, it will be pleasant to start with a proposition with which, I feel confident, all teachers will cordially agree; and that is, that they all work much too hard and have far too many things to do. One has only to look at any school or examination syllabus to see that it is cluttered up with a great variety of exhausting subjects which they are called upon to teach, and the teaching of which sadly interferes with what every thoughtful mind will allow to be their proper duties, such as distributing milk, supervising meals, taking cloak-room duty, weighing and measuring pupils, keeping their eyes open for incipient mumps, measles and chicken-pox, making out lists, escorting parties round the Victoria and Albert Museum, filling up forms, interviewing parents, and devising end-of-term reports which shall combine a deep veneration for truth with a tender respect for the feelings of all concerned.

Upon these really important duties I will not enlarge. I propose only to deal with the subject of teaching, properly so-called. I want to inquire whether, amid all the multitudinous subjects which figure in the syllabuses, we are really teaching the right things in the right way; and whether, by teaching fewer things, differently, we might not succeed in "shedding the load" (as the fashionable phrase goes) and, at the same time, producing a better result.

This prospect need arouse neither hope nor alarm. It is in the highest degree improbable that the reforms I propose will ever be carried into effect. Neither the parents, nor the training colleges, nor the examination boards, nor the boards of governors, nor the Ministry of Education would countenance them for a moment. For they amount to this: that if we are to produce a society of educated people, fitted to preserve their intellectual freedom amid the complex pressures of our modern society, we must turn back the wheel of progress some four or five hundred years, to the point at which education began to lose sight of its true object, towards the end of the Middle Ages.

Before you dismiss me with the appropriate phrase—reactionary, romantic, mediaevalist, *laudator temporis acti,* or whatever tag comes first to hand—I will ask you to consider one or two miscellaneous questions that hang about at the back, perhaps, of all our minds, and occasionally pop out to worry us.

When we think about the remarkably early age at which the young men went up to the university in, let us say, Tudor times, and thereafter were held fit to assume responsibility for the conduct of their own affairs, are we altogether comfortable about that artificial prolongation of intellectual childhood and adolescence into the years of physical maturity which is so marked in our own day? To postpone the acceptance of responsibility to a late date brings with it a number of psychological complications which, while they may interest the psychiatrist, are scarcely beneficial either to the individual or to society. The stock argument in favour of postponing the school leaving-age and prolonging the period of education generally is that there is now so much more to learn than there was in the Middle Ages. This is partly true, but not wholly. The modern boy and girl are certainly taught more subjects—but does that always mean that they are actually more learned and know more? That is the very point which we are going to consider.

Has it ever struck you as odd, or unfortunate, that today, when the proportion of literacy throughout Western Europe is higher than it has ever been, people should have become susceptible to the influence of advertisement and mass-propaganda to an extent hitherto unheard-of and unimagined? Do you put this down to the mere mechanical fact that the Press and the radio and so on have made propaganda much easier to distribute over a wide area? Or do you sometimes have an uneasy suspicion that the product of modern educational methods is less good than he or she might be at disentangling fact from opinion and the proven from the plausible?

Have you ever, in listening to a debate among adult and presumably responsible people, been fretted by the extraordinary inability of the average debater to speak to the question, or to meet and refute the arguments of speakers on the other side? Or have you ever pondered upon the extremely high incidence of irrelevant matter which crops up at committee-meetings, and upon the very great rarity of persons capable of acting as chairmen of committees? And when you think of this, and think that most of our public affairs are settled by debates and committees, have you ever felt a certain sinking of the heart?

Have you ever followed a discussion in the newspapers or elsewhere and noticed how frequently writers fail to define the terms they use? Or how often, if one man does define his terms, another will assume in his reply that he was using the terms in precisely the opposite sense to that in which he has already defined them?

Have you ever been faintly troubled by the amount of slipshod syntax going about? And if so, are you troubled because it is inelegant or because it may lead to dangerous misunderstanding?

Do you ever find that young people, when they have left school, not only forget most of what they have learnt (that is only to be expected) but forget also, or betray that they have never really known, how to tackle a new subject for themselves? Are you often bothered by coming across grown-up men and women who seem unable to distinguish between a book that is sound, scholarly and properly documented, and one that is to any trained eye, very conspicuously none of these things? Or who cannot handle a library catalogue? Or who, when faced with a book of reference, betray a curious inability to extract from it the passages relevant to the particular question which interests them?

Do you often come across people for whom, all their lives, a "subject" remains a "subject", divided by watertight bulkheads from all other "subjects", so that they experience very great difficulty in making an immediate mental connection between, let us say, algebra and detective fiction, sewage disposal and the price of salmon, cellulose and the distribution of rainfall—or, more generally, between such spheres of knowledge as philosophy and economics, or chemistry and art?

Are you occasionally perturbed by the things written by adult men and women for adult men and women to read? Here, for instance, is a quotation from an evening paper. It refers to the visit of an Indian girl to this country:

> Miss Bhosle has a perfect command of English ("Oh, gosh", she said once), and a marked enthusiasm for London.

Well, we may all talk nonsense in a moment of inattention. It is more alarming when we find a well-known biologist writing in a weekly paper to the effect that: "It is an argument against the existence of a Creator" (I think he put it more strongly; but since I have, most unfortunately, mislaid the reference, I will put his claim at its lowest)—"an argument against the existence of a Creator that the same kind of variations which are produced by natural selection can be produced at will by stock-breeders." One might feel tempted to say that it is rather an argument *for* the existence of a Creator. Actually, of course, it is neither: all it proves is that the same material causes (re-combination of the chromosomes by cross-breeding and so forth) are sufficient to account for all observed variations—just as the various combinations of the same thirteen semitones are materially sufficient to account for Beethoven's *Moonlight Sonata* and the noise the cat makes by walking on the keys. But the cat's performance neither proves nor disproves the existence of Beethoven; and all that is proved by the biologist's argument is that he was unable to distinguish between a material and a final cause.

Here is a sentence from no less academic a source than a front-page article in the *Times Literary Supplement*:

The Frenchman, Alfred Epinas, pointed out that certain species (e.g. ants and wasps) can only face the horrors of life and death in association.

I do not know what the Frenchman actually did say: what the Englishman says he said is patently meaningless. We cannot know whether life holds any horror for the ant, nor in what sense the isolated wasp which you kill upon the window-pane can be said to "face" or not to "face" the horrors of death. The subject of the article is mass-behaviour in *man*; and the human motives have been unobtrusively transferred from the main proposition to the supporting instance. Thus the argument, in effect, assumes what it sets out to prove—a fact which would become immediately apparent if it were presented in a formal syllogism. This is only a small and haphazard example of a vice which pervades whole books—particularly books written by men of science on metaphysical subjects.

Another quotation from the same issue of the *T.L.S.* comes in fittingly here to wind up this random collection of disquieting thoughts—this time from a review of Sir Richard Livingstone's *Some Tasks for Education*:

> More than once the reader is reminded of the value of an intensive study of at least one subject, so as to learn "the meaning of knowledge" and what precision and persistence is needed to attain it. Yet there is elsewhere full recognition of the distressing fact that a man may be master in one field and show no better judgement than his neighbour anywhere else; he remembers what he has learnt, but forgets altogether how he learned it.

I would draw your attention particularly to that last sentence, which offers an explanation of what the writer rightly calls the "distressing fact" that the intellectual skills bestowed upon us by our education are not readily transferable to subjects other than those in which we acquired them: "he remembers what he has learnt, but forgets altogether how he learned it."

Is not the great defect of our education today—a defect traceable through all the disquieting symptoms of trouble that I have mentioned—that although we often succeed in teaching our pupils "subjects", we fail lamentably on the whole in teaching them how to think? They learn everything, except the art of learning. It is as though we had taught a child, mechanically and by rule of thumb, to play *The Harmonious Blacksmith* upon the piano, but had never taught him the scale or how to read music; so that, having memorized *The Harmonious Blacksmith*, he still had not the faintest notion how to proceed from that to tackle *The Last Rose of Summer*. Why do I say, "As though"? In certain of the arts and crafts we sometimes do precisely this—requiring a child to "express himself" in paint before we teach him how to handle the colours and the brush. There is a school of thought which believes this to be the right way to set about the job. But observe—it is not the way in which a trained craftsman will go about to teach himself a new medium. *He,* having learned by experience the best way to economise labour and take the thing by the right end, will start off by doodling about on an odd piece of material, in order to "give himself the feel of the tool".

Let us now look at the mediaeval scheme of education—the syllabus of the schools. It does not matter, for the moment, whether it was devised for small children or for older students; or how long people were supposed to take over it. What matters is the light it throws upon what the men of the Middle Ages supposed to be the object and the right order of the educative process.

The syllabus was divided into two parts; the Trivium and Quadrivium. The second part—the Quadrivium—consisted of "subjects", and need not for the moment concern us. The interesting thing for us is the composition of the Trivium, which preceded the Quadrivium and was the preliminary discipline for it. It consisted of three parts: Grammar, Dialectic, and Rhetoric, in that order.

Now the first thing we notice is that two at any rate of these "subjects" are not what we should call "subjects" at all: they are only methods of dealing with subjects. Grammar, indeed, is a "subject" in the sense that it does mean definitely learning a language—at that period it meant learning Latin. But language itself is simply the medium in which thought is expressed. The whole of the Trivium was, in fact, intended to teach the pupil the proper use of the tools of learning, before he began to apply them to "subjects" at all. First, he learned a language; not just how to order a meal in a foreign language, but the structure of language—*a* language, and hence of language itself—what it was, how it was put together and how it worked. Secondly, he learned how to use language: how to define his terms and make accurate statements; how to construct an argument and how to detect fallacies in argument (his own arguments and other people's). Dialectic, that is to say, embraced Logic and Disputation. Thirdly, he learned to express himself in language; how to say what he had to say elegantly and persuasively. At this point, any tendency to express himself windily or to use his eloquence so as to make the worse appear the better reason would, no doubt, be restrained by his previous teaching in Dialectic. If not, his teacher and his fellow-pupils, trained along the same lines, would be quick to point out where he was wrong; for it was they whom he had to seek to persuade. At the end of his course, he was required to compose a thesis upon some theme set by his masters or chosen by himself, and afterwards to defend his thesis against the criticism of the faculty. By this time he would have learned— or woe betide him—not merely to write an essay on paper, but to speak audibly and intelligibly from a platform, and to use his wits quickly when heckled. The heckling, moreover, would not consist solely of offensive personalities or of irrelevant queries about what Julius Caesar said in 55 B.C.—though no doubt mediaeval dialectic was enlivened in practice by plenty of such primitive repartee. But there would also be questions, cogent and shrewd, from those who had already run the gauntlet of debate, or were making ready to run it.

It is, of course, quite true that bits and pieces of the mediaeval tradition still linger, or have been revived, in the ordinary school syllabus of today. Some knowledge of grammar is still required when learning a foreign language—perhaps I should say, "is again required"; for during my own lifetime we passed through a phase when the teaching of declensions and conjugations was considered rather reprehensible, and it was considered better to pick these things up as we went along. School debating societies flourish; essays are written; the necessity for "self-expression" is stressed, and perhaps even over-stressed. But these activities are cultivated more or less in detachment, as belonging to the special subjects in which they are pigeonholed rather than as forming one coherent scheme of mental training to which all "subjects" stands in a subordinate relation. "Grammar" belongs especially to the "subject" of foreign languages, and essay-writing to the "subject" called "English"; while Dialectic has become almost entirely divorced from the rest of the curriculum, and is frequently practised unsystematically and out of school-hours as a separate exercise, only very loosely related to the main business of learning. Taken by and large, the great difference of emphasis between the two conceptions holds good: modern education concentrates on *teaching subjects*, leaving the method of thinking, arguing and expressing one's conclusions to be picked up by the scholar as he goes along; mediaeval education concentrated on first *forging and learning to handle the tools of learning*, using whatever subject came handy as a piece of material on which to doodle until the use of the tool became second nature.

"Subjects" of some kind there must be, of course. One cannot learn the use of a tool by merely waving it in the air; neither can one learn the theory of grammar without learning an actual language, or learn to argue and orate without speaking about something in particular. The debating subjects of the Middle Ages were drawn largely from Theology, or from the Ethics and History of Antiquity. Often, indeed, they became stereotyped, especially towards the end of the period, and the far-fetched and wire-drawn absurdities of scholastic argument fretted Milton and provide food for merriment even to this day. Whether they were in themselves any more hackneyed and trivial than the usual subjects set nowadays for "essay-writing" I should not like to say: we may ourselves grow a little weary of "A Day in my Holidays", "What I should like to Do when I Leave School", and all the rest of it. But most of the merriment is misplaced, because the aim and object of the debating thesis has by now been lost sight of. A glib speaker in the Brains Trust once entertained his audience (and reduced the late Charles Williams to helpless rage) by asserting that in the Middle Ages it was a matter of faith to know how many archangels could dance on the point of a needle. I need not say, I hope, that it never was a "matter of faith"; it was simply a debating exercise, whose set subject was the nature of angelic substance: were angels material, and if so, did they occupy space? The answer usually adjudged correct is, I believe, that angels are pure intelligences; not material, but limited, so that they may have location in space but not extension. An analogy might be drawn from human thought, which is similarly non-material and similarly limited. Thus, if your thought is concentrated upon one thing—say, the point of a needle—it is located there in the sense that it is not elsewhere; but although it is "there", it occupies no space there, and there is nothing to prevent an infinite number of different people's thoughts being concentrated upon the same needle-point at the same time. The proper *subject* of the argument is thus seen to be the distinction between location and extension in space; the *matter* on which the argument is exercised happens to be the nature of angels (although, as we have seen, it might equally well have been something else); the practical lesson to be drawn from the argument is not to use words like "there" in a loose and unscientific way, without specifying whether you mean "located there" or "occupying space there". Scorn in plenty has been poured out upon the mediaeval passion for hair-splitting: but when we look at the shameless abuse made, in print and on the platform, of controversial expressions with shifting and ambiguous connotations, we may feel it in our hearts to wish that every reader and hearer had been so defensively armoured by his education as to be able to cry: *Distinguo.*

For we let our young men and women go out unarmed, in a day when armour was never so necessary. By teaching them all to read, we have left them at the mercy of the printed word. By the invention of the film and the radio, we have made certain that no aversion to reading shall secure them from the incessant battery of words, words, words. They do not know what the words mean; they do not know how to ward them off or blunt their edge or fling them back; they are a prey to words in their emotions instead of being the masters of them in their intellects. We who were scandalized in 1940 when men were sent to fight armoured tanks with rifles, are not scandalized when young men and women are sent into the world to fight massed propaganda with a smattering of "subjects"; and when whole classes and whole nations become hypnotised by the arts of the spell-binder, we have the impudence to be astonished. We dole out lip-service to the importance of education—lip-service and, just occasionally, a little grant of money; we postpone the school leaving-age, and plan to build bigger and better schools; the teachers slave conscientiously in and out of school-hours, till responsibility becomes a burden and a nightmare; and yet, as I believe, all this devoted effort is largely frustrated, because we have lost the tools of learning, and in their absence can only make a botched and piecemeal job of it.

What, then, are we to do? We cannot go back to the Middle Ages. That is a cry to which we have become accustomed. We cannot go back—or can we? *Distinguo.* I should like every term in that proposition defined. Does "Go back" mean a retrogression in time, or the revision of an error? The first is clearly impossible *per se*; the second is a thing which wise men do every day. "Cannot"—does this mean that our behaviour is determined by some irreversible cosmic mechanism, or merely that such an action would be very difficult in view of the opposition it would provoke? "The Middle Ages"—obviously the twentieth century is not and cannot be the fourteenth; but if "the Middle Ages" is, in this context, simply a picturesque phrase denoting a particular educational theory, there seems to be no *a priori* reason why we should not "go back" to it—with modifications—as we have already "gone back", with modifications, to, let us say, the idea of playing Shakespeare's plays as he wrote them, and not in the "modernized" versions of Cibber and Garrick, which once seemed to be the latest thing in theatrical progress.

Let us amuse ourselves by imagining that such progressive retrogression is possible. Let us make a clean sweep of all educational authorities, and furnish ourselves with a nice little school of boys and girls whom we may experimentally equip for the intellectual conflict along lines chosen by ourselves. We will endow them with exceptionally docile parents; we will staff our school with teachers who are themselves perfectly familiar with the aims and methods of the Trivium; we will have our buildings and staff large enough to allow our classes to be small enough for adequate handling; and we will postulate a Board of Examiners willing and qualified to test the products we turn out. Thus prepared, we will attempt to sketch out a syllabus—a modern Trivium "with modifications"; and we will see where we get to.

But first: what age shall the children be? Well, if one is to educate them on novel lines, it will be better that they should have nothing to unlearn; besides, one cannot begin a good thing too early, and the Trivium is by its nature not learning, but a preparation for learning. We will, therefore, "catch 'em young", requiring only of our pupils that they shall be able to read, write and cipher.

My views about child-psychology are, I admit, neither orthodox nor enlightened. Looking back upon myself (since I am the child I know best and the only child I can pretend to know from inside) I recognize in myself three stages of development. These, in a rough-and-ready fashion, I will call the Poll-parrot, the Pert, and the Poetic—the latter coinciding, approximately, with the onset of puberty. The Poll-parrot stage is the one in which learning by heart is easy and, on the whole, pleasurable; whereas reasoning is difficult and, on the whole, little relished. At this age, one readily memorizes the shapes and appearances of things; one likes to recite the number-plates of cars; one rejoices in the chanting of rhymes and the rumble and thunder of unintelligible polysyllables; one enjoys the mere accumulation of things. The Pert Age, which follows upon this (and, naturally, overlaps it to some extent), is only too familiar to all who have to do with children : it is characterized by contradicting, answering-back, liking to "catch people out" (especially one's elders) and in the propounding of conundrums (especially the kind with a nasty verbal catch in them). Its nuisance-value is extremely high. It usually sets in about the Lower Fourth. The Poetic Age is popularly known as the 'difficult" age. It is self-centred; it yearns to express itself; it rather specializes in being misunderstood; it is restless and tries to achieve independence; and, with good luck and good guidance, it should show the beginnings of creativeness, a reaching-out towards a synthesis of what it already knows, and a deliberate eagerness to know and do some one thing in preference to all others. Now it seems to me that the lay-out of the Trivium adapts itself with a singular appropriateness to these three ages : Grammar to the Poll-parrot, Dialectic to the Pert, and Rhetoric to the Poetic age.

Let us begin, then, with Grammar. This, in practice, means the grammar of some language in particular; and it must be an inflected language. The grammatical structure of an uninflected language is far too analytical to be tackled by anyone without previous practice in Dialectic. Moreover, the inflected languages interpret the uninflected, whereas the uninflected are of little use in interpreting the inflected. I will say at once, quite firmly, that the best grounding for education is the Latin grammar. I say this, not because Latin is traditional and mediaeval, but simply because even a rudimentary knowledge of Latin cuts down the labour and pains of learning almost any other subject by at least fifty per cent. It is the key to the vocabulary and structure of all the Romance languages and to the structure of all the Teutonic languages, as well as to the technical vocabulary of all the sciences and to the literature of the entire Mediterranean civilization, together with all its historical documents. Those whose pedantic preference for a living language persuades them to deprive their pupils of all these advantages might substitute Russian, whose grammar is still more primitive. (The verb is complicated by a number of "aspects"—and I rather fancy that it enjoys three complete voices and a couple of extra aorists—but I may be thinking of Basque or Sanskrit.) Russian is, of course, helpful with the other Slav dialects. There is something also to be said for Classical Greek. But my own choice is Latin. Having thus pleased the Classicists among you, I will proceed to horrify them by adding that I do not think it either wise or necessary to cramp the ordinary pupil upon the Procrustean bed of the Augustan age, with its highly elaborate and artificial verse-forms and oratory. The post-classical and mediaeval Latin, which was a living language down to the end of the Renaissance, is easier and in some ways livelier, both in syntax and rhythm; and a study of it helps to dispel the widespread notion that learning and literature came to a full-stop when Christ was born and only woke up again at the Dissolution of the Monasteries.

However, I am running ahead too fast. We are still in the grammatical stage. Latin should be begun as early as possible— at a time when inflected speech seems no more astonishing than any other phenomenon in an astonishing world; and when the chanting of "amo, amas, amat" is as ritually agreeable to the feelings as the chanting of "eeny, meeny, miney, mo".

During this age we must, of course, exercise the mind on other things besides Latin grammar. Observation and memory are the faculties most lively at this period; and if we are to learn a contemporary foreign language we should begin now, before the facial and mental muscles become rebellious to strange intonations. Spoken French or German can be practised alongside the grammatical discipline of the Latin.

In *English*, verse and prose can be learned by heart, and the pupil's memory should be stored with stories of every kind— classical myth, European legend, and so forth. I do not think that the Classical stories and masterpieces of ancient literature should be made the vile bodies on which to practise the technics of Grammar—that was a fault of mediaeval education which we need not perpetuate. The stories can be enjoyed and remembered in English, and related to their origin at a subsequent stage. Recitation aloud should be practised—individually or in chorus; for we must not forget that we are laying the ground work for Disputation and Rhetoric.

The grammar of *History* should consist, I think, of dates, events, anecdotes and personalities. A set of dates to which one can peg all later historical knowledge is of enormous help later on in establishing the perspective of history. It does not greatly matter *which* dates: those of the Kings of England will do very nicely, provided that they are accompanied by pictures of costume, architecture, and other "everyday things", so that the mere mention of a date calls up a strong visual presentment of the whole period.

Geography will similarly be presented in its factual aspect, with maps, natural features and visual presentment of customs, costumes, flora, fauna and so on; and I believe myself that the discredited and old-fashioned memorizing of a few capital cities, rivers, mountain ranges, etc., does no harm. Stamp-collecting may be encouraged.

Science, in the Poll-parrot period, arranges itself naturally and easily round collections—the identifying and naming of specimens and, in general, the kind of thing that used to be called "natural history", or, still more charmingly, "natural philosophy". To know the names and properties of things is, at this age, a satisfaction in itself; to recognize a devil's coach-horse at sight, and assure one's foolish elders that, in spite of its appearance, it does not sting; to be able to pick out Cassiopeia and the Pleiades, and possibly even to know who Cassiopeia and the Pleiades were; to be aware that a whale is not a fish, and a bat not a bird—all these things give a pleasant sensation of superiority; while to know a ring-snake from an adder or a poisonous from an edible toadstool is a kind of knowledge that has also a practical value.

The grammar of *Mathematics* begins, of course, with the multiplication table, which if not learnt now will never be learnt with pleasure; and with the recognition of geometrical shapes and the grouping of numbers. These exercises lead naturally to the doing of simple sums in arithmetic; and if the pupil shows a bent that way, a facility acquired at this stage is all to the good. More complicated mathematical processes may, and perhaps should, be postponed, for reasons which will presently appear.

So far (except, of course, for the Latin), our curriculum contains nothing that departs very far from common practice. The difference will be felt rather in the attitude of the teachers, who must look upon all these activities less as "subjects" in themselves than as a gathering-together of *material* for use in the next part of the Trivium. What that material actually is, is only of secondary importance; but it is as well that anything and everything which can usefully be committed to memory should be memorized at this period, whether it is immediately intelligible or not. The modern tendency is to try and force rational explanations on a child's mind at too early an age. Intelligent questions, spontaneously asked, should, of course, receive an immediate and rational answer; but it is a great mistake to suppose that a child cannot readily enjoy and remember things that are beyond its power to analyse—particularly if those things have a strong imaginative appeal (as, for example, *Kubla Khan*), an attractive jingle (like some of the memory-rhymes for Latin genders), or an abundance of rich, resounding polysyllables (like the *Quicunque Vult*).

This reminds me of the Grammar of *Theology*. I shall add it to the curriculum, because Theology is the mistress-science, without which the whole educational structure will necessarily lack its final synthesis. Those who disagree about this will remain content to leave their pupils' education still full of loose ends. This will matter rather less than it might, since by the time that the tools of learning have been forged the student will be able to tackle Theology for himself, and will probably insist upon doing so and making sense of it. Still, it is as well to have this matter also handy and ready for the reason to work upon. At the grammatical age, therefore, we should become acquainted with the story of God and Man in outline—i.e. the Old and New Testament presented as parts of a single narrative of Creation, Rebellion and Redemption—and also with "the Creed, the Lord's Prayer and the Ten Commandments". At this stage, it does not matter nearly so much that these things should be fully understood as that they should be known and remembered. Remember, it is material that we are collecting.

It is difficult to say at what age, precisely, we should pass from the first to the second part of the Trivium. Generally speaking, the answer is: so soon as the pupil shows himself disposed to Pertness and interminable argument (or, as a schoolmaster correspondent of mine more elegantly puts it: "When the capacity for abstract thought begins to manifest itself"). For as, in the first part, the master-faculties are Observation and Memory, so in the second, the master-faculty is the Discursive Reason. In the first, the exercise to which the rest of the material was, as it were, keyed, was the Latin Grammar; in the second the key-exercise will be Formal Logic. It is here that our curriculum shows its first sharp divergence from modern standards. The disrepute into which Formal Logic has fallen is entirely unjustified; and its neglect is the root cause of nearly all those disquieting symptoms which we have noted in the modern intellectual constitution. Logic has been discredited, partly because we have fallen into a habit of supposing that we are conditioned almost entirely by the intuitive and the unconscious. There is no time now to argue whether this is true; I will content myself with observing that to neglect the proper training of the reason is the best possible way to make it true, and to ensure the supremacy of the intuitive, irrational and unconscious elements in our make-up. A secondary cause for the disfavour into which Formal Logic has fallen is the belief that it is entirely based upon universal assumptions that are either unprovable or tautological. This is not true. Not all universal propositions are of this kind. But even if they were, it would make no difference, since every syllogism whose major premise is in the form "All A is B" can be recast in hypothetical form. Logic is the art of arguing correctly: "If A, then B"; the method is not invalidated by the hypothetical character of A. Indeed, the practical utility of Formal Logic today lies not so much in the establishment of positive conclusions as in the prompt detection and exposure of invalid inference.

Let us now quickly review our material and see how it is to be related to Dialectic. On the *Language* side, we shall now have our Vocabulary and Morphology at our finger-tips; henceforward we can concentrate more particularly on Syntax and Analysis (i.e. the logical construction of speech) and the history of Language (i.e. how we came to arrange our speech as we do in order to convey our thoughts).

Our Reading will proceed from narrative and lyric to essays, argument and criticism, and the pupil will learn to try his own hand at writing this kind of thing. Many lessons—on whatever subject—will take the form of debates; and the place of individual or choral recitation will be taken by dramatic performances, with special attention to plays in which an argument is stated in dramatic form.

Mathematics—Algebra, Geometry, and the more advanced kind of Arithmetic—will now enter into the syllabus and take its place as what it really is: not a separate "subject" but a sub-department of Logic. It is neither more nor less than the rule of the syllogism in its particular application to number and measurement, and should be taught as such, instead of being, for some, a dark mystery, and for others, a special revelation, neither illuminating nor illuminated by any other part of knowledge.

History, aided by a simple system of ethics derived from the Grammar of Theology, will provide much suitable material for discussion; Was the behaviour of this statesman justified? What was the effect of such an enactment? What are the arguments for and against this or that form of government? We shall thus get an introduction to Constitutional History—a subject meaningless to the young child, but of absorbing interest to those who are prepared to argue and debate. *Theology* itself will furnish material for argument about conduct and morals; and should have its scope extended by a simplified course of dogmatic theology (i.e. the rational structure of Christian thought), clarifying the relations between the dogma and the ethics, and lending itself to that application of ethical principles in particular instances which is properly called casuistry. *Geography* and the *Sciences* will all likewise provide material for Dialectic.

But above all, we must not neglect the material which is so abundant in the pupils' own daily life. There is a delightful passage in Leslie Paul's *The Living Hedge* which tells how a number of small boys enjoyed themselves for days arguing about an extraordinary shower of rain which had fallen in their town—a shower so localized that it left one half of the main street wet and the other dry. Could one, they argued, properly say that it had rained that day *on* or *over* the town or only *in* the town? How many drops of water were required to constitute rain? and so on. Arguments about this led on to a host of similar problems about rest and motion, sleep and waking, *est* and *non est*, and the infinitesimal division of time. The whole passage is an admirable example of the spontaneous development of the ratiocinative faculty and the natural and proper thirst of the awakening reason for definition of terms and exactness of statement. All events are food for such an appetite. An umpire's decision; the degree to which one may transgress the spirit of a regulation without being trapped by the letter; on such questions as these, children are born casuists, and their natural propensity only needs to be developed and trained—and, especially, brought into an intelligible relationship with events in the grown-up world. The newspapers are full of good material for such exercises; legal decisions, on the one hand, in cases where the cause at issue is not too abstruse; on the other, fallacious reasoning and muddle-headed argument, with which the correspondence columns of certain papers one could name are abundantly stocked.

Wherever the matter for Dialectic is found, it is, of course, highly important that attention should be focused upon the beauty and economy of a fine demonstration or a well-turned argument, lest veneration should wholly die. Criticism must not be merely destructive; though at the same time both teacher and pupils must be ready to detect fallacy, slipshod reasoning, ambiguity, irrelevance and redundancy, and to pounce upon them like rats.

This is the moment when précis-writing may be usefully undertaken; together with such exercises as the writing of an essay, and the reduction of it, when written, by 25 or 50 per cent.

It will, doubtless, be objected that to encourage young persons at the Pert Age to browbeat, correct and argue with their elders will render them perfectly intolerable. My answer is that children of that age are intolerable anyhow; and that their natural argumentativeness may just as well be canalised to good purpose as allowed to run away into the sands. It may, indeed, be rather less obtrusive at home if it is disciplined in school; and, anyhow, elders who have abandoned the wholesome principle that children should be seen and not heard have no one to blame but themselves. The teachers, to be sure, will have to mind their step, or they may get more than they bargained for. All children sit in judgement on their masters; and if the Chaplain's sermon or the Headmistress's annual Speech-day address should by any chance afford an opening for the point of the critical wedge, that wedge will go home the more forcibly under the weight of the Dialectical hammer, wielded by a practised hand. That is why I said that the teachers themselves would need to undergo the discipline of the Trivium before they set out to impose it on their charges.

Once again: the contents of the syllabus at this stage may be anything you like. The "subjects" supply material; but they are all to be regarded as mere grist for the mental mill to work upon. The pupils should be encouraged to go and forage for their own information, and so guided towards the proper use of libraries and books of reference, and shown how to tell which sources are authoritative and which are not.

Towards the close of this stage, the pupils will probably be beginning to discover for themselves that their knowledge and experience are insufficient, and that their trained intelligences need a great deal more material to chew upon. The imagination —usually dormant during the Pert Age—will re-awaken, and prompt them to suspect the limitations of logic and reason. This means that they are passing into the Poetic Age and are ready to embark on the study of Rhetoric. The doors of the storehouse of knowledge should now be thrown open for them to browse about as they will. The things once learned by rote will be seen in new contexts; the things once coldly analysed can now be brought together to form a new synthesis; here and there a sudden insight will bring about that most exciting of all discoveries: the realization that a truism is true.

It is difficult to map out any general syllabus for the study of Rhetoric: a certain freedom is demanded. In literature, appreciation should be again allowed to take the lead over destructive criticism; and self-expression in writing can go forward, with its tools now sharpened to cut clean and observe proportion. Any child that already shows a disposition to specialize should be given his head: for, when the use of the tools has been well and truly learned, it is available for any study whatever. It would be well, I think, that each pupil should learn to do one, or two, subjects really well, while taking a few classes in subsidiary subjects so as to keep his mind open to the inter-relations of all knowledge. Indeed, at this stage, our difficulty will be to keep "subjects" apart; for as Dialectic will have shown all branches of learning to be inter-related, so Rhetoric will tend to show that all knowledge is one. To show this, and show why it is so, is pre-eminently the task of the Mistress-science. But whether Theology is studied or not, we should at least insist that children who seem inclined to specialize on the mathematical and scientific side should be obliged to attend some lessons in the Humanities and vice versa. At this stage also, the Latin Grammar, having done its work, may be dropped for those who prefer to carry on their language studies on the modern side; while those who are likely never to have any great use or aptitude for mathematics might also be allowed to rest, more or less, upon their oars. Generally speaking: whatsoever is *mere* apparatus may now be allowed to fall into the background, while the trained mind is gradually prepared for specialization in the "subjects" which, when the Trivium is completed, it should be perfectly well equipped to tackle on its own. The final synthesis of the Trivium —the presentation and public defence of the thesis—should be restored in some form; perhaps as a kind of "leaving examination" during the last term at school.

The scope of Rhetoric depends also on whether the pupil is to be turned out into the world at the age of sixteen or whether he is to proceed to public school and/or university. Since, really, Rhetoric should be taken at about fourteen, the first category of pupil should study Grammar from about nine to eleven, and Dialectic from twelve to fourteen; his last two school years would then be devoted to Rhetoric, which, in his case, would be of a fairly specialized and vocational kind, suiting him to enter immediately upon some practical career. A pupil of the second category would finish his Dialectical course in his preparatory school, and take Rhetoric during his first two years at his public school. At sixteen, he would be ready to start upon those "subjects" which are proposed for his later study at the university : and this part of his education will correspond to the mediaeval Quadrivium. What this amounts to is that the ordinary pupil, whose formal education ends at sixteen, will take the Trivium only; whereas scholars will take both Trivium and Quadrivium.

Is the Trivium, then, a sufficient education for life? Properly taught, I believe that it should be. At the end of the Dialectic, the children will probably seem to be far behind their coevals brought up on old-fashioned "modern" methods, so far as detailed knowledge of specific subjects is concerned. But after the age of fourteen they should be able to overhaul the others hand over fist. Indeed, I am not at all sure that a pupil thoroughly proficient in the Trivium would not be fit to proceed immediately to the university at the age of sixteen, thus proving himself the equal of his mediaeval counterpart, whose precocity astonished us at the beginning of this discussion. This, to be sure, would make hay of the public-school system, and disconcert the universities very much—it would, for example, make quite a different thing of the Oxford and Cambridge Boat Race. But I am not here to consider the feelings of academic bodies: I am concerned only with the proper training of the mind to encounter and deal with the formidable mass of undigested problems presented to it by the modern world. For the tools of learning are the same, in any and every subject; and the person who knows how to use them will, at any age, get the mastery of a new subject in half the time and with a quarter of the effort expended by the person who has not the tools at his command. To learn six subjects without remembering how they were learnt does nothing to ease the approach to a seventh; to have learnt and remembered the art of learning makes the approach to every subject an open door.

It is clear that the successful teaching of this neo-mediaeval curriculum will depend even more than usual upon the working together of the whole teaching staff towards a common purpose. Since no subject is considered as an end in itself, any kind of rivalry in the staff-room will be sadly out of place. The fact that a pupil is, unfortunately, obliged, for some reason, to miss the History period on Fridays, or the Shakespeare class on Tuesdays, or even to omit a whole subject in favour of some other subject, must not be allowed to cause any heart-burnings—the essential is that he should acquire the method of learning in whatever medium suits him best. If human nature suffers under this blow to one's professional pride in one's own subject, there is comfort in the thought that the end-of-term examination results will not be affected; for the papers will be so arranged as to be an examination in method, by whatever means.

I will add that it is highly important that every teacher should, for his or her own sake, be qualified and required to teach in all three parts of the Trivium; otherwise the Masters of Dialectic, especially, might find their minds hardening into a permanent adolescence. For this reason, teachers in preparatory schools should also take Rhetoric classes in the public schools to which they are attached; or, if they are not so attached, then by arrangement in other schools in the same neighbourhood. Alternatively, a few preliminary classes in Rhetoric might be taken in preparatory schools from the age of thirteen onwards.

Before concluding these necessarily very sketchy suggestions, I ought to say why I think it necessary, in these days, to go back to a discipline which we had discarded. The truth is that for the last 300 years or so we have been living upon our educational capital. The post-Renaissance world, bewildered and excited by the profusion of new "subjects" offered to it, broke away from the old discipline (which had, indeed, become sadly dull and stereotyped in its practical application) and imagined that henceforward it could, as it were, disport itself happily in its new and extended Quadrivium without passing through the Trivium. But the scholastic tradition, though broken and maimed, still lingered in the public schools and universities: Milton, however much he protested against it, was formed by it—the debate of the Fallen Angels and the disputation of Abdiel with Satan have the tool-marks of the schools upon them, and might, incidentally, profitably figure as set passages for our Dialectical studies. Right down to the nineteenth century, our public affairs were mostly managed, and our books and journals were for the most part written, by people brought up in homes, and trained in places, where that tradition was still alive in the memory and almost in the blood. Just so, many people today who are atheist or agnostic in religion, are governed in their conduct by a code of Christian ethics which is so rooted in their unconscious assumptions that it never occurs to them to question it. But one cannot live on capital for ever. A tradition, however firmly rooted, if it is never watered, though it dies hard, yet in the end it dies. And today a great number—perhaps the majority—of the men and women who handle our affairs, write our books and our newspapers, carry out research, present our plays and our films, speak from our platforms and pulpits—yes, and who educate our young people, have never, even in a lingering traditional memory, undergone the scholastic discipline. Less and less do the children who come to be educated bring any of that tradition with them. We have lost the tools of learning—the axe and the wedge, the hammer and the saw, the chisel and the plane—that were so adaptable to all tasks. Instead of them, we have merely a set of complicated jigs, each of which will do but one task and no more, and in using which eye and hand receive no training, so that no man ever sees the work as a whole or "looks to the end of the work". What use is it to pile task on task and prolong the days of labour, if at the close the chief object is left unattained? It is not the fault of the teachers—they work only too hard already. The combined folly of a civilization that has forgotten its own roots is forcing them to shore up the tottering weight of an educational structure that is built upon sand. They are doing for their pupils the work which the pupils themselves ought to do. For the sole true end of education is simply this: to teach men how to learn for themselves; and whatever instruction fails to do this is effort spent in vain.

CHAPTER VIII

THE TEACHING OF LATIN: A NEW APPROACH

HAVING RECEIVED FROM your Society[1] an invitation no less courteous than pressing, I accepted with alacrity the opportunity of coming to speak to you. I stand here prepared, not, I fear, to increase your information or improve your minds, nor yet to offer you any very lively entertainment; but only to pour into your sympathetic ears the story of my life. It is not a sensational story, nor one calculated to appeal to the headline writers of the *Local Gossip* and the *Daily Ghoul*, eager though they always are for the personal angle on every subject from the habits of the liver-fluke to the higher mathematics. Yet you may agree with me that it has, after all, its tragic aspects.

Infandum regina, jubes renovare dolorem

as the old Latin poet puts it:

Sed si tantus amor casus cognoscere nostros... incipiam

or, as a later poet puts it in a younger Italian tongue:

Dizò come colui che piange e dice.

It is not without deliberate purpose that I have begun with those two notorious tags; for it is part of the contemporary tragedy that one can no longer call them notorious.

I was born at Oxford, in the fourth year before Queen Victoria's Diamond Jubilee. My father was at that time Headmaster of the Cathedral Choir School, where it was part of his duty to instruct small demons with angel-voices in the elements of the ancient Roman tongue. When I was four-and-a-half years old, he was presented with the living of Bluntisham-cum-Earith, in Huntingdonshire—an isolated country parish, which was one of the ancient ports or bridges to the Isle of Ely, and which

[1] The Association for the Reform of Latin Teaching.

contains to this day the bulwarks of a Roman camp. I recollect very well my first arrival at the Rectory, wearing a brown pelisse and bonnet trimmed with feathers, and accompanied by my nurse and my maiden aunt, who carried a parrot in a cage. It was January, and the winter must have been mild that year, for the drive near the gate was already bright yellow with winter aconites—a plant which is said never to grow except where the soil has been watered by Roman blood. For all I know, this is true; for they grow thickly in my present garden in Essex, which lies along the road by which the Emperor Claudius marched upon Colchester.

I do not know whether my father missed his small choristers amid the new duties of a country parish, or whether he was actuated only by a sense of the fitness of things and a regard for his daughter's intellectual welfare. I know only that I was rising seven when he appeared one morning in the nursery, holding in his hand a shabby black book, which had already seen some service, and addressed to me the following memorable words: "I think, my dear, that you are now old enough to begin to learn Latin."

And should the representatives of the *Local Gossip* and the *Daily Ghoul* think this matter for a headline: "Began Latin at Six, says Author Sayers," one would have to rebuke their ignorance. There was nothing unusual about my father's action, neither did it argue any remarkable aptitude in me. In those dark ages, half a century ago, before modern educational improvements had set in, that was the age at which one did begin to learn Latin. My father, seeing his offspring approach that age, reacted automatically to the situation. In the absence of little boys, he seized upon such infant material as was at hand, and went to work with the customary tool, which was, in fact, Dr. William Smith's *Principia*.

I was by no means unwilling, because it seemed to me that it would be a very fine thing to learn Latin, and would place me in a position of superiority to my mother, my aunt, and my nurse—though not to my paternal grandmother, who was an old lady of parts, and had at least a nodding acquaintance with the language. My father sat down in the big chair, put his arm round me to restrain me from wriggling and, opening the book, confronted me with the mysterious formula:

THE TEACHING OF LATIN

mensa:	a table
mensa:	O table!
mensam:	a table
mensae:	of a table
mensae:	to or for a table
mensā:	by, with, or from a table

Presumably at this point he explained that the ancient Romans had had the un-English habit of altering the endings of their nouns according as the case was altered. I have no recollection of finding anything particularly odd about this: I was far too young. Life was full of odd things which one accepted without protest, as simple facts. A dog had four legs, a beetle six, a spider eight: why not? I do remember wondering why anybody should ever want to say "O table"; and I also remember finding it, at some later point, entertaining that a sailor, a poet, or a husbandman should have feminine endings. However, the first three sentences of Exercise I raised none of those social problems, consisting as they did of the simple statements, *Filia currit, Filiae currunt, Puellae rosas habent.* The book has now vanished into Limbo along with many other familiar objects of my childhood; but I think that in the course of that first morning's work we arrived at a slightly more complicated and romantic situation, in which *Poeta puellae rosas dat.* The exercise had an English counterpart, which began, I think, for a change, "The woman runs". I do not, by the way, altogether believe the report of a friend who in later life assured me that the Latin Grammar on which she had been brought up contained the assertion, "The King's daughters wash the sailor with their right hands". It certainly is not in Dr. William Smith, all of whose examples were characterized by the strictest propriety.

When we had rendered Exercise I, Part 2, into Latin, my father rose up and went away, leaving the book with me, and recommending that I should commit the declension of *mensa* to memory. This I immediately did, being at that time of life when the committing to memory of meaningless syllables and inconsequent lists of things is as easy as "Hey-diddle-diddle". I chanted the rigmarole aloud until I was familiar with it, and hastened away to show off my prowess in the kitchen.

From that time on, the Latin lesson became a daily event. I will not pretend that the first fine careless rapture of achievement endured for ever. *Dominus,* I seem to remember, was well-received, though slightly complicated by neuters; and a new and highly satisfactory chant was soon added to the repertory, which went with a noble swing:

> *bonus, bona, bonum*
> *bonum, bonam, bonum*
> *boni, bonae, boni*

and so forth, reaching a fine galumphing crescendo in

> *bonorum, bonarum, bonorum,*

before declining into a softly reiterated burden of

> *bonis, bonis, bonis.*

With the Third Declension, the high and austere order of Imperial Rome seemed to lose grip a little. Irregularities set in: there were nouns like *rex*, and *mus*, and *caput*, whose nominatives seemed to have lost their roots, and there was a tiresome difference of opinion between noun and adjective about the correct termination of the ablative singular. On the whole, however, the lack of symmetry was atoned for by a certain whimsicality and coloratura. The Fourth and Fifth Declensions remained rather exotic: one never got sufficient opportunities for using those fascinating terminations in *-uum, -ubus*, and *-erum*; on the other hand, there was always the perilous but exciting adventure of the double-barrelled declensions of *respublica* and, later on, of *jusjurandum*, where, alas! pride in the two-handed engine nearly always betrayed one into saying *juremjurandum*, and being scolded for *not thinking*.

And here, in passing, let us pay tribute to the memory of A. D. Godley, Public Orator in Oxford University, when I was an undergraduate, and to that noble poem which begins:

> What is it that roareth thus?
> Can it be a motor-bus?
> Yes! the reek and hideous hum
> *Indicant motorem bum.*

But the motor-bus was still in the future when I was trudging my way through the conjugations: the Active Voice, always friendly, except for a tendency to confusion between the Future Indicative and Present Subjunctive of the Third and Fourth Conjugations (the rot always seemed to set in at the Third

Anything); the Passive Voice always lumbering and hostile; the Deponents lurking meanly about, hoping to delude one into construing them as Passives; verbs like *fero*, so triumphantly irregular as to be permanently unforgettable; verbs with reduplicated perfects of a giggling absurdity—*peperi* was always good for a hearty Victorian pun—and defectives, which were simply a mess. It is a nostalgic memory that I could at one time recite the whole table of irregulars without more than an occasional side-slip; and I still remember that *utor, fruor, vescor, fungor* are followed by the ablative, when many more generally useful fragments of knowledge have slipped into Lethe and vanished.

By this time, of course, the girls, the poets and the roses had slipped into the background. We marched with Caesar, built walls with Balbo, and admired the conduct of Cornelia, who brought up her children diligently in order that they might be good citizens. The mighty forest of syntax opened up its glades to exploration, adorned with its three monumental trees—the sturdy Accusative and Infinitive, the graceful Ablative Absolute, and the banyan-like and proliferating Ut and the Subjunctive. Beneath their roots lurked a horrid scrubby tangle of words beginning with u, q and n, and a nasty rabbit-warren of prepositions. There was also a horrid region, beset with pitfalls and mantraps, called *Oratio Obliqua*, into which one never entered without a shudder, and where, starting off from a simple Accusative and Infinitive, one tripped over sprawling dependent clauses and bogged one's self down in the consecution of tenses, till one fell over a steep precipice into a Pluperfect Subjunctive, and was seen no more.

I do not know why the recollection of all this is pleasant to me. Why, for example, did I in those days greatly prefer Latin to the French, of which I later became a master? I do not think my father was a particularly inspired teacher; his methods would now be called unimaginative and old-fashioned to the last degree. One reason may, I fancy, have been that the pronunciation, being flat-footedly English, gave me no trouble; another, that the complications of the morphology and syntax released in me some kind of low cunning which today finds expression in the solving of crossword puzzles.

By the time I was thirteen, the French had hauled up hand over fist upon the Latin, and overtaken it. I had a French governess with whom I conversed, and I read Molière and *The Three Musketeers*. I was not trained to converse in Latin, and the Augustan age produced no Dumas. This was, I think, a pity.

I was, indeed, introduced to the Latin authors. The day arrived on which, toiling very slowly with a vocabulary, I began to work my way line by line through the episode of Pyramus and Thisbe from the *Metamorphoses*. After which we embarked, at the same snail's pace, upon the second book of the *Aeneid*.

My father's way with the involutions of the classic hexameter was calculated to lighten the labour of the student, though I am not sure whether it was the best approach to the literary beauties of Virgil. Having explained the construction of the verse and brought me to the point of at least grasping the rhythm of the concluding dactyl and spondee, he would then kindly take my brief daily portion, tear it word from word, and rearrange the *disjecta membra* in the order in which Virgil would have written them had he been writing simply English prose for use in lower forms. The consequence is that to this day I find it very difficult to assemble the clauses in any classic verse, or to decide which adjective belongs to which noun, or to see what principle, other than the brute necessity of getting the quantities in the right place, governs the order of the words in a line. In the end, of course, these props and crutches were taken away from me, and I was left to grope my way about the verse for myself; but it never seemed more than a kind of jig-saw. I cannot recollect what prose passages I read, if any, with my father. Memory throws up the name of Cornelius Nepos, but with nothing attached to it. The great trouble, I am sure, was the appalling slowness with which I proceeded. The shape of the thing as a story or a poem was lost in the slow grubbing over the ground. I could not then, much less since, ever read any passage of classical Latin swiftly, or by the eye; although in my early teens I could read and write French almost as quickly and correctly as English; and was not far behind in German.

[*Miss Sayers lost more than she gained at school, largely owing to the confusion caused in her mind by a change of pronunciation.*]

As soon as I took up residence in Oxford, I was sent to a warrior called Mr. Herbert May, with instructions that I was to be crammed through Smalls. Mr. May lived in a narrow, semi-detached house in the gloomier purlieus of Oxford, in a perpetual atmosphere of snuff. With this he refreshed himself all through his coachings; and I would not grudge him a single pinch of it, for his life must have been a hard one. So far as I know, he spent all his time with people like me. He was the indefatigable seagull, forever winging his way through the clashing rocks of Latin Prose and Greek Unseens with a fleet of dismal and inexperienced Argonauts thrashing the seas at his tail. A kindlier and more imperturbable man I never met. In two terms he accomplished what my school-teachers had not ventured to undertake in four years. We pounded our way through the *Hecuba* and the *Alcestis*; we coped with the Aorist; we mowed down under our feet that weedy growth of repulsive particles with which the Greek language is infested. Oddly enough, I cannot recall what the Latin set books were, if any; but from the fact that I still remember a few lines of the Sixth Aeneid, I am inclined to think that we may have had to tackle it. My only distinct recollection is of making my way through a series of Latin Proses, and of Mr. May, choking with laughter and snuff over some more than usually preposterous howler, recovering himself to say encouragingly: "Well, Miss Sayers, you do make the most elementary errors, but I will say for you that what you write is Latin." By which I took him to mean that I did instinctively frame the sentence after the high Roman fashion, collecting everything into a vast articulated complex of clauses and sub-clauses before proceeding to adorn the structure with passive deponents and the non-existent parts of defective verbs. And I conclude from this that it was not my linguistic sense that was at fault, but that with more imaginative teaching I might have made as good a job of Latin as of German or French.

I got through Responsions, and that was the end of that. The Degree course allowed me to do my Mods. in Modern Languages. The Latin I no longer required began to slip away through the sieve of preoccupation. The Greek lingered only long enough to steer me through a couple of Testaments for the now obsolete Divinity Mods., and then followed the Latin down the drain.

Two contacts only remained. I was reading French, and the Old French required for the Language Papers demanded a minimum acquaintance with the Latin roots, morphology and syntax. And as a member of the Bach Choir I learned to sing the Latin Mass and a number of mediaeval hymns and carols.

This added yet another pronunciation to my collection—the ecclesiastical. I had been brought up to say "Pleeni sunt ceeli"; school had commanded me to say "Playnee soont koilee"; I now sang "Playnee soont chaylee". I had never, and I have never, been able to dissociate the written word from the spoken sound; if I cannot pronounce I cannot read. With the fragmentation of the sounds the disintegration of control followed so fast that at this stage in my career I could scarcely have read ten consecutive Latin words aloud in a consistent pronunciation and without false quantities, or construed ten consecutive lines. Yet I believe that it was about this time that a dim glamour which had haunted me all my childhood, and haunts me to this day, began to shine into my mind like the sun rising through a mist—the shimmering, spell-binding magic of the mediaeval Latin.

Everybody is, I suppose, either Classic or Gothic by nature. Either you feel in your bones that buildings should be rectangular boxes with lids to them, or you are moved to the marrow by walls that climb and branch, and break into a inflorescence of pinnacles. And however successfully you educate yourself to a just appreciation of the other kind, it will never have the same power to capture you soul and body in your unguarded moments.

In the same way, you either have the austere taste which delights in the delicate interplay of stress and quantity in the hexameter—only you must remember that nobody had ever once thought of showing me how that worked—or you have the more (if you like) twopence-coloured taste that reacts powerfully to:

> *Tuba mirum spargens sonum*
> *Per sepulchra regionum*
> *Coget omnes ante tronum.*

Augustine was moved to tears by the sorrows and death of Dido, and with good reason:

> *illa, graves oculos conata attollere, rursus*
> *deficit, infixum stridet sub pectore volnus.*
> *ter sese attollens cubitoque adnixa levavit:*
> *ter revoluta toro est, oculisque errantibus alto*
> *quaesivit caelo lucem, ingemuitque reperta.*

A more plangent and piercing cry goes up from the foot of the Cross:

> *Pro peccatis sui gentis*
> *vidit Jesum in tòrmentis*
> *et flagellis subditum;*
> *vidit suum dulcem natum*
> *moriendo desolatum*
> *dum emisit spiritum.*

But I want to come back to this later. For the moment I will only leave on record that my Latin education ended upon this note.

It ended, I say, there, leaving me, after close on twenty years' teaching, unable to read a single Latin author with ease or fluency, unable to write a line of Latin without gross error, unfamiliar with the style and scope of any Latin author, except as I had taken refuge in English translations, and stammering of speech because by this time all three pronunciations were equally alien and uncertain. And this was a thing that never ought to have happened to me, because I was born with the gift of tongues.

I call this a very lamentable history. Yet there are two things I feel bound to say with all the emphasis I can command. First: if you set aside Classical specialists and the products of those public schools which still cling to the great tradition, I, mute and inglorious as I am, and having forgotten nearly all I ever learned, still know more Latin than most young people with whom I come in contact. Secondly: that if I were asked what, of all the things I was ever taught, has been of the greatest practical use to me, I should have to answer: the Latin Grammar.

As to the first point, I can only say that I do not blame the modern methods of teaching Latin: I do not know what they are. The trouble is that the allegedly literate and educated population of this country is no longer composed of public school boys and parsons' daughters, but of a vast mass of young persons who have been turned loose on the world at the age of sixteen, and very many of whom have learnt no Latin at all. And that most of them, and of their parents, and apparently of the persons who decide what educational fodder shall be sponsored by the State, and quite certainly of those who provide the popular literature and journalism which influences their thinking, are under the impression that Latin is a bit of antiquated upper-class trimming, of no practical value to anyone.

Which brings me to my second point: the practical uses of Latin. It is not to you that I need preach a sermon about them: or you would not be at this conference. But I think that in this utilitarian age those who are concerned to keep Latin in the school curriculum would be well advised to insist upon them more frequently than they do. In a correspondence a little time ago in the *Daily Telegraph,* arguments about cultural background, class privilege and mental discipline wandered along for weeks before one correspondent had the wits to up and say that the learning of Latin had, after all, a certain practical value in the saving of time and labour, even if that was all one cared about. To you, therefore, and at this point, I will only say briefly that, in my experience, an early grounding in the Latin Grammar has these advantages:

1. It is the quickest and easiest way to mastery over one's own language, because it supplies the structure upon which all language is built. I never had any formal instruction in English grammar, nor have I ever felt the need of it, though I find I write more grammatically than most of my juniors. It seems to me that the study of English grammar in isolation from the inflected origins of language must be quite bewildering. English is a highly sophisticated, highly analytical language, whose forms, syntax and construction can be grasped and handled correctly only by a good deal of hard reasoning, for the inflections are not there to enable one to distinguish automatically one case or one construction from another. To embark on any complex English construction without the Latin Grammar is like trying to find one's way across country without map or signposts. That is why so few people nowadays can put together an English paragraph without being betrayed into a false concord, a hanging or wrongly attached participle, or a wrong consecution; and why many of them fall back upon writing in a series of short sentences, like a series of gasps, punctuated only by full stops.

2. Latin is the key to fifty per cent. of our vocabulary—either directly, or through French and other Romance languages. Without some acquaintance with the Latin roots, the meaning of each word has to be learnt and memorised separately—including, of course, that of the new formations with which the sciences are continually presenting us. Incidentally, the vocabulary of the common man is becoming more and more restricted, and this is not surprising.

3. Latin is the key to all the Romance languages directly, and indirectly to all inflected languages. The sort of argument which continually crops up in correspondence upon the teaching of Latin is: "Why should children waste time learning a dead language when Spanish or what-have-you would be much more useful to him in business?" The proper answer, which is practically never given, is the counter-question: "Why should a child waste time learning half a dozen languages from scratch, when Latin would enable him to learn them all in a fraction of the time?" When I wanted to work on Dante, I taught myself to read the mediaeval Italian in a very few weeks' time, with the aid of Latin, an Italian Grammar, and the initial assistance of a crib. To learn to speak and write the modern tongue correctly would demand tuition and more time—but not much and not long. Old as I am, I would back myself to learn Spanish, Portuguese or Provençal with equal ease. But knowing French would not have helped me very much to read Italian, and I doubt whether, without the Latin substructure, Italian would help me very far with Portuguese; although, of course, the more languages one knows, the easier it is to learn more. It is difficult to be sure, because it is impossible for me to empty my mind of the Latin, even in imagination. But I know how very different a task it would be to start upon a language like Czech or Chinese, which would not open to the Latin key. And I remember, too, in my own school-teaching days, being confronted by a class of girls of fifteen or sixteen, who had to have some German pumped into them for an exam. They had done French in the ordinary way, but now had to offer a second language. I remember saying—stupidly and without thinking, for I was still young—"No, you can't say, '*Ich bin gegeben ein Buch*'—'I have been given' isn't a true Passive". I remember their bewildered faces. And I remember realizing that we had come to the Wood where Things have no Names, and that everything would have to be laboriously thought out and explained from the very beginning. And that they hadn't got much time.

4. The literature of our own country and of Europe is so studded and punctuated with Latin phrases and classical allusions that without some knowledge of Latin it must be very difficult to make anything of it. Here we are getting away from the uses of grammar to the benefits of background and culture. I will therefore not say very much about it at this point, except

to point out that the student of English history or English literature or English law is always encountering the odd tag, the Latin title, the isolated phrase, and that it must be quite maddening to have to stop and look them up every time in a reference book.

5. There is also the matter of derivation, as distinct from vocabulary. I cannot help feeling that it is wholesome, for example, to know that "civility" has some connection with the *civitas*; that "justice" is more closley akin to righteousness than to equality; and that there was once some dim and forgotten connection between reality and thought.

But I do not want to dwell too long on these things which, to us, are commonplaces. I will only repeat that this particular set of values is very difficult to put across to those on whom there rests at present the ultimate responsibility for educating the young.

In the time that remains to me, I will rather sort over my own experience and see what it offers in the way of constructive suggestions for the teaching of Latin. I must repeat that I do not know what you are actually doing about this. It will be for you to say whether your practice agrees anywhere with my theory, and, where it does not, whether and why you consider my suggestions impracticable or undesirable.

To begin, then, at the beginning: I am convinced that the age at which I began was the right one. An acquaintance of mine whose boy is just starting life at a grammar school tells me that the boys there do not begin Latin till they are eleven. I am sure that this it too late. In acquiring the Accidence, everything depends upon getting declensions and conjugations firmly fixed in the memory during the years when the mere learning of anything by rote is a delight rather than a burden. The jingle of "*mensa, mensa, mensam*" or "*amo, amas, amat*" belongs properly to the same mental age as "eeny, meeny, miney, mo", or "This is the house that Jack built". By the time that the reasoning and arguing faculty is awake, the capacity for assembling sounds by aural memory is weakening, and by the age of puberty it is practically lost. One can, of course, learn by heart at all ages if one earnestly puts one's mind to it—in the sense that one can memorize a thing *ad hoc,* as an actor memorizes a part. But the thing learnt at a later age does not abide graven upon the very foundations of the memory like the thing learnt in childhood. And the more rational one becomes, the more tedious and difficult it is to learn strings of sounds which are not logically associated.

> Abstract nouns in *-io* call
> *Feminina* one and all;
> Masculine will only be
> Things that you can touch or see,
> As *curculio, vespertilio,*
> *Pugio, scipio,* and *papilio,*
> With the nouns that number show,
> Such as *ternio, senio.*

The first four lines of that mnemonic make sense, and so do the last two; if I had not known them from the cradle, I could learn them tomorrow. But the fifth and sixth lines are different. If I had to learn them fresh today, I should have forgotten them by tomorrow, because they make no connected sense. But I remember them now, although I have not the faintest recollection of what any one of the words means, except *papilio*. I could not possibly forget them, any more than I could forget *hic, haec hoc*. And it is all nonsense to pretend that small children hate and are bored by learning things by heart. They like it. They have a passion for it. If they are given no outlet for this passion in school, they will devote themselves to memorizing number-plates or cricket averages. The love of memorizing for memorizing's sake is the hall-mark of the sub-rational intellect, and it is simply silly not to take advantage of it while the going's good. What is, I am sure, a strain and vexation to the young mind is to be compelled to *reason* before the time; just as it is a strain and vexation to have to memorize after the best time for that kind of thing is past. It is (as Wordsworth rightly pointed out) extremely unwise to keep bothering a young child with "Why, Edward, tell me why?" Wait till Edward asks "Why?" before burdening his mind with reasons. And meanwhile let him chant *"mensa, mensa, mensam"* at the top of his voice. His grown-ups will get tired of it before he does. But do not on any account *waste* those precious years when declension and conjugation can be learned without difficulty and without boredom.

Now, as to the vexed question of pronunciation. I will say here and now that I have never discovered, nor can I see, any reasonable use or excuse for the "waynee, weedee, weekee" convention. It is not merely that I have a profound sympathy with one of my friends who says he just cannot believe that Caesar was the kind of man to talk in that kind of way. Caesar may, indeed, have done so, but what then? We do not, except experimentally at the Mermaid Theatre, or in a Third Programme broadcast by Neville Coghill, insist on pronouncing the English of Shakespeare and Chaucer as Shakespeare and Chaucer pronounced it. Antiquarian research is useful and enlightening; but for the general use and enjoyment of literature we adopt other standards. And if we have succeeded (which is not certain) in discovering the pronunciation used in the Augustan age, it is probable that that pronunciation did not endure very long—no pronunciation does. It had certainly gone by the time that the Romance languages began to issue out of the Latin matrix. And the "New", or Antiquarian pronunciation, has serious disadvantages. It is the remotest of all from the modern English pronunciation, whether of common words or of proper nouns, and therefore to us the least helpful for derivations and for feeling the continuity of linguistic development. You cannot sing it. And it does not link us with our fellow-Latinists on the Continent, who all tend to assimilate the Latin to the vernacular in the traditional way. Indeed, I think the only person I have heard casually using the Antiquarian Latin was a young American whom I once encountered at lunch; and even he, if I had replied with the ecclesiastical pronunciation, would probably have understood me. The really important thing, however, is that there should be, at any rate during the period of schooling, a uniform usage.

If one rejects the Antiquarian school of thought, there remain two other possibilities for English students. There is the "Old" or "Protestant" usage. This probably began to be used in this country during the fifteenth century, perhaps partly as an anti-Papist and anti-foreign measure; but chiefly in order to keep the pronunciation of Latin in line with that of the vernacular, which was also changing rapidly at about that period. This harnessing of the Latin to the vernacular is traditional in every country, and has very much to be said for it. It enables the child to learn Latin with rapidity and ease, just because it does not require him to load his tongue and memory with a new set of vowel-and-consonant associations. It assists him greatly to discover for himself the derivations and history of his own native words. It makes no confusing discrepancies between the pronunciation of proper names and their derivations—between, for instance, Keekero and Ciceronian, Kysar and Caesarism; and it makes for a decent uniformity in the pronunciation of Latin names that have been anglicized. This last consideration may seem trivial, but you will not think so if you have had anything to do with the theatre, where I recently had to spend much time and energy hammering it into the heads of actors that the English form of Constantinus, or "Constanteenoos", is Constantine, and not Constanteen. It is maddening to any sensitive ear to hear the same person in the same production called alternately Coriolanus and Coriolahnus, and to find Virgilia and Valaria going together to meet him, with sporadic variations of Vairgheelia and Valeria. Generally speaking, also, the "Old" pronunciation sounds better when introducing a Latin quotation into an English speech, since it slides in more readily, and does not stand out so conspicuously from the vowel-texture of its context.

The "Old" pronunciation had, however, two very grave drawbacks. It did not pay any attention to the intrinsic quantity of vowels. One was brought up to decline $b\breve{o}s$, $b\breve{o}vis$, which made it peculiarly hard to remember that the "o" of bos is in fact long, and the "o" of $bovis$ short when it came to actually scanning them. This also greatly increased the difficulty of appreciating the music and pattern of quantitative verse, let alone, I should imagine, of writing it. If the English people had nobody but themselves to consider, I should feel strongly inclined to advocate a return to the "Old" pronunciation, but with a readjustment of the conventional vowel-sounds to coincide with their quantitative values, pronouncing $m\bar{a}ter$, but $p\bar{a}ter$, $l\bar{o}cus$, $m\bar{a}nus$, $m\breve{i}h\breve{i}$ (instead of $m\bar{i}h\bar{i}$) and so on, with all consonant and vowel sounds as in English (e.g. the soft "c" and "g" before "i" and "e", and the "j" and "v" as "j" and "v"). The only awkwardness that I can see would arise with first and second declension dative and ablative plurals: *mensis* would give a false quantity—*mensees* would introduce a foreign vowel sound, and *mensice* might need some getting used to. I am quite sure that for the average child, for whom it is important not to spend too much time and trouble (not to mention tears) upon the rudiments, this would be by far the quickest, easiest, and most generally helpful pronunciation to adopt.

Unfortunately, there would still remain the other very serious drawback, arising out of the fact that the modern English values of a, e, i and u have developed in a direction which isolates them completely from the values given to those vowels on the Continent. The more closely we follow the tradition of assimilating the Latin to the vernacular, the less possible does it become to restore the use of Latin as a *lingua franca*. If it appeared in any way possible so to restore it, then I think it might be better to plump from the start for the ecclesiastical pronunciation, which can be understood in every country where Latin Mass is sung, even by those who do not attend Mass. The ecclesiastical Latin is beautiful, singable, and cosmopolitan; neither does it demand from English Catholics a divided allegiance. Moreover, although equally with the "Antiquarian" usage, it disguises the connection between the modern English speech and its Latin roots, yet it links us up with our own history; for it is to all intents and purposes the Latin spoken by our own countrymen up to the time of the great vowel-shift.

But, putting the question of pronunciation aside, and supposing that my own experience in this matter had been less unfortunate, where did my Latin education, starting so well as it did, go wrong? Looking back upon it, I feel sure that the trouble was simply that the whole process was far too slow. Why did the French, which I began by hating, haul up so fast upon the Latin, which I began by loving? For two reasons: I was encouraged—not to say compelled—to speak it every day and for a great part of the day. And, more important still, as soon as I had got a hold of the grammar, it presented me with works of literature which were not only in themselves such as to hold a child's attention, but which were easy enough to be read fluently and quickly, by pages instead of paragraphs at a time, and were written in the same language which I was learning to speak.

All this was, of course, made easy for me by the fact that I was brought up at home with a French governess. The problem of learning *any* language conversationally in school, with little time and large classes, is a baffling one. You cannot possibly hope to get the same results as by individual teaching. You can give French lessons in French to the more advanced forms; and you can encourage the acting of French plays. You can, no doubt, do as much for Latin, if the number of periods in the week allotted to this study allows it, and if everybody's energies are not taken up by preparing set books for examinations. You cannot, unhappily, send pupils abroad to Latin-speaking countries to brush up their spoken Latin in the holidays. I do not know whether there is much hope of ever establishing conversational Latin even on the same scale as conversational French. I suspect that much depends on the type of school and on the sex and social background of the scholars. So I will not dwell on this aspect of the matter, except to say that I think it would have helped me very much if I had ever been got into the habit of speaking Latin, if only to say "Please" and "Thank you" and "Pass the mustard".

Even without conversation, reading might have stimulated the enthusiasm which leads to ease and fluency. But here was the trouble—I could not get on fast enough. And it is my belief that the classical texts of the Augustan Age are simply far too difficult.

They were difficult even in their own day, in the sense that they were elaborate, literary, and highly artificial. The language of Cicero was not spoken in the streets, nor even, I fancy, in the drawing-rooms, of ancient Rome. The legions did not tramp their way to victory chanting the Hellenic, quantitative measures which delighted the ears of the cognoscenti assembled at poetry-readings or exchanging culture in the baths. The ordinary educated Roman could appreciate Virgil and Horace or Cicero because he came to them through his own daily speech, as we come through our own modern speech to the elaborations of Joyce and Eliot. And as time went on and the language changed, they could still go back through their own speech to the writings of the Golden Age, as we, through our speech, go back to the Metaphysicals and to *Euphues*—if we ever do go back to *Euphues*, which is perhaps a little doubtful. But teachers do not, as a rule, ask foreign children to plunge immediately into the study of English by way of Donne and *Euphues* without any help at all from the current English, whose syntax and vocabulary are so much nearer to their own. Doubtless, when the time comes, they are put on to Shakespeare; but they are not, from the start, confined exclusively to the highly compressed and elliptical language of the later Shakespeare, on the grounds that this represents the Golden Age of English from which every later development is a debasement and a degeneration of the language. Yet this is the way in which, for the last four hundred years or so, we have started English boys on the learning of Latin.

It can, of course, be done. It was done—in a more leisured

age, and for one sex only of a privileged professional class, and in schools which concentrated on the teaching of classical languages and on uncommonly little else. But I doubt if it is the right way of going about it today. And it is not the way in which it was done for the first fifteen centuries of our era.

It is being borne in upon me with more and more force and with every year I live that the greatest single defect of my own Latin education, and that (I expect) of many other people, is the almost total neglect of those fifteen Christian centuries. The great reproach cast up against Latin by those who would drive it altogether from the schools is that it is a dead language. But if it is dead today, it is because the Classical Scholars killed it by smothering it with too much love. Up to the time of the Revival of Learning, it was a living language, growing and developing like a living language alongside of its children and grandchildren and, like many a hearty and lively grandparent today, picking up much of their speech and slang as it went along. It is fascinating to watch it from the first century onwards, assimilating syntax and vocabulary from the vernacular Greek, weaving in the Hebrew through the Vulgate—after the same manner, though perhaps not to the same extent, as Anglo-Saxon assimilated the Norman-French; to see it renewing itself by contact with its own Romance languages as English renews itself by contact with American, becoming more analytic as they become more analytic, and developing a new vocabulary to express current ideas. Contamination and barbarism are one set of names for this sort of thing: another name is vitality. Everything which is alive tends to break out into vulgarity at times. Only the dead and embalmed can preserve for ever their changeless marmoreal dignity.

The extent to which the legend of a sculpturesque classicism has fastened upon the popular English mind is curious and interesting. I find, for example, that the thing in my own plays which excites most outrage and contempt—not from scholars, who know better, but from the average semi-educated reviewer —is that I make the Roman common soldier talk British Army slang. It would, I imagine, be vain to point out that what Roman soldiers in fact talked was Roman Army slang. It is rooted in the popular mind that not merely the native Praetorians but also the mixed ranks of fourth-century foreign mercenaries conversed about the camp-fire in the periods of Cicero, or at the very least in those of Caesar—for which the correct equivalent is supposed to be Victorian Wardour Street. It was when I was digging down at Oxford for the roots of the French language that the origin of the word *tête* was first revealed to me: *testa*, a potsherd. In that disreputable period when the spoken word was passing into Romance, the Latin man-in-the-street was unregenerately referring to his pal's face as his "mug". That, I think, was the day on which I first saw the light. *Tempora mutantur*, but certain tendencies seem to be ingrained in the human race, and are preserved in philology as flies are preserved in amber. Yet *chief* long remained current side by side with *tête*, as the once-vulgar "donkey" still holds its place beside the reverend and biblical "ass". Perhaps time will eventually ennoble "mug" and "moke" also.

There is another and profounder sense in which the Augustan Latin is felt to be dead. Our civilization, such as it is, remains in its living bones a Christian civilization—and the Augustan Latin was never Christian. Even those who most roundly assert that Christianity is dead bring it to the bar of their inherited Christian values, and by the concentrated rage which they bring to its obsequies proclaim that it is in many ways disconcertingly alive. Nobody is either annoyed or delighted over the assertion that Great Pan is dead and the Olympians only myths. And the language in which Augustine of Hippo fought the Manichees and—later, but without breach of continuity—Aquinas defended Aristotle, and Galileo fought Rome for the movement of the earth, is, if dead, dead with a different deadness from that of a language which officially recognizes only the Olympians. To set up a great gap in learning and literature between the days of Augustus and the Renaissance is not true to life or history.

And—to go back to my former point—the mediaeval Latin is much easier than the Classical. Not all of it; some of it is very crabbed, and there were always, in every age, men who tried to conform their living Latin to the Latin of the Augustans. But the true mediaeval Latin is akin to us, with its simplified construction and modern analytical syntax. The proof of that is that I, who cannot read a page of Virgil or Cicero or Horace without the pains of the damned, can read Aquinas without more difficulty than is involved in understanding what he is talking about. When I read Benvenuto da Imola on Dante, I can pass from Italian text to Latin commentary and scarcely notice the change-over. In short, my training in the Latin Grammar, while it left me still unfitted to cope with the Augustans, did fit me to cope with the Mediaevals, whom I could have read easily and fluently, had anybody directed my attention to them in time.

And lest you should think I know too little to know what I am talking about, I will quote from the preface of a book which I met with only the other day—after I had decided what I was going to say to you. I wish I had known of its existence earlier: it would have solved half my problems for me. That is H. P. V. Nunn's *Introduction to the Study of Ecclesiastical Latin.* He says:

> Much of Classical Latin is highly artificial, not to say unnatural, in its modes of expression. The authors whose works are most generally read wrote for a fastidious and highly cultivated society of littérateurs... and especially under the early Empire, they wrote with a view to reading their works to admiring circles of friends, whose applause they hoped to arouse by some novel or far-fetched term of expression.

And, having said that those who intend to use his book "should possess at the least a knowledge of the conjugations of Latin verbs and the declensions of Latin nouns such as may be got from any primer"—and that was what I had, before I was in my 'teens—he goes on:

> The author feels confident from experience that those who begin with the Latin Bible and the easier Ecclesiastical authors, will be able to go on to the study of the Classics, if they desire to do so, with far more intelligence and profit than if they had tried to approach them without some previous preparation.

Well, I had begun to think that, but should have been afraid to say it, because I had never tried it, nor known anybody else who had. But his experience, it seems, confirms my instinct. And, after all, that is the natural way of learning any language—to begin with the more modern and go back to the more ancient, even if the ancient is the more noble and curial.

It is true that many people, if started upon the Mediaevals, would, in this hurried century, never have time to go further. Even so, would half a loaf not be better than no bread? Their training in the Vulgate would not enable them to write like Cicero; but it would be *something* to be able to write Vulgate Latin. After all, few of us actually ever succeed in writing like Milton or Dr. Johnson; but to write like Conan Doyle or Eleanor Farjeon is better than never learning to write at all: a plain, homely prose and a tripping verse have their uses. And the Mediaeval Latin at its worst is seldom ignoble; at its best, it is noble indeed.

At twenty years of age, the old-fashioned schooling turned me out helpless, ignorant and dissatisfied. Forty years later I encounter the product of the new schooling—still more helpless, still more ignorant, and possibly not even dissatisfied.

But ignorance has seldom prevented anybody from laying down the law about how other people ought to run their jobs, and proposing impracticable solutions. So I will proceed to offer a few "constructive suggestions", as they say, for getting boys and girls reasonably well Latinized with the least possible waste of time and energy.

1. Catch 'em young and get the Accidence into them along with the multiplication-table (if they still learn that). Eleven years old is too late—they are beginning to think.

2. Throw that dreary man Cicero out of the window, and request the divine Virgil (with the utmost love and respect) to take a seat along with his fellow-Augustans and the First Consul, until your pupils are ready to be ushered into the presence.

3. Choose a pronunciation and stick to it.

4. Start your youngsters off upon the mediaeval syntax and the easiest and simplest mediaeval texts. (Books? No, I know there are no books. I will come to that later.) Let the readings go as fast as possible, getting on to long, sustained extracts as soon as may be, and using a crib if necessary (except, of course, for Unseens).

5. If possible, let them speak Latin in class. Let them write simple proses—not about Caesar's Gallic Wars, but about their cats and dogs and what they do at home. Don't bother too much about style, so long as they get something down; and if they ask what is the Latin for "Skye Terrier" or "motor-scooter", bear in mind that a trifle of that kind would not have flummoxed Abelard or Roger Bacon. The singing of Latin hymns and carols would help too. And they might write and act their own Latin Nativity Play.

6. Let them get up their classical myths and general background in English. It would do no harm to introduce them to Ovid and Virgil in a good translation, if you can find one. Caesar, if you like (though the girls won't care much about him). How about the letters of the Younger Pliny, which cover the

link-up with Christianity? The most important thing is to display the people who spoke Latin as real people, living right on from Caesar's time into the Middle Ages.

7. When the time comes—that is, when they can read with ease and have a decent vocabulary—let them go on to the Augustans in the original, pointing out that these are works of literature and intended to be enjoyed as such. Pick the really exciting, moving and memorable bits, and let them express themselves freely about the sportsmanship displayed at the Funeral Games in honour of Anchises! This is your moment for wrestling with the quantitative metres, and with the difference between Mediaeval and Classical syntax. It should at worst offer little more difficulty than the difference between modern English and the English of Chaucer.

Now as to books. The trouble is, as you rightly say, that even if you could bear to teach the Mediaeval Latin, there are no annotated texts. Mr. Nunn's book, which I have mentioned, contains a useful guide to syntax, and a number of short extracts from Christian authors covering the period I have in mind, i.e. from the Vulgate to the Renaissance. (Post-Renaissance texts should be avoided at first, being quite as hard as the Classical and more derivative. And, indeed, all the writers who at any period were being consciously Augustan should be avoided in the early stages.)

Being primarily intended for the use of theological students, Mr. Nunn's extracts are rather too exclusively ecclesiastical for our purpose, and need supplementing by some secular texts. Being myself very ignorant, I asked C. S. Lewis about this, and here are his suggestions:

> For an intelligible narrative poem, what about a chunk out of *Waltharius*, by Ekkehard, of St. Gall (tenth century). See a delightful account of it in W. P. Ker's *Dark Ages*.
> For prose: Saxo Grammaticus (give them the Hamlet story); Jordanes (vel Jornandes) *De Rebus Geticis* (lots about Attila); Gregorius Turonensis *Historia Francorum*; the anonymous *Gesta Francorum* (on the First Crusade); Geoffrey of Monmouth (some Arthurian bit); and—if you want to include something of the Renaissance—Kepler's *Somnium*, which is the first real instance of "scientifiction".

To this list one could add immediately a number of the Mediaeval Latin Lyrics, of which Helen Waddell has given us a selection (though her translations are rather loose and over-romanticized), and one or two odd things which have an interest of their own, such as Dante's "Letter to a Friend in Florence"; and there should be some fun in the mediaeval Bestiaries. Other things should turn up—few people have explored mediaeval texts with this purpose in mind. But keep things simple—don't wrestle with the complications of the *cursus*!

If you can get your colleagues in the History and English schools to lend a hand with the game by linking these various authors up with their background, so much the better.

What you would need, in addition to Mr. Nunn's book, is:

(a) A book of exercises, to go with the grammar.

(b) A more extended selection of "Late and Mediaeval Latin Unseens for the use of Middle and Upper Forms", with vocabulary and annotations.

(c) A series of annotated texts, for reading *in extenso*. These things do not exist; but they could be written. Nobody, by the way, need be afraid of setting pupils passages from the Vulgate, on the grounds that it would be over-familiar. In my experience, the Bible is unknown country to most young people nowadays

Let me end with the famous heart-cry from Augustine—him who wept for Dido:

> *Cur ergo Graecam etiam grammaticam oderam talia cantantem? Nam et Homerus peritus texere tales fabulas, et dulcissime vanus est, et mihi tamen amarus erat puero.*
>
> *Credo etiam Graecis pueris Virgilius ita sit, cum eum sic discere coguntur, ut ego illum. Videlicet difficultas, difficultas omnio ediscendae peregrinae linguae, quasi felle aspergebat omnes suavitates Graecas fabulosarum narrationum. Nulla enim verba illa noveram, et saevis terroribus ac poenis ut nossem instabatur mihi vehementer.*
>
> (We have abolished the cruel threats and punishments, but boredom is quite as frustrating.) *Nam et Latina aliquando infans nulla noveram; et tamen advertendo didici sine ulla metu et cruciatu, inter etiam blandimenta nutricum et joca arridentium et laetitias alludentium.*
>
> *Didici vero illa sine poenali onere urgentium cum me urgeret cor meum ad parienda concepta sua, quae non possem, nisi aliqua verba didicissem, non a docentibus sed a loquentibus, in quorum et ego auribus parturiebam quidquid sentiebam. Hinc satis elucet majorem habere vim ad discenda ista liberam curiositatem, quam meticulosam necessitatem.*

CHAPTER IX

THE WRITING AND READING OF ALLEGORY

ALLEGORY, OF LATE years, has been suffering from what is popularly known as "a bad Press". Almost any reference to it in contemporary critical writing tends to be both slighting and superficial, and to use such expressions as: "artificiality", "chilly abstractions", "frigid allegorical conceits", "tedious didacticism", "conventional and bloodless personifications". Still more significantly, the term itself is often used as a mere pejorative; thus, a reviewer may say: "The book never *degenerates* into allegory, but is, *on the contrary*, a rich and evocative work of the imagination." Or finally, the word may be applied, quite at random, to something which is not allegory at all, but which happens to contain some religious or moral teaching which the critic dislikes or fails to understand. When C. S. Lewis published his novel *Perelandra* (since re-issued under the title *Voyage to Venus*), which is a fantasy of the kind we now call "space-fiction", recounting quite straightforwardly the beginnings of rational life on that planet, and how a new "fall of man" was prevented by the intervention of a voyager from our own Earth, to prevent misunderstanding he wrote in his preface: "All the human characters in this book are purely fictitious, and none of them is allegorical." Notwithstanding, one reviewer, after describing the actual journey through space, abruptly concluded his review: "Then the allegory begins." Having, that is, deliberately filed away the book in the wrong pigeonhole, he took it for granted that about a work of that kind there was nothing useful to be said.

Now, when a whole department of literature is thus unanimously and, as it were, automatically condemned for the mere crime of being itself, and excluded from serious critical attention, it is pretty safe to say that we have simply forgotten how to judge it. It is extremely improbable, to say the least of it, that a genre which, in the past, produced such acknowledged masterpieces as *The Divine Comedy*, *The Faerie Queene*, and *The Pilgrim's Progress* is altogether worthless. Neither is it probable that a genre which enjoyed so many hundreds of years of popularity corresponds to no fundamental need in human nature. It is much more likely that we have fallen out of touch with it, so that we no longer remember how this particular literary game should be played—what its intention is or what its rules are— and thus are in no position to tell whether it is well or badly done, or what it is all about. We are in the same situation as an American who, not knowing the first thing about cricket, is planked down in the pavilion at Lord's to watch a Test Match. The only impression he is likely to carry away is that this is a slow and formal game, and not in the least like baseball. He will only have a very vague notion of what everybody is so earnestly trying to do, and the finer points of the play will escape him altogether.

So with allegory. Most of us are, to be sure, a little more advanced than the reviewer of Dr. Lewis's novel: we know that an allegory is a story which says one thing, and means another— whereas, on that occasion, Dr. Lewis meant exactly what he said, neither more nor less. But we may well wonder why a writer should choose what seems to us this very roundabout way of expressing himself. And further, the whole question is obscured for us by a great deal of argument about myth and symbol, imagery and fantasy, figures and archetypes, and so on, which gets mixed up with the subject, and makes it difficult to see the wood for the trees.

Perhaps the simplest way is to start by saying that Allegory is a distinct literary form, whose aim and method is to dramatize a psychological experience, so as to make it more vivid and more comprehensible. Parable and Fable are two other literary forms which do much the same thing. Each of them tells a literal story which is complete in itself, but which also presents a likeness to some spiritual or psychological experience, so that it can be used to signify and interpret that experience; and the story is told, not for its own sake, but for the sake of what it signifies. At the bottom of all such stories there lies this perception of a *likeness* between two experiences, the one familiar and the other unfamiliar, so that the one can be used to shed light on the other. "Whereunto shall we *liken* the Kingdom of God; or with what *comparison* shall we compare it? . . . And another parable spake he unto them: The Kingdom of Heaven is *like* unto leaven, which a woman took, and hid in three measures of meal, till the whole was leavened." Usually the story is a good deal more elaborate than this, as for example the Parable of the Sower: a number of events occur, each one of which can be interpreted with reference to the real (i.e. the figurative) meaning; but throughout the two stories remain distinct and parallel—corresponding at all points, but never intruding on one another.

In the Fable, which is usually a story ostensibly about animals but actually about human beings, the figurative meaning is as a rule compressed into a Moral at the end:

> The mice held a meeting to decide how they could best protect themselves against the cat. A young mouse proposed that a bell should be tied to the cat, so that they might hear her coming. "That is all very well", said an old mouse, "but who is to bell the cat?"
>
> *Moral*: It is easy to propose impossible remedies.

Both these forms of figurative narrative are, of course, very ancient—more ancient than Allegory, whose distinctive feature is that the personages of the literal story are *personified abstractions*. Here is a little tale which sits, as it were, on the fence, halfway between Fable and Allegory.

> Fire, Water, and Reputation went on a journey together. Before starting, they thought it would be well to arrange how they should find one another, in case they should get separated. Fire said: "Wherever you see smoke, there you will find me." Water said: "Wherever the grass is greenest, there you will find me." But Reputation said: "Beware how you lose me, for a lost reputation is not easily recovered."

It is evident that the third speaker in this dialogue is of a different kind from the others. Fire and Water are concrete things, however much personified, but Reputation is not a *thing* at all; it is a personified abstraction.

Since this is the sort of personification with which Allegory characteristically deals, it is fairly evident that it is not likely to appear except in an advanced civilization: one in which people are already learning to think in terms of abstract concepts.

It is in the reign of Augustus, at the latter end of the period which we call "B.C.", that we begin to notice something rather peculiar happening to those Olympian deities whom the Romans had taken over from the Greeks. Instead of being fully characterized, self-sufficient, super-human personages, enjoying a communal life, with emotions and interests and adventures and somewhat unedifying love affairs of their own, they are beginning to turn into abstractions. Mars, for example, in the old days, though he was the patron of war, was never simply and solely War: he had leisure and interest to spare for other things. He had a love affair with Venus; and when Vulcan, her husband, caught them at it and cast a net over the erring pair and dragged them into the presence of the other gods, there was much merriment on high Olympus. If he interfered in a human war, he did so by coming in to support one side or the other for personal reasons—to avenge an injury or to assist some hero in whom he was interested. But in the *Thebaid* of Statius, who wrote in the beginning of the Christian era, we find Mars fulfilling quite another function. Jupiter wants a war started to punish the city of Thebes; accordingly he sends for Mars and tells him to go and stir one up. Mars does so, and, having carried out this order, departs to stir up wars elsewhere. In all this, Jupiter is still behaving like a mythological deity: he has personal reasons for being offended with Thebes. But Mars has no interest in Thebes one way or the other: he simply exists in order to stir up strife at the command of fate. He has ceased to be the God of War: he has become the personification of Warfare. Later in the poem, semi-divinized attributes enter in their own persons, to play the kind of part that would formerly have been played by some god or other. Allegory has come into being.

Our natural reaction is to say that this is a great pity. The mythological Mars is clearly much more picturesque and poetical than an abstraction called Warfare. But human souls cannot live by picturesqueness and poetry. Under the Empire, the old gods were already dying; they had been dying for many years. It was no longer possible to interpret human destinies and human behaviour in terms of the Olympians. The Romans were, in fact, developing a new kind of moral consciousness.

The Greeks, incurably intellectual, had in their philosophy always tended to take it for granted that, to *be* good, it was sufficient to *know* the good. Like certain more recent thinkers, they rather took the line that all evil dispositions could be cured by education. But in this period of crisis and confusion, the Romans, always incurably moral, were discovering within themselves that inner dislocation between knowing and doing right which we call the "divided will" and sometimes "the sense of sin". They knew, with the painful conviction of experience, what it meant to say: "I see and approve the better, but follow the worse." In this dilemma, neither the ancient cult-religions of Rome nor the newer gods of Greece could give them any help. They turned to the Eastern mysteries, with their offer of release and redemption from the self and integration in the One. Christianity, arriving literally, one might say, at the "psychological moment", with this "divided will" at the very centre of its doctrine of human nature, spoke to their condition. But Christianity did not induce that condition in them: it was there already.

It is thus not surprising that man, becoming acutely aware of a conflict within himself, should look for a literary mode of expressing these new feelings. He feels his life to be, not so much a battle against forces without as a battle between forces within him; and he begins to personify those forces and dramatize the conflict. Allegory becomes his poetic medium; and the Allegories of this period most frequently take the form of a *Psychomachia*, a Soul-battle, fought between the Vices and the Virtues. The tradition of the *Psychomachia* proved exceedingly tough and vital: indeed it has so passed into our current speech that we can scarcely get away from it today. When we use expressions such as "he was torn between greed and fear", or "his curiosity overcame his sense of decency", we are making a *Psychomachia*— an Allegorical combat between personified qualities. We may tell ourselves, in our more philosophical moments, that abstractions like "fear" and "curiosity" have no independent existence —there is only one actual person who fears or is inquisitive; but it is very difficult not to speak, or even to think, as though our personality were a battle-ground for emotions distinct from and stronger than ourselves.

There are, of course, certain technical difficulties about writing a *Psychomachia* on a big scale. The personified qualities, having no personal existence outside those qualities which they personify, are apt to be somewhat limited in their activities and conversation. This is a disability of all Allegory, which occasions and to some extent justifies the charges of "frigidity" and "artificiality"; we shall see later how the great masters of Allegory got over it. Moreover, while warfare is an occupation well suited to such vices as Wrath, Jealousy, and Cruelty, and to such virtues as Courage, Fortitude, Loyalty, and the like, there are other qualities—especially such mild and Christian virtues as Patience, Meekness, Humility, Pity and so on—which do not take kindly to the profession of arms. Some of the combats in Prudentius, for instance, turn out rather grotesquely. Other suitable subjects had to be found for Allegory—for example, the *Epithalamion* or Marriage between selected virtues, each accompanied by a suitable train of followers. And so forth. We should undoubtedly find these early experiments very tedious to read, and should sigh for the elasticity and many-sided humanity of the old gods. But to these pioneer writers, Allegory was no dull convention— it was a new and exciting medium by which to explore undiscovered regions of the soul, and to make their first adventure into analytical psychology.

They found also another use for it. Allegory became an instrument for interpreting not only the present but the past. By its help, pious pagans could find a satisfying meaning for those mythological tales which had begun to shock thoughtful men by their immorality and inconsequence; and pious Christians could perform a like office for the mythical and historical portions of the Old Testament. Thus seen, the old stories glowed with a new light. Indeed, the allegorical interpretation of Scripture enjoyed a surprisingly long life; modern theology has found a better way of dealing with religious myths, but there can be few people of my age, who were brought up to hear sermons, who have not been made familiar with spiritual exercises of this kind. To be sure, many of the interpretations were tasteless and unconvincing—but it does not do to judge any literary form by its sufferings at the hands of devout persons intent on edification. And if one insists on allegorizing a story which was not originally written with that end in view, there are bound to be moments when the interpretation becomes forced and unnatural. Nevertheless, this business of, as it were, allegorizing backwards must have been of great assistance to those who were writing original allegory for its own sake: it enlarged the field of experiment, and suggested a wider variety of literal story to carry the allegorical signification.

From what we have been saying, we should be led to expect that Allegory, as a literary fashion, would tend always to accompany any profound change in men's psychological outlook. And this does indeed turn out to be the case. The golden age of Allegory in Europe sets in with that remarkable psychological upheaval which was produced in the twelfth century by the discovery of Romantic Love.

We are so much accustomed nowadays to take it for granted that romantic love between the sexes is one of the most important and sacred things in life, that it is hard to believe that, before the twelfth century, such an idea never entered anybody's head —and, if it had, would have been considered not only immoral but ridiculous. That human beings did in fact fall in love, with very disturbing effects, was of course a fact that nobody in any age could possibly overlook; but it had never been customary to admire them for it. On the contrary, passion, as distinct from a decent conjugal affection, had always been held to be a bad thing, both in men and in women—but especially in men, since it overthrew their sovereign reason, made them behave like lunatics, and (still worse) caused them to submit to the caprices of the inferior sex. On this point, pagan and Christian were agreed. The passionate adoration of woman was a weakness, and worse. Ovid had written a satire on the subject called *The Art of Love*, in which he scarified the foolish lover who made himself a woman's slave, and sarcastically advised him as to the best methods of making a public fool of himself:

> Go early ere the appointed hour to meet
> The fair, and long await her in the street.
> Through shouldering crowds on all her errands run;
> Though graver business wait the while undone.
> If she commands your presence on her way
> Home from the ball to lackey her, obey!
> Or if from rural scenes she bids you, "Come",
> Drive if you can, if not, then walk, to Rome.
>   *Ars Amatoria* ii. 223 (*trans*. C. S. Lewis).

And so on.

At the same time, Christian preachers never wearied of warning young men against the wiles of women and the snares of love. To be sure, they disagreed somewhat as to whether the pleasures of sex were evil in themselves. Sex, as such, could scarcely be evil, since God had ordained it; but it should perhaps be accepted merely as a necessary means for keeping up the population, and not enjoyed—for that was to know no better than the beasts. Some theologians took the more cheerful view that the pleasures of love were all right so long as they were confined to the senses and did not get the upper hand of one's reason. But all were agreed that the sort of passion which overthrows a man soul and body, making him indifferent to all other earthly (and indeed heavenly) considerations, was altogether evil and shameful. And every layman, gentle or simple, while doubtless holding matrimony profitable and wenching excusable, would heartily have agreed with the fathers of the Church that the very idea of a man prostrate with devotion before the feet of a young woman was silly, degrading, and a reversal of the proper order of things.

And then, almost unimaginably, starting among the troubadours of Provence, and singing its way across Europe in all the Romance languages, came the new cult of courtly love. We cannot now stop to inquire what brought it into being; it is enough that it came, that it spread like wild-fire, and established itself, changing the whole aspect of men's lives, and effecting one of the very few genuine social revolutions in history. It sprang from, and registered, and in so doing helped to produce, profound psychological changes, which demanded poetical expression. Writers were concerned to examine and dissect this entirely novel interior experience, and allegory, which had already proved itself useful in the spiritual laboratory, was again pressed into the service. By a curious irony, Ovid's *Art of Love*, written as a satire, was accepted as a serious textbook for the correct conduct of a love-affair and, with this in their hands, the courtly poets settled down to work out a complete art and science of the passion of love. Whole poems were devoted to debates in the Court of Love, in which the niceties of amorous conduct were thrashed out with as much earnest hair-splitting as prevails in a court of law; and a correct ritual of devotion to one's lady was devised, with so perilous a likeness to the devotions prescribed by the Church as to occasion scandal and accusations of blasphemy.

Not that the poets confined themselves to mere didacticism; they by no means neglected the duty of telling an exciting story. The literary material on which they laid hands for this purpose was that rich traditional deposit of wonder and adventure which we call the "matter of Britain", or, more popularly, "'Arthurian romance". Tales like that of Tristram and Iseult, or or Owain, which dealt with such matters as love-potions, or the carrying-off and rescue of distressed ladies, obviously provided just the kind of basic material that was needed. The tales were ruthlessly modernized, expanded, and added to when required, and made a vehicle for the new and fashionable ideas. Most of the time, the poet was content to tell a straightforward story; but when a character has to choose between two possible courses of action, we find a tendency to drop into Allegory. Thus, in Chrestien de Troyes's *Romance of Lancelot,* the hero, who has lost his horse, is told that if he wants news of his lady Queen Guinevere he must submit to be carried in a common cart. Lancelot hesitates a moment before mounting upon this unknightly and undignified conveyance; and his hesitation takes the form of a debate between Love and Reason:

> Reason, who does not judge like Love,
> Bids him not mount, and warns him off
> By chiding and admonishing
> That he should ne'er do anything
> Whence he might get shame or disgrace.
> The mouth and not the heart's the place
> Where Reason dwells, that dares him chide.
> But Love sits closeted inside
> His heart, and doth command and say
> He ought to mount the cart straightway.
> Love wills it so; so must it be;
> For of the shame nought recketh he
> When such is Love's command and will.
>
> *Charrette* 369.

It is interesting that the *Tristan* of Thomas the Anglo-Norman, in which the poet attempts long passages of direct psychological analysis, with scarcely any resort to allegory, seems never to have achieved any very great popularity in its own day. To us, Thomas's approach appears more "modern" and straightforward than Chrestien's; but his contemporaries probably found it obscure and lacking in drama, in the absence of those personifications which we stigmatize as tedious and unreal. Thomas, in fact, was ahead of his time; for from the twelfth to the fourteenth century Allegory is preparing to take its place as the dominant form in literature.

So, from Romances of adventure, with allegorical passages, we come to poems which are conceived as Allegories from start to finish. Some are allegories of courtly love, some are religious allegories, others again are huge and confused compendia dealing with everything which an educated person ought to know. Fortunately, one of the best and most influential examples of pure allegorical form presents itself very handily for our study, since it was translated for us by Chaucer. This is the First Part of the *Romance of the Rose*, written by Guillaume de Lorris about the middle of the thirteenth century. Its allegorical significance is as simple as possible: it is the story of a young man falling in love with a girl. In the *literal* story, the girl never appears at all: she is only made known to us by the allegorical personages who typify various aspects of her character. The only actual human being who appears in the poem is the Lover himself. Like so many mediaeval allegories, the story is cast into the form of a dream, told to us by the dreamer. The Lover dreams, then, that he is just getting up on a fine May morning,

> In time of love and jolitie
> That all thing ginneth waxen gay.

He washes his hands and dresses himself, lacing up his sleeves with a silver bodkin, and goes out to amuse himself in a meadow "soft, sweet, and green", through which runs a clear river. Presently he comes to a garden by the waterside, full of beautiful trees in which the birds make melody, and surrounded by high walls. This garden represents the courtly life, and on the outside of the walls are painted figures of those qualities which unfit one to live that life—vices such as Hate, and Felony, and "Villainy" (which means Churlishness), Covetousness and Avarice (for a courtier must be free with his money), and Envy, and Prudery —and also Sorrow, Old Age, and Poverty, for these are not welcome in the playground of noble youth. The Lover is, of course, eager to get into this delightful place and, finding at last a wicket gate, he knocks repeatedly. At length the door is opened by an elegant lady called Idleness. She is beautifully dressed and looks like a person unaccustomed to work, for, says the poet, when she has done combing her hair and arranging herself to perfection, she "calls it a day".[1] Idleness informs the Lover that the garden belongs to the Lord of Mirth, and at his earnest prayer lets him in. The place is so enchanting, and so melodious with birds, that it seemed to him like an earthly paradise; and here he finds a goodly company engaged in dancing— Courtesy, who welcomes him as he approaches, and Mirth with

[1] Thenne had she don al hir journé.

his lady Gladness; Beauty and Riches with their lovers; Largesse, and Franchise, and Youth; and among them is the God of Love himself with his squire, Sweet-Looking, who carries his bow and arrows. There is no time to read the descriptions of all these attractive people, nor yet of the many trees and fresh flowers adorning the garden which the Dreamer now sets out to explore. He comes eventually to a fountain, at the bottom of which are two crystal stones. And the crystal is a magic crystal, for, gazing into it, one can see reflected the whole garden and everything that is in it. And there he sees a rose-bed full of roses, which so much attracts him that he immediately sets off in search of it. When he comes there, he says:

> The savour of the roses swote
> Me smote right to the heartë roote,
> As I had all embalmed be.

One particular rose—a half-opened crimson bud—overwhelms him with desire to pluck it; but the rose-bed is set about with a thick and thorny hedge, and he does not know how to come near the rose.

Now, all this while, unseen by him, the God of Love has been following him, bow in hand. And when he sees the Lover's desire thus fixed upon the Rose:

> He took an arrow full sharply whet,
> And in his bowe when it was set,
> He straight up to his ear drough,
> The strongë bowe that was so tough,
> And shot at me so wonder smart
> That through mine eye into mine heart
> The tackle smote, and deep it went.

The arrow is called Beauty; and the god follows it up with four others: Simplicity, Courtesy, Company and finally Fair-Semblance,

> The which in no wise will consent
> That any lover him repent
> To serve his love with heart and all,
> For any peril that may befal.

Thus stricken, the Dreamer surrenders to Love, who binds him to his service and admonishes him, in a speech of considerable length, on the whole duty of a lover.

So far, the allegory is very easy to follow. A young man goes to court and enjoys the gay and luxurious life there. He is rash enough to gaze into a lady's eyes (this is the episode of the crystal stones in the fountain), and sees there the promise of further delights (the rose-bed). In particular, he feels that it would be delightful to win the lady's love (the Rose). While he is light-heartedly pleasing himself with these thoughts, he falls deeply and genuinely in Love.

Now we come to something a good deal more subtle. As the heart-smitten Lover is gazing wistfully through the hedge, there comes up to him a cheerful young man called Bialacoil (Fair-Welcome), who says that, provided he behaves himself like a gentleman, he will be charmed to let him through the hedge to see the Rose closer, and do him any service in his power. This obliging youth is the first of the Lady's personal qualities; and here we begin to see the advantage of the allegorical device, for, though we can sense immediately what Bialacoil represents, we can hardly put it into words without a lot of clumsy periphrasis. He is, one may say, the Lady's instinct to be pleasant to people : she thinks it agreeable of the Dreamer to be so obviously attracted and she receives his attentions amiably—to put it in one word, she shows him "Fair-Welcome", Bialacoil. The allegory, which looks like the longest way round, is really, you see, the shortest way home in these matters.

So Bialacoil lets the Lover through the hedge. He cannot, he explains, do as much for him as he would like to do, for fear of the three guardians whom Chastity has set to keep watch on the rose-bed. The first of these is Shame, the daughter of Reason and Trespass; and once again, this parentage seems to me to convey very accurately our curiously ambiguous attitude to sexual modesty. The others are Malebouche (Wicked-Tongue)—the fear of slander; and Danger, of whom more in a moment. Bialacoil ventures, however, to present the Lover with—not the Rose, but a leaf which has grown near it : the Lady, that is, grants some favour, or token of kindness or compassion. This emboldens the Lover to ask if he may pluck the rose. But at this, poor Bialacoil is terrified, and out of the grass where he has been lurking there starts up Danger—a hideous black-faced churl who frightens Bialacoil away and thrusts the Lover back through the hedge. The young man, in fact, has gone too far : the girl is seriously shocked and affronted, and rebuffs him with that kind of primitive roughness and brutality which can easily be roused in any woman by a sudden, direct approach which presumes upon her kindness.

This is, of course, only the beginning of the story, which soon becomes more complicated. Reason tries in vain to dissuade the Lover from his attempt; Venus (physical passion) intervenes on his behalf to undermine the Lady's resistance; Suspicion (Jalousie) is aroused; a wall is built about the rose-bed and Bialacoil is banished to a dungeon. Guillaume de Lorris never finished his poem: it was completed later at unwieldy length by Jehan de Meung—a poet of much greater power, but much less skill in handling allegory. But the fragment we have shows how delicate and accurate an instrument Allegory could be in the right hands. It is also remarkable for the extreme purity of its form: there is no confusion between the figure and the thing figured—no intrusion of flesh-and-blood persons upon the personified abstractions who play all the roles in its tiny drama.

And here we are reminded of two cautions which Dante gave about the proper way to read and write Allegory. Defending this allegorical handling of Love in his early book, the *Vita Nuova*, he says that a reader "might be in a difficulty as to what I say concerning Love, as if he were a thing in himself, and not only an intelligent being but a corporeal being. Which thing, according to truth, is false; for Love exists not as a being in itself but is a *quality of a being* (an accident in a substance)". And he goes on to say that those who write Allegory "should not speak this without having some interpretation in their minds of what they say; for deep shame it were to him who should rhyme under cover of a figure or of rhetorical colouring, and afterwards could not, if required, strip such vesture from his words, in such a way that they should have a real meaning" (*Vita Nuova* xxv). We must not, that is, be led away by our own eloquence into attributing to abstractions the kind of reality that belongs to actual persons. And we must also take care that the literal and the figurative meanings can be so separated as to form two independent stories, corresponding at all points, but each coherent and complete in itself.

Dante himself is, of course, the greatest of all allegorists; but his is a special case. In *The Divine Comedy* he invented a method so individual that no one has ever really succeeded in using it on the grand scale again. All his characters do, indeed, represent "qualities in a person"; but he has used, instead of personified abstractions, actual historical or mythical personages who are fitted to serve as natural symbols of those qualities. Thus the various kinds of Pride are represented, not by a lady called "Superbia", or by a giant called "Orgoglio", but by such people as Capaneus, Farinata, Umberto Aldobrandesco, Oderisi the Painter, and Provenzan Salvani. Thus at one stroke Dante abolishes the limitations which fetter the conversation and behaviour of abstractions, and regains something of the freedom which belonged to the mythological treatment of the gods. Yet, although so penetrated with symbolism, and set in a great symbolic framework, *The Comedy* can be interpreted allegorically at no fewer than three levels, without any encroachment of the figure upon the thing figured, or vice versa. But nobody has ever been able to bend Dante's bow, and it is easier to study the pure classic outline of Allegory in the works of the lesser masters. We may notice, however, that for his literal story Dante has chosen a scheme which was to become very popular and very rewarding —that of a journey or pilgrimage.

It is in the fourteenth century that Allegory becomes a Dominant Form in literature. Almost anything that a writer wanted to say, on any subject whatever, was crammed, as though into a hold-all, into an allegorical romance of some kind. Similarly, in the nineteenth century, a writer's heterogeneous views on life in general emerged, almost automatically, from his mind in the shape of a sentimental novel; that is, whatever the book was really about, it *purported* to be the sentimental history of Jack and Jill. Whenever any literary form achieves dominance, the result is the production of a huge mass of works, some bad, some good and many mediocre; and the classical outline of the form becomes distorted—bulging, like the hold-all, under the pressure of bulky contents which strain it out of shape.

By the time we get to Spenser's *Faerie Queene*, Allegory has got about as much as it can carry, and is already falling out of fashion. This Spenser knew, as he showed by making deliberate use of an archaic style of language. For his literal story he uses a background of the old Arthurian Romance—not as the twelfth century knew it, but in the fantasticated development it had undergone in the hands of Boiardo and Ariosto, in which adventure is piled upon adventure, story interlocked with story, in a way which allows of immense richness of description and variety of detail. Spenser's method is genuinely allegorical, and often contains allegory within allegory—as where the House of Alma presents us with a self-contained allegorical picture of the human body, packed within the Allegory of Temperance which forms the subject of the Second Book. He has also interwoven with the moral allegory the strands of a political allegory—and the very word "interwoven" is a way of saying that the pure form of Allegory is becoming blurred. One cannot strip the poetic lendings from the political sense of *The Faerie Queene* and present it as a complete and coherent entity; it makes its appearance only in patches: the levels of interpretation are becoming confused. Nor is it always possible to distinguish clearly between person and personification, between the figure and the thing figured. Is Sir Guyon, for instance, a temperate man, or the virtue of temperance *in* a man? His Palmer seems certainly to be rather a quality than a person: but when Guyon suddenly produces an iron lock, a stake, and a hundred iron chains with which to bind Occasion and Furor, we cannot help wondering how these objects came to be in the possession of a knight and a palmer wandering on foot through open country: the allegory is intruding into the literal story, with disquieting results. Not that such things need trouble our enjoyment very much, so long as we keep in mind while we read that the allegorical meaning is the real and important meaning. But if we try to forget the Allegory, and read only for the story, or for what people call "the poetry", we shall be faintly disturbed by a kind of incongruity which we never feel in reading either the *Comedy* or the *Romance of the Rose* on the one hand, or the irresponsible absurdities of the *Orlando Furioso* on the other. In Spenser, the flower of Allegory has opened to the full, and the petals are beginning to fall apart, though its scent and its beauty are incomparable. After this, sustained Allegory disappears as a narrative genre; though in many Moralities the pure allegorical form contrives to hold the stage to a surprisingly late date: *Everyman*, at the end of the fifteenth century is as "unmixed" as *The Romance of the Rose* three hundred and fifty years earlier, and its personified qualities are as humanly, though perhaps not quite as subtly, characterized. "What!" says Beauty, aghast to find herself accompanying Everyman on a journey that ends in a grave, "Should I smother here?" and when assured that this is so, she adds hastily:

> I cross out all this; adieu by St. John!
> I take my cap in my lap and am gone.

Whereas Strength plays the part of the common-sense candid friend:

> Yea, I have you far enough conveyed;
> Ye be old enough, I understand,
> Your pilgrimage to take on hand;
> I repent me that I hither came.

But for the most part as we move on into the sixteenth and seventeenth centuries, men have grown sufficiently aware of their conscious mental processes to be able to represent them directly, without allegorical simplifications. There was, however, one region of the psychological field in which the simple, if not the learned, came to need help in making themselves clear to themselves.

The great theological disturbance which had its centre at Geneva transferred the sensitive area of religious experience from confrontation with a transcendent God without, to the workings of the Spirit within the Soul. As always, a strong sense of sin—a vivid awareness of the divided personality—called for some kind of dramatic expression. In England the acute consciousness of this inward crisis induced by the struggles and persecutions of the late seventeenth century bore fruit in the works of John Bunyan—especially in *The Holy War* and *The Pilgrim's Progress*.

It is difficult to say what were Bunyan's "models" for these books. To say that he was steeped in the Bible explains nothing; for the Bible, though rich in myth and parable, is almost barren of Allegory. It is doubtful whether Bunyan ever read an allegorical poem or saw a morality play—yet if these had never been, his own books would have been different. For all the characteristic features are there: the personifications, the pilgrimage or psychomachia, the "debates" between abstractions, the dream framework. Probably the tradition of Allegory, fixed in men's minds through many generations, was handed down in sermons from preacher to preacher. *The Holy War* is as classically "pure" in form as *The Romance of the Rose*; *The Pilgrim's Progress* is of the "mixed" Spenserian type, in that there are moments (as with Mr. Greatheart or the Interpreter) when we cannot be perfectly sure whether we are dealing with persons or abstractions, and moments when (as with the martyrdom of Faithful at Vanity Fair) there is a slight confusion between the literal and the allegorical story.

The Holy War has never enjoyed the same prestige, or evoked the same affection, as *The Pilgrim's Progress*; but this, I think, is due not so much to its austerity of form as to the obvious fact that warfare, particularly siege-warfare, cannot possibly provide such a variety of entertaining incidents as a journey. The Psychomachia, though the most obvious machinery for an analysis of the divided will, has never in the long run proved satisfying. But the one book displays just as brilliantly as the other Bunyan's supreme gift as an allegorist—his genius for investing abstractions with a homespun, humorous and convincing humanity. Consider, for instance, the defence of Mr. Incredulity when he is put on trial as a prisoner of war for resisting the forces of the divine King Shaddai. Incredulity is not an original inhabitant of Mansoul, but a member of the occupation forces of Diabolus, settled there when Diabolus first took over the town.

> Then said Incredulity: "I know not Shaddai; I love my old prince; I thought it my duty to be true to my trust, and to do what I could to possess the minds of the men of Mansoul to do their utmost to resist strangers and foreigners, and with might to fight against them. Nor have I, nor shall I, change mine opinion for fear of trouble, though you at present are possessed of place and power."

The defence is disallowed; but it is the defence of a human being, not a frigid and abstract conceit; and we have heard many very like it, in recent war trials.

Bunyan is the last of the English allegorists in the great tradition. After him, we get a hundred and fifty years of rationalism and common sense, the integrated mind, and the omnipotence of education. Or if there were men like William Blake, or groups like the Romantics, who were aware of their own inner dissensions, their protests did not voice themselves in formal allegory, but in symbolism, or prophecy, or in direct exposition and argument.

But towards the end of the nineteenth century, the sense of spiritual cleavage and insecurity produced by disturbing new scientific views of man's place in nature, evoked a fresh attempt at Allegory on the large scale—Tennyson's *Idylls of the King*

This is a most interesting work, whch has been treated with absurd frivolity by twentieth-century critics who, ignoring its claim to be Allegory, and ignorant or contemptuous of allegorical form as such, have consistently mistaken its virtues for defects and condemned it accordingly.

It is indeed very fumbling and uneven in its allegorical technique. This is partly because by that time the art of writing and reading allegory had been forgotten, and partly because the composition of the *Idylls* extended over forty years, and the first few stories were not undertaken with any definite allegorical intention in mind. It was only as he went along that Tennyson became fully conscious that he was writing, as he says in the *Dedication*, an allegory "of sense at war with soul". On the whole, Tennyson is at his worst when he is merely re-writing Malory, and at his best when he is deliberately allegorizing on his own account. In the opening Idyll, *The Coming of Arthur*, which stands first, but was one of the latest to be written, both allegory and poetry are at their best.

Like Dante (whom he knew well) he has chosen to use not personified abstractions but traditional personages in whom those abstractions may be symbolized; and like the twelfth-century romancers, and Spenser, he has chosen the "matter of Britain" for the subject of his literal story. He has been sneered at for turning Arthur's knights into "Victorian ladies and gentlemen" —but here Tennyson is right and his critics wrong. An allegorist must write in terms of contemporary problems: Tennyson is doing with the Arthurians what the Romancers did when they turned them into mediaeval devotees of courtly love, and what Spenser did when he turned them into Elizabethans with a sound Protestant morality. No writer can in fact really assume the whole habit of mind of another age—or, if he could, he would merely produce pastiche. However we may dress the production, Shakespeare's *Lear* is no legendary king of folk-tale, but a complicated man of the Renaissance.

Neither is it very sensible to talk contemptuously about "the painful snuffle of Tennyson's blameless king".[1] We may not find King Arthur very lovable—but then, neither did Guinevere; and that is what the allegory is about. For the central image which dominates the poem is the marriage of Arthur and Guinevere. Unless (this is the whole argument) the Soul (Arthur) can retain

[1] Graham Hough: *The Last Romantics*.

the allegiance of the Heart (Guinevere), it cannot consolidate its rule over man's nature (Logres), for the realm will be "betrayed by what is false within". The fault is indeed in Guinevere; yet it is necessary that her treason should not be merely perverse. There is in Arthur, as there is indeed in all idealism, something which the undisciplined heart may easily find repellent. Tennyson's real error here has been to fall at one point into the allegorist's besetting sin of confusing the figurative with the literal story. The sexual relations between Arthur and Guinevere are only the image of the relations between Soul and Heart; but in the Idyll called *Guinevere* he has slipped into treating the problem as though it were *really* only a question of sexual ethics—of whether a man holding a public position would be justified in openly condoning his wife's adultery. But it is difficult to see how the Soul can publicly repudiate the Heart for the sake of setting a good example—unless on a dualistic and ascetic view of life which Tennyson certainly did not accept. I do not say it would be impossible to make out a case for the allegorical interpretation here: but it would require a good deal of ingenuity, and would still seem strained and unnatural. The whole tone of the passage rather suggests that Tennyson, confronted with the facts of the literal story as he finds them in Malory, has slid aside from his main allegory into discussing a different problem—that of forgiving the sinner and, at the same time, not only condemning the sin but making it clear that one does so. It is wrong, I think, to stigmatize Arthur as a sanctimonious prig: he is concerned (as we are today perhaps too little concerned) with maintaining public standards of conduct; and we cannot dismiss a very real dilemma by merely using words like "smug" and "hypocritical". But I think it is fair to say that the story, as Tennyson handles it, does not quite fit in with the main allegorical structure of the poem as a whole.

On the other hand, in *The Coming of Arthur*, the long argument about Arthur's parentage—whether he is

>   the child of shamefulness,
> Or born the son of Gorlois after death,
> Or Uther's son, and born before his time—

is a fine and imaginative translation, into the terms of the traditional allegorical debate, of the heart-searchings aroused by evolutionary theory. What was the soul? Was it of heavenly descent, or evolved out of animal instincts, or the offspring of self-delusion? Has it any right at all to claim sovereignty over the rest of man's nature, or is that claim mere usurpation? And the debate ends in Merlin's account of Arthur's mysterious arrival at Tintagel—the storm, and the ship like a winged dragon, and the naked babe carried to the shore in a whirl of fire and water—

> ... and presently thereafter follow'd calm,
> Free sky and stars.

Tennyson is too honest a writer to answer his own question, except by implication. Merlin, who stands for the intellect, will not pronounce:

> Where is he who knows?
> From the great deep to the great deep he goes.

The whole Idyll is a magnificent piece of allegorical writing, precise, subtle, and on the very highest plane of technical accomplishment. Equally good, though thinner in allegorical texture, are *Lancelot and Elaine,* and *The Holy Grail,* both dealing with the morbid effects of an unbalanced idealism; on the one hand, retreat into a fantasy of egotistical emotion; on the other, flight into an over-spiritualized religion.

I have chosen *The Idylls of the King* to represent this period for two reasons. In the first place, because the issue there is a simple one, and we need not be confused, as we are in discussions about, for example, *Peer Gynt,* with talk about myth, imagery, and symbolism. In the second place, because the poem and its present status illustrate so clearly what happens when the whole habit of writing and reading Allegory has fallen into decay. Tennyson's own touch is uncertain, he is seldom quite sure what kind of poem he is writing, or whether he ought not to apologize for writing Allegory at all. And the effect on critical appreciation has been disastrous, since, too ignorant or too contemptuous of Allegory to take it seriously, writers have based their judgement on totally irrelevant standards. For we have now reached the period when it is sufficient to give a thing the bad name of Allegory and leaving it without further ado. Thus, a recent writer quotes Yeats as saying: "I find that though I love symbolism, which is often the only fitting speech for some mystery of disembodied life, I am for the most part bored by allegory, which is made, as Blake says, by 'the daughters of memory', and coldly, with no wizard frenzy." And he comments: "Symbolism is the only possible expression of some otherwise inexpressible spiritual essence, while allegory is *an arbitrary translation of some principle that is already familiar*, of something that has *already been expressed in other terms*."[1]

Historically, we have seen that this is quite untrue. Allegory, in a journeyman's hands, may (like symbol itself) come to be used to translate the already familiar; but it always *begins* as an effort to express something for which terms have not yet been invented.

So long as we remember this, we may readily agree that symbolism springs from, and stirs, profounder and more primitive levels of the soul; indeed, as we said to begin with, Allegory is not primitive, neither is it possible for primitive minds to produce it.

If there is any truth in the contention, which we have been so far putting forward, that a strong and disturbing awareness of psychological dislocation tends to result in the production of Allegory, what are we to say about our own times? For we have seen that Allegory is despised and misunderstood as a literary form—and yet there can never have been a period in which our sense of the divided psyche was so acute. Ought we not to be experiencing a vigorous revival of Allegory? Why should it obstinately stay dead under the very conditions which ought to give it life?

The answer is, quite simply, that we *are* experiencing a revival of Allegory, though not quite in the place where we are accustomed to look for it. The resurrection in fact took place before the critics had got around to burying the body, and was brought about, not by the poets, but by the psycho-analysts, particularly those of the Freudian school. I am not now referring to the odd and sometimes perverse use which they have made of primitive myth, but to the interesting vocabulary which they have found themselves driven to use in expressing their experimental conclusions about the psychology of the Unconscious. This vocabulary is not scientific, but poetical, and imposes a poetical and indeed fictional form on the whole presentation of their subject.

[1] Graham Hough: *The Last Romantics* p. 228.

[Freud's] conception of the mind (says Professor J. C. Flügel) is essentially dynamic. He regards striving or conation (to use the generally accepted psychological term) as the real function of mind, and the opposition between different parts of the mind can, he thinks, best be expressed as a conflict between inconsistent and opposing mental tendencies or "wishes".

Outline of Modern Knowledge, p. 375.

This is plain enough. Like the pioneer explorers of the Conscious, the pioneer explorer of the Unconscious can only think and express himself effectively in terms of a *Psychomachia*. This device is taken up and used by his successors, Adler and Jung. A whole rout of personified abstractions take part in the "conflict", some new to us; others already familiar under other names: the Libido (who in some aspects corresponds closely to the mediaeval Cupidon), the Censor (who in Dante sits at the Threshold of Assent but in Freud at the lower Threshold of Consciousness), Eros and Agape (again closely corresponding to the earlier Venus and Amor), the Will-to-Life, the Will-to-Death, and the Will-to-Power (who form a kind of family group, like Spenser's Sansfoy, Sansloy, and Sansjoy, though of course bearing no other resemblance to them), and that other allied trinity, the Ego, the Super-Ego, and the Id. The assault of disreputable Wishes upon the House of Consciousness, their encounter with the Censor, who firmly opposes their entrance and repressively imprisons them in the dungeons below the Threshold, their escape in disguise through the ivory gate into the Garden of Dreams, the impish tricks which they play upon those respectable inhabitants, Mind and Behaviour, and the long process by which the good magicians Analysis, Transference and Sublimation unmask them, convert them, and eventually bring them under control of the Conscious and make them swear fealty to Person (the integrated personality) forms an exciting episode worthy to adorn the pages of any Allegory. It *is*, in fact, Allegory, with all the illuminating persuasiveness, and some of the dangers, of Allegory. The chief danger of Allegory, as Dante was careful to point out, is that we should be led into mistaking its poetic truth for concrete fact. The writer previously quoted says, speaking of the "unconscious morality" by which we tend to conform to received conscious standards of thought and conduct:

This morality is [now] regarded as a definite entity within the mind and is called the *Super-Ego*. It is, as it were, at the behest of the Super-Ego that the Censor does its work.

His loose employment of the philosophic term "entity" must not mislead us—and if we are trained in the interpretation of Allegory it will not mislead us—into supposing that the *Super-Ego* or any other personified quality really is an *entity*: i.e. an independently existing being.

Which thing, according to truth, is false; for Love (or any other such personification) exists not as a being, but is a quality of being (an accident in a substance).

Provided that we remember this, and do not attribute a self-existing, objective and daemonic reality to each of the complex activities of the single psyche, we can easily accept these modern Allegories as helpful pictures of our interior difficulties. If not, the allegories of modern psychology will end by becoming as stereotyped and unreal as those of the older faculty-psychology, or as dangerous to the personality as the Manichaean duality between matter and spirit.

It would be strange if the allegorical apparatus of the new psychology did not, after all, find its way into literature. And so in fact it does. A great deal of modern poetry and fiction teases us by seeming to carry some kind of allegorical significance; but we find it very hard to "strip", in Dante's phrase, "the vesture from the words in such a way that they shall have a real meaning". For one thing, the images are not the traditional ones; neither does the writer help us as a rule by giving his characters explanatory names, as the old allegorists did when they personified Bialacoil, Duessa, or Giant Despair; they do not even use openly the allegorical figures of the psycho-analysts. Further, both the writers themselves and their apologists seem to avoid the label "Allegory", as though it were an obscene word, preferring expressions like "myth" or "symbol", which, when accurately used, mean something different.

As an outstanding example of the modern allegorist, we may take Franz Kafka, who died in 1924. His two longest and most important novels, *The Trial* and *The Castle,* are efforts to find a satisfactory allegorical expression for man's awareness of a relation to some power beyond himself. He feels, obscurely, that this power claims his entire allegiance, and that it claims to sit in absolute judgement upon his thoughts and actions; but he cannot understand its claims, or the values by which it judges him. He can never get into direct touch with it; and all the intermediaries who purport to provide channels of communication with it only lead him into labyrinths of nonsense, frustration, disorder, or mere filth. Yet the compulsion to find the way and establish the relationship persists, and makes any easy accommodation with the life of everyday things impossible. Throughout, there is a suggestion that it is precisely the man's determination to intellectualise his situation and justify himself that stands in the way of his success. Both books were left incomplete by their author; and no complete solution to this heartbreaking mystery is offered.

A key to Kafka's enigmatical writings has been furnished by Herbert Tauber (*Franz Kafka: An Interpretation of his Works*). It is perhaps not complete; it may here and there be mistaken (after all, it has taken us some six hundred years to wrestle with the problem of Dante, and we are not out of the wood yet!)—the point which concerns us now is that this key treats the books frankly as Allegories. Tauber says: "Kafka avails himself of the old rights of poetic licence, using landscapes to symbolize states of mind, houses and rooms as symbols of personality, men and animals to symbolize aspects of their own ego, and even representing Fate as a function of character." He then goes on: "All these characteristics, particularly extolled by the surrealists as a new discovery and used by them as a polemic deliberately opposed to the 'old' world of reality, are to be found in Kafka's work." He might have added that, though these characteristics are not to be found in the "realistic" novel, they are so far from being a new discovery as to be found in all allegorists from the first century onwards. Any work of fiction which personifies "states of mind" and "aspects of the ego" is in fact an Allegory, whether or not it also avails itself of myth and symbol.

There are, I think, three chief errors to avoid when reading Allegory. The first is a finicking insistence on finding a significance for every word in the text, even in passages which are obviously only put in to give vividness and verisimilitude to the literal story. If Dante says that he took no more than three paces to come up with somebody, it is quite unnecessary to attach allegorical importance to the number three, and an allegorical significance to each separate step; nor is it sensible to try and find a particular meaning for every tree that grows in Guillaume de Lorris's garden. Flat-footed literalism of this kind, much indulged in by many mediaeval and some modern commentators, has been largely to blame for the disgust and irritation which the very word "Allegory" excites in people's minds. Common-sense and a sensitiveness to poetic expression will usually tell us whether we are dealing with figurative speech or mere décor; and it is a sound rule that any significance which seems forced or arbitrary is probably not in accordance with the writer's intention.

The second error is that of confusing the allegorical with the literal meaning. This may sometimes, we have seen, be the fault of the writer; but it is also an error into which the reader may slip on his own account. A little practice in reading the great masters of allegorical form will soon enable one to avoid being drawn away by red herrings, and also to detect where the writer has accidentally crossed his own trail.

The third error is much more fundamental, and is an infallible recipe for weariness of the flesh and vexation of spirit. I mean the very widespread notion that the best way to enjoy Allegory is to read for the sake of the "poetry", or the literal story, and not bother about what it signifies. That is the direct opposite of the truth. If we read, for instance, Dante's *Inferno* merely as a description of literal torments in a physical Hell, we are likely to find ourselves baffled and repelled before we are halfway through, and in no mood to appreciate its rare moments of pure lyricism. But if we see it as, primarily, an exploration into the infinite possibilities of evil which lurk in the depths of the psyche, we shall discover its unexpected relevance to the human situation and its uncomfortably piercing insight. This is true, not only of poems as austere as Dante's, but also of those which, like *The Romance of the Rose,* or *The Faerie Queene,* are gaily adorned with "quaint and pleasant devices"; it is only when we see what the whole thing is really about that we can take intelligent pleasure in the thousandfold beauties which accompany and enhance the significant figures of the story. For we are so made that we soon grow weary of ornament for the sake of ornament, and even of beauty which makes no appeal to the heart or the understanding.

CHAPTER X

THE FAUST LEGEND AND THE IDEA OF THE DEVIL

IT IS NOTORIOUS that one of the great difficulties about writing a book or play about the Devil is to prevent that character from stealing the show. Any actor will tell you that the role of the Devil in any handling of the subject is sure-fire. And it is apt to be sure-fire—not only in the sense that the Devil is a picturesque figure full of colour and action; that is true of any vigorous villain. But it is also true in the sense that the Devil is only too apt to capture the sympathy of the house.

This is a serious matter, either for the artist, or the audience, or both. Or perhaps it would be better to say that it is always a serious matter for the audience; for the artist, it may be serious in one of three ways. Either he knows what he is doing and intends it (in which case there is something wrong with him spiritually as a man), or else he is, as Blake said of Milton, "of the Devil's party without knowing it" (in which case the spiritual evil is deeper and more incurable), or there is simply a failure of communication in his art.

It is not, of course, surprising that the Devil should appear attractive, nor that he should be made to appear so in a work of the imagination. It is precisely the Devil's business to appear attractive: that is the whole meaning of temptation to sin. And unless the artist conveys something of this attraction, his Devil will be a mere turnip-ghost, exciting either boredom or derisive laughter, and in no way conveying or communicating the power of evil. But it is important artistically as well as theologically to ascertain whether the artist is able to view his own creation critically, or whether he has fallen, consciously or unconsciously, under the power of his own spell-binding.

There is, indeed, a grave theological difficulty about the Devil, which we had better look at first and clear out of the way (so far as that is possible) before going on to the artistic side of the subject. It is the old difficulty about omnipotence and free-will. If God is almighty and created everything, how do we account for the existence of the evil power, or of any sort of evil in creation? One answer—that of the Manichaeans—is to deny that God is omnipotent and to allow the co-existent presence of two powers: good and evil, light and darkness. Even in this scheme of things, it is generally supposed that the good will eventually conquer the evil. But the supposition behind it is that the evil and the darkness are as *primary* as the good and the light. A variation of this is that the darkness is primary: that it existed in chaos or the abyss before the light got to work upon it, and that the light—what we mean by God—is continually engaged in building up creation towards the good against the backward drag which seeks to reduce all things to the primeval chaos. This position is unorthodox and, strictly speaking, heretical. It lies behind a good deal of Berdyaev's philosophy; and it seems to have a good deal also to do with the fashionable doctrine of Emergent Evolution, by which God is supposed to be evolving Himself out of chaos in an enormous time-process.

The orthodox Christian conception is more subtle and less optimistic; it is also much less involved in the time-process. For it, the light and the light only is primary: creation and time and darkness are secondary and begin together. When you come to consider the matter, it is strictly meaningless to say that darkness could precede light in a time-process. Where there is no light, there is no meaning for the word "darkness"; for darkness is merely a name for that which is without light. Light, by merely existing, creates darkness, or at any rate the possibility of darkness. In this sense, it is possible to understand that profound saying: "I form the light, and create darkness; I make peace, and create evil; I the Lord do all these things." (*Isaiah, xlv.* 7.)

But it is at this point that it becomes possible for the evil and the darkness and the chaos to boast: "We are that which was before the light was, and the light is a usurpation upon our rights." It is an illusion: evil and darkness and chaos are pure negation, and there is no such state as "*before* the light", because it is the primary light that creates the whole time-process. It is an illusion; and that is the primary illusion inside which the Devil lives and in which he deceives himself and others. That primary illusion is stated with perfect clarity by Goethe's Mephistopheles:

> Ich bin ein Teil des Teils, der Anfangs alles war,
> Ein Teil der Finsternis, die sich das Licht gebar,
> Das stolze Licht, das nun der Mutter Nacht
> Den alten Rang, den Raum, ihr streitig macht.

That is the Devil's claim: the exact statement of the pride by which he fell from Heaven. It sounds extremely fine, and when it is set forth in attractive language, it is sometimes difficult to remember that the Devil is a liar and the father of lies. In *Paradise Lost*, we find Satan making the same claim: he "feels himself impaired" because of the authority of the Son of God. He believes, or affects to believe, that he himself is anterior to the Son, and ought not, therefore, to be subject to Him. In the subsequent argument with Abdiel he shows himself a poor logician, but we may, if we like, suppose that by this time he really believes in his own claim, or has argued himself into the illusion of belief—for the corruption of the will saps the intellect, and the Devil is ultimately a fool as well as a villain. He is, let us believe by all means, the victim of his own illusion. But Milton is not; Milton knows, and says, that the Son is anterior to Satan, and is, in fact, the very power by whom Satan was created.

In the orthodox Christian position, therefore, the light is primary, the darkness secondary and derivative; and this is important for the whole theology of evil. In *The Devil to Pay* I tried to make this point; and I remember being soundly rapped over the knuckles by a newspaper critic, who said in effect that after a great deal of unintelligible pother, I had worked up to the statement that God was light, which did not seem to be very novel or profound. Novel, it certainly is not: it is scarcely the business of Christian writers to introduce novelties into the fundamental Christian doctrines. But profundity is another matter: Christian theology is profound, and since I did not invent it, I may have the right to say so. These are the lines, spoken by Mephistopheles, in the presence of the Judge before whom a lie cannot live:

> *Faustus:* Who made thee?
> *Mephistopheles:* God; as the light makes the shadow.

That is the acknowledgment of derivation. Later follows:

Faustus: What art thou, Mephistopheles?
Mephistopheles: I am the price that all things pay for being,
The shadow on the world, thrown by the world
Standing in its own light, which light God is.

And whether or not those lines are good verse, they do bring us up against the fundamental problem. Evil is "the price that all things" (i.e. all created things—God is not a "thing") "pay for being"—that is, for existing in created and material form. There is, for them, along with the reality of God, the possibility of not-God. For things inorganic, this is only known as change, and not as evil; for creatures organic but not self-conscious, there is both change and pain—and here there is a very great mystery, which we are scarcely in a position to solve, because we know nothing of what pain may be like to the unselfconscious organism. But to the self-conscious creature the not-God is known as change, as pain, and *also* an intellectual error and moral evil; and it is at this point that it becomes evil in the profoundest sense of the word, because it can be embraced and made active by the will. The *possibility* of evil exists from the moment that a creature is made that can love and do good because it chooses and not because it is unable to do anything else. The *actuality* of evil exists from the moment that that choice is exercised in the wrong direction. Sin (moral evil) is the deliberate choice of the not-God. And pride, as the Church has consistently pointed out, is the root of it: i.e. the refusal to accept the creaturely status; the making of the *difference* between self and God into an antagonism against God. Satan, as Milton rightly shows, "thinks himself impaired," and in that moment he chooses that evil shall be his good.

That is what the orthodox Catholic doctrine is; I do not want to argue it here, because that would lead us away from our subject; but I want to make clear what it *is*. Evil is the soul's choice of the not-God. The corollary is that damnation, or hell, is the permanent choice of the not-God. God does not (in the monstrous old-fashioned phrase) "send" anybody to hell; hell is that state of the soul in which its choice becomes obdurate and fixed; the punishment (so to call it) of that soul is to remain eternally in that state which it has chosen.

In the Christian *mythos* the original head and front of this offending is not placed among mankind. It happened first among another order of created beings. The devils are fallen angels. Satan and his followers chose the not-God, and when they had it, they found that it was hell. In that obduracy they suffer; and into that suffering they endeavour to drag the rest of creation—of which man in particular concerns us. Their whole will is to hatred and negation and destruction, and if they could accomplish that will wholly they would be none the happier, since happiness is not in them—they have destroyed their own capacity for happiness. The lust for destruction in no way increases the happiness of those who indulge in it—if anything, the more successful they are in it, the more miserable they are—but they persist in it because they have destroyed their own will for anything else. This is, of course, a witless state of mind; but then the intellect is one of the first things that the evil will destroys. That it is not an impossible state of mind is quite apparent—for we can see it existing in human beings today —and sometimes can find it only too clearly in our virtuous selves: for example, in jealousy, that searches avidly for fresh occasions of the distrust which torments it: or in our savage resentment against those we have injured, which prompts us to renew the injury and so increase the miserable resentment.

I apologize for this long theological preliminary, which seemed necessary in order that we might examine the subject of the Devil in literature. Because one of the most important things we have to do is to distinguish the Devil as (in the sight of God) he is, and the thing which may be called the "diabolic set-up". The underlying actuality is miserable, hideous, and squalid; the "set-up" is the façade which the Devil shows to the world—and a very noble façade it often is, and the nobler, the more dangerous. The Devil is a spiritual lunatic, but, like many lunatics, he is extremely plausible and cunning. His brain is, so to speak, in perfectly good working order except for that soft and corrupted spot in the centre, where dwells the eternal illusion. His method of working is to present us with the magnificent set-up, hoping we shall not use either our brains or our spiritual faculties to penetrate the illusion. He is playing for sympathy; therefore he is much better served by exploiting our virtues than by appealing to our lower passions; consequently, it is when the Devil looks most noble and reasonable that he is most dangerous. And here the poets have sometimes become his unconscious or even his conscious allies. And in order to be fair to the poets, it is very necessary that we should find out whether the illusion is in them or in us.

I should like to take two or three examples of the Satanic set-up from the work of the poets who have dealt with the subject—including those who have dealt with the Faustus-legend and the theme of the Devil's Bargain.

In the original Faustus-legend there is no set-up, except of the most obvious kind. It is a plain story of the man who barters his hope in the next world for success or power in this, knowing quite well what he is doing. Such set-up as there is in this and in the mediaeval mystery-plays may be found in the traditional clowning and horse-play of which the Devil is always the centre. The theology is correct enough—the Devil is a fool and is outwitted in the end—but I suspect that he was, for the audience, a "favourite character" for the sake of the comic relief. On the whole, this was probably wholesome; at any rate, at the time. Laughter is a blessed thing, and the Devil's pride does not easily endure it; "The devil, the proud spirit cannot endure to be mocked" (Sir T. More). It was only much later that the Devil was to make his profit out of these mediaeval floutings. But in Marlowe's *Dr. Faustus* we begin to come to something different.

Marlowe is said to have been, or claimed to be, an atheist; but his handling of the legend is orthodox enough. Faustus makes his bargain with open eyes and is duly damned. And it is interesting to see what the bargain is. A nineteenth-century editor[1] of *Faust* has remarked : "The Devil of any age or people is the enemy of what that age or people regards as supremely good." That is only partly true. In *Dr. Faustus,* the Devil's offer is precisely of something which Marlowe's age regarded, or was coming to regard as supremely good—knowledge and especially the power acquired by knowledge. Sensual pleasures are, indeed, included—Faustus demands "girls and gold", but above all, adventure, romance, and power in their most splendid forms; and knowledge as a means to these things :

> emperors and kings
> Are but obeyed in their several provinces,
> Nor can they raise the wind or rend the clouds;
> But his dominion that exceeds in this
> Stretcheth as far as doth the mind of man,
> A sound magician is a mighty god.

[1] Calvin Thomas.

That is Faustus coming to the study of magic; and then:

> Had I as many souls as there be stars,
> I'd give them all for Mephistopheles.
> By him I'll be great Emperor of the world,
> And make a bridge thorough the moving air,
> To pass the ocean with a band of men :
> I'll join the hills that bind the Afric shore,
> And make that country continent to Spain,
> And both contributory to my crown.
> The Emperor shall not live but by my leave.

And when the bargain is struck, Faustus—soon wearying of the merely academic learning of astronomy (which he dismisses as trifles) is next found touring the world. What the Devil is actually offering him is the immediate future—the splendours of the Renaissance, the triumph of power politics, the opening of the economic era—the New Humanism—the exaltation of the mind of man. The Devil is on the side of all the grand new things—of expansion and progress, and all the gods of the age to come. But on which side is Marlowe?

Formally, on God's side. The gifts are the Devil's gifts, and Faustus goes to hell. Faustus proclaims that "This word *damnation* terrifies not him,/ For he confounds hell in Elysium;/ His ghost be with the old philosophers!" But in the end he is both damned and terrified. His own sympathies may be with Faustus, but in fact he condemns his own sympathies. So far, so orthodox. But a new note comes in in the presentation of Mephistopheles:

> F. Where are you damned?
> M. In hell.
> F. How comes it then that thou art out of hell?
> M. Why this is hell, nor am I out of it :
> Think'st thou that I who saw the face of God,
> And tasted the eternal joys of Heaven,
> Am not tormented with ten thousand hells,
> In being deprived of everlasting bliss?

To which, so grand is the language, the audience is moved to rejoin heartily, "Oh, poor creature!" Faustus, it is true, sneers at Mephistopheles and adjures him

> "Learn thou of Faustus manly fortitude,
> And scorn those joys thou never shalt possess."

That advice will be taken by Milton's Satan. But in the meanwhile, we observe the structure of the Satanic façade already going up. It is true that Mephistopheles is comparatively frank about the origin of his sufferings:

> F. Was not that Lucifer an angel once?
> M. Yes, Faustus, and most dearly loved of God.
> F. How comes it then that he is Prince of devils?
> M. O, by aspiring pride and insolence;
> For which God threw him from the face of Heaven.

But somehow the suggestion is already there that Satan and his followers are rather noble in their suffering. It is only a suggestion, conveyed rather by the sound than by the sense of the lines; but the suggestion is there. It is the beginning of what we may call the Promethean set-up—the sympathetic picture of the sad, proud sufferer defying omnipotence.

In Milton's Satan, this set-up is magnificently completed. "Nobility" is Satan's line, and he runs it for all it is worth. He is "impaired", his pride is hurt, he has been deprived of his rights, his sufferings are acute, but he bears them superbly, he presents himself as the champion of all noble rebels, he is the indomitable spirit

> "Who durst defy th'Omnipotent to arms"—

and the whole thing is so grand, and sad, and stoical as to deceive the very elect. What Satan does not mention (though Milton does) is that Satan did not in fact suffer any wrongs, and undergoes no torments except those he has deliberately chosen. He plays for sympathy, and he gets it. As a friend of mine observed on this subject: "One can't help admiring anybody who fights so courageously a battle he knows to be hopeless, against somebody else who is omnipotent." Indeed, one is so lost in admiration, that one is led to overlook the fact that the battle was undertaken without any necessity and in a totally unworthy cause.

It has for some time been the fashion to pretend that Milton was the dupe of his own eloquence, and really *was* "of Satan's party without knowing it". I hope that Charles Williams and C. S. Lewis have sufficiently disposed of that pretence. Milton was no dupe. It is true that he could summon up sufficient imaginative sympathy with Satan to present his case with a diabolic plausibility—but imaginative sympathy is not moral approval. Milton knew very well that the set-up of the "grand infernal peers" was only a set-up—the reality was the hideous obscenity

"Squat like a toad, close at the ear of Eve"—

the hissing serpent crawling on its belly, the monstrous paramour of sin and father of Death. Milton did not deceive himself.

I think, however, there is some excuse for those who imagine that he did—and it is simply a literary excuse. I think that the magnificent and ordered grandeur of Milton's style was perhaps not quite a satisfactory instrument for communicating squalor and beastliness. It communicates beauty in spite of its author. Flexible as it is within its own compass, it cannot sink quite so far as to the real deep of Hell. But I do not want to enter upon the great Milton row, with which the older universities are still ringing. I will only note that within the last couple of centuries this particular Satanic set-up has been accepted at its face-value by a great number of critics who should know much better.

The noble sufferer set-up achieved its most forcible-feeble expression when it became the Byronic set-up, and stormed and attitudinized through the *Sturm und Drang* period of heroic Satans and Satanic heroes. By this time the poets themselves had become thoroughly duped. Their poetry was hardly the better for it, and the set-up (in that form) has now become a laughing-stock, though it is still naïvely accepted, in another form, by a number of simple-minded people who suppose that there is something noble in being agin' the government of the universe, and that heresy is in itself a proof of superior understanding.

With Goethe, we come to a different form of the set-up, and one which has the merit of raising a very central theological difficulty. It is integral to Christianity to affirm that Christ (and, in Him, all Christians) can so redeem evil as to make of it a greater good. *O felix culpa!* The sin of Adam is the occasion of the Incarnation; redeemed man is something more poignantly blessed than innocent man could ever have been. That is the glory of the God who was made man, and that is Catholic doctrine. But at the same time, evil is no less evil because it can be in the literal sense made good. "The Son of Man goeth ... but woe unto that man by whom the Son of Man is betrayed." Evil may be made the occasion of good, but in itself it remains evil and damnable.

That is the doctrine. But from this it is but a single false step to making the assertion that evil is a good thing because it is the occasion of good. And from that assertion the new façade is built up. In this set-up, the Devil becomes, as it were, a part of the Divine process, playing the same part in the cosmic constitution as the advocates of the Party System assign to the Opposition: his job is to stir up the people on the government side of the house and keep them from going to sleep on the job.[1] This view of the matter is put by Goethe plainly enough into the mouth of God,

> Des Menschen Thätigkeit kann allzuleicht erschlaffen,
> Er liebt sich bald die unbedingte Ruh;
> Drum geb' ich gern ihm den Gesellen zu,
> Der reizt und wirkt und muss als Teufel schaffen.

We must therefore suppose that to that extent Goethe himself was "of the Devil's party"—and not without knowing it.

The new kind of Devil is certainly a most happy relief from the Byronic Devil, and a very great deal healthier. We have got rid of the notion that obstinate opposition to the order of life is something to be proud of. The spirit of negation is exposed in its barrenness, its futility, and also in its vulgarity—for Goethe's Mephistopheles, for all his cynical charm, is at bottom a low-minded person. The bubble of the Satanic nobility is well and truly pricked. And on this occasion it is true to say that the Devil is taken to represent the enemy of what the period accepts as its best good. The era of progress and perfectibility is coming in; and the Devil is seen either as the grit which clogs and stops the wheels, or—and here we must vary the metaphor—as the "roughage" which irritates and stimulates the system to perform its work of metabolism. It is the optimistic view of an optimistic age, stirring with all the vigour of a new life and confident in its own power to assimilate the toughest morsels and turn them into vital sustenance.

Something, however, has been lost, and dangerously lost. We may perhaps see what it is if we compare the Devil's Bargain

---

[1] cf. the Book of Job, in which "Satan" appears to exercise precisely this function. Here, however, he is not represented as a spirit of evil in the sense in which we use the words when we speak of "the Devil".

in *Faust* with that in *Dr. Faustus*. Faustus makes a choice; Faust only makes a wager. Faustus may *say* that he does not believe in the immortality of the soul; but in reality he knows what he has done and that it is a thing irrevocable. Faust makes a bet, confident that he will win it, and is very little tormented with the fear of hell—for he has not chosen hell; he has merely defied it. The author sees to it that the Devil is cheated of his bargain—correctly enough in one sense, seeing that the will of Faust does not consent to evil. But what is getting lost is the sense of the dignity and finality of choice, and of the reality and evilness of evil. Faust gains Heaven by striving—and in the end by striving to do some good in the world; but, for all his remorse about Margarete, there is little real conviction of the ravage of evil, or of the cost of its redemption. The price of accepting the Progressive set-up is that in the end it persuades us not to take evil very seriously.

I must be fair to Goethe: in the famous speech which I have already quoted, there is a reservation:

> Von allen Geistern, die verneinen,
> Ist mir der Schalk am wenigsten zur Last.

It is suggested that there may be other and worse spirits of evil than the irritant Mephistopheles. But the suggestion is not, I think, elaborated; and it is certainly fair to say that Mephistopheles never for one moment is represented to us as a spirit in torment, and that the appearance of Hell-mouth in the final scene is, almost admittedly, pure décor. Mephistopheles does, in fact, admit it:

> Ihr hut sehr wohl, die Sünder zu erschrecken;
> Sie halten's doch für Lug und Trug und Traum.

Hell has become a picture to frighten sinners with; it is not felt as a real possibility.

Whatever our theological views about the possibility of final damnation may be, it is, I think, true to say that the age of progress and perfectibility from which we are now emerging did bear certain marks of this particular Satanic set-up. It did hold to a belief that "somehow good" would emerge of itself from the world-process so long as we kept on going on; it did "play down" the actuality of sin and the intolerable nature of evil; it did deprecate the idea that any act or choice could be final or irrevocable; and the result of these things was, in fact, a slackening of the rigid sense of personal responsiblity in the face of eternal fact.

If I now say a word or two about my own *Devil to Pay* it is not because I think that I am suitable company for poets like Marlowe and Milton and Goethe, but because it was an endeavour to bring the fable of the Devil's Bargain to the interpretation of the inter-war period. In my play, Faustus's transactions with the Devil go through two phases. In the first, the idea that evil is a means to good reaches its almost inevitable conclusion: i.e. it is *consciously* accepted and exploited. Faustus, sickened by the human suffering about him, tries to take the short cut to a remedy, and to cast out bodily evil by invoking the aid of spiritual evil. Many builders of earthly utopias and new orders seem prepared to do the like. When this endeavour to make Satan cast out Satan fails, he reacts into the next phase, which is to repudiate the actuality of evil, and, with it, the whole personal responsibility for the redemption of evil. The illusion of Helen is the illusion that it is possible to go back before the Fall and regain the simple animal innocence which Walt Whitman admired, or pretended to admire—the innocence which does not *know* evil:

> Serpent of Eden, take thy curse again,
> Undo the sin of Adam, turn the years
> Back to their primal innocence.

But the years cannot be turned back. We cannot, as Mr. Charles Williams has said, return to primal innocence by simply removing our aprons of fig-leaves. When the human will consented to sin, and so called evil into actual existence, it learnt to know the existing good as evil; and the corollary was that, in the absence of the knowledge of evil, it could no longer know either good or evil. Faustus bargains for animal innocence—that is his choice, and he gets it. His soul becomes the soul of an animal, knowing neither good nor evil, and irresponsible. In this irresponsible mood, he is the instrument of all mischief—as the whole of innocent and inorganic nature is the instrument of the evil will. The evil will uses him for the making of war; as it uses all nature's innocent and irresponsible forces. In the moment of death he calls upon Christ and upon Lisa, and in that last lucid moment is saved—but so as by fire, having to undergo in Purgatory that redemptive suffering which he repudiated.

It is not for me to say whether I have been the dupe of my own set-up—I hope not; but of course, if I have, I do not know it. My Mephistopheles starts as a plausible humanitarian, breathing contempt upon the inefficiency of God: that is his set-up. In the sequel, he is vulgar and cruel—and he is fooled, because the bargain into which he entered destroyed the identity of the soul he wanted for his own: he falls himself into the inefficiency to which he claimed superiority. He is made to work God's will, but in spite of himself. So far as it goes, the theology is, I think, sound—though in a play so short it would be impossible for even a great writer to plumb the deeper issues.

As to whether the idea of the play was suited to the time in which it appeared, I will say only this: first; that a great number of people expressed the opinion that it would have been *better* had Faustus chosen to remain in his animal state to all eternity, rather than redeem his human soul by purgation. Secondly; that the play only ran for a few weeks in London—largely because of the imminence of the war which we had been largely instrumental in bringing about, through a refusal of responsibility, and through a determined refusal to believe in the possibility of a deliberate will to evil.

From this very brief and hasty sketch, there is one poet whom I have very conspicuously left out. You are probably wondering why—at least, you ought to be—and wriggling in your seats with anxiety to shout at me (but that courtesy restrains you) that from this portrait-gallery of the Devil the most important example of all is missing.

I had not forgotten. The greatest poet, the most exact theologian, the most adult intellect of all ought, chronologically, to have been taken first; but I have left him to the last, because if, now, we are going to begin once more to take evil seriously, he is the one with whom we shall have to reckon. He was never taken in by the Satanic set-up; nor did his verse—that amazing and flexible instrument which could move at will and almost in a breath from the raptures of Paradise, "all air and fire", through the homeliest earthiness, to the extreme of infernal dirt and squalor and beastliness—nor did his verse ever offer his readers the smallest excuse for finding the Devil anything else but diabolical. Down the great sterile circles of perverse and petrified choice, Hell goes narrowing to its frozen centre, deep after deep; at the top are the irresponsibles, who refused choice; below them, the people who incontinently lapsed into evil through failure to control their choice, blown on the winds or sodden in the march-water of their passions; then the deliberate hardening of the will to the choice of the wrong made in full knowledge— the will to violence, the will to deceit—circle below circle of fire and filth and disease, down to the ultimate treachery in which all feeling, all intellect, every conception, is frozen. And, fixed in the ice at the bottom, the ultimate corruption, resentful and despairing, passive and rebellious, petrifying and petrified, fixed for ever in a misery without dignity, the grotesque and ghastly reality behind the façade. In a sense he still appears not less than archangel ruined; but the ruin is here complete; the beauty does not shine through the corruption: it is the corruption of beauty itself:

> S'el fu sì bello com'elli è or brutto,
> e contra 'l suo fattore alzò le ciglia,
> ben dee da lui procedere ogni lutto.

"If once he was beautiful as now he is hideous, and lifted up his brows against his Maker, well may he be the origin of all sorrow." He chose to ape the glory of the Trinity, and he has his choice: the monstrous three-headed parody lies fixed there in his inimitable self-will, champing the traitors in its jaws; the six wings of his immortal seraphhood beat savagely, powerless to lift him out of the ice of his obduracy, and increasing that ice by the wind of their beating:

> quindi Cocito tutto s'aggelava.
> Con sei occhi piangea, e per tre menti
> gocciava 'l pianto e sanguinosa bava.

"Hereby all Cocytus was frozen; with six eyes he wept, and down his three chins gushed tears and bloody foam."

That is the thing at the bottom: the idiot and slobbering horror. At the entrance to his realm stand the two dreadful sentences:

> "Here dwell the wretched people who have lost the good of the intellect."

and the fearful paradox of the corrupted will:

"All their fear is changed into desire."

That is the picture seen by the poet who took evil seriously. And we cannot evade Dante by saying that we do not believe in that particular kind of judgement after death. For he himself said that his poem was indeed, *literally*, an account of what happens in the world beyond the grave, but *allegorically* an account of what happens within the soul. His Hell is the picture of an eternal possibility within the heart of man; and he adds that the gate to that Hell always stands wide open.

CHAPTER XI

OEDIPUS SIMPLEX: FREEDOM AND FATE IN FOLK-LORE AND FICTION

So POWERFUL IS the impression made upon our minds by the devotional literature of the Freudian cult that if you were to ask the first person you met what the story of Oedipus was about, he would quite probably reply that it was a story about incest. And indeed it is natural enough that in this legend of the man who, quite unwittingly and altogether unwillingly, killed his father and married his own mother, Freud and his followers should have seen an allegory of the alleged unconscious impulse in the human male to do that very thing. But this is an allegorical interpretation of the story; it is not the story itself. The psycho-analysts have allegorized the myths in exactly the same way that Christian preachers and mystics have allegorized the Old Testament, seeing in Leah and Rachel types of the active and the contemplative life, in Noah's Ark a type of baptism, in the *Songs of Songs* a signification of the love of Christ for the Church. This allegorizing tendency is something thought to be peculiarly mediaeval, but it is in fact found whenever a new trend in psychology, lacking a ready-made technical vocabulary, is forced to express itself indirectly in poetic images. The allegorizing of the Old Testament begins with the Early Fathers; Julian the Apostate, struggling with the problems of a new, conscious morality, allegorized the Olympians; the Renaissance allegorized Virgil; Freud and Jung, wrestling with the problems of an unconscious immorality, have allegorized the folk-tales. The practice is ancient and highly respectable, and it is based on an assumption fundamentally sound, namely, that all art and myth-making disclose the universal pattern of things and may therefore be taken as symbolic presentments of truths greater than themselves. But this kind of interpretation belongs to the sphere of devotion and edification and not of historical criticism. The modern Bible-critic will not permit us to suppose that the story of Jacob's two wives was originally written about a couple of abstractions, or that the writer of *The Song of Songs* was proleptically thinking about Christ when he composed his love-poem. The allegorical interpretation of Scripture has fallen out of fashion, and so it is easy for us to distinguish between the story and the symbolism imposed upon it; but where the allegorical method is still in force the distinction is less readily made. It is quite easy to slip into the belief that the Oedipus story really is about the Oedipus Complex.

But it is not. No incestuous passions are displayed in action; it is not *about* incest as the tale of Phaedra or Myrrha is about incest. No parricidal passions are displayed in action; it is not *about* parricide as the story of Orestes is about matricide. It is *about* something which lies upon the very surface of the story, and may for that reason appear, at first sight, to be simpler. That is why I have called it the "Oedipus Simplex". But it is really far from simple. Philosophically, it goes beneath the roots of the great riddle of fate and free will to the most unfathomable of all mysteries—the inscrutable nature of time. And to the writer it presents, as we shall see, a literary problem of a very peculiar and exacting kind.

Oedipus belongs, in fact, to a very widespread group of folk-tales whose theme may be compendiously summed up as man's vain attempt to cheat the oracle. It is very noticeable that from the majority of these tales the incest-motif is completely absent, and that when the parricide-motif occurs it does not always involve the killing of an actual father. One is tempted to say that these atrocities have been put into the Oedipus legend "just to make it horrider"—as though the story-teller had deliberately set himself to discover the most revolting consequences that could possibly be extracted from his theme. I do not seriously suggest that he did anything so self-conscious, and it is a curious fact that the earlier version of the story lacks both the appalling sense of guilt and also the catastrophic ending which to us seem inseparable from it. Oedipus kills his father, and marries his mother, and yet survives to rule in peace over Thebes. But to a tragic poet bent on arousing pity and terror in his audience, the legend (however it first started) is a gift. No more horrid situation could well be devised by the wit of man, and, exploited as Sophocles exploits it, with a brilliant detective-story technique which unfolds one ghastly *anagnorisis* after another until the tension is well-nigh unbearable, it leaves us with an oppressive sense of doom and agony, frustration, and above all of bodily and spiritual pollution. But the *Oedipus* is unique of its kind; nearly all the other members of its group are cheerful stories with happy endings.

The outline of the plot is invariable. A child is born, of whom it is prophesied that he (or she) will bring about some disaster. The prophecy is duly fulfilled despite every effort to avert it, the disaster being often precipitated by the very precautions taken against it.

The details vary considerably. The child is usually (though not invariably) a boy, and the predestined disaster is frequently (though not always) the killing of a king, who may be the child's father, grandfather, or no relation at all. The attempts made to avert the doom may be by imprisoning or exposing the child (seldom by killing it outright, which would involve the pollution of infanticide, though this variant does sometimes occur as in the very primitive type-tale of Kronos and Zeus). The fulfilment of the prophecy is brought about frequently by accident, or in ignorance; though sometimes the subject of it is fully aware of what he or she is doing.

In *Oedipus*, the Delphic Oracle foretells that a son will be born to Laius King of Thebes who will slay his father. According to Sophocles, this is the whole content of the original prophecy—the further prediction, that the boy will marry his mother, is made only at the second consultation of the oracle, when the separation of the child from his parents has made it possible for this catastrophe to come about without his knowledge. In the Perseus legend, it is prophesied to King Acrisius that his daughter Danae will bear a son who will kill his grandfather. Acrisius imprisons Danae in a brazen tower, and here she bears a son to Zeus, who visits her as a shower of gold. Acrisius sets mother and child adrift on the sea in an open chest, and they are rescued by Dictys the fisherman. This very common exposure-and-rescue motif is found also in the story of Oedipus, who is exposed upon the mountains, rescued by a shepherd, and taken to Polybus King of Corinth, who brings him up as his own son. The legend told by Herodotus about Cyrus the Persian has close affinities with the Perseus-legend. King Astyages dreams that his daughter Mandane will have a son who will usurp his throne. He tries to avert this by marrying her to a commoner, but after the birth of her son he has a second warning dream. He tells his steward Harpagus to destroy the child; Harpagus hands it over to the herdsman Mitradates with orders to expose it; but Mitradates takes it home and brings it up as his own. In the German folk-tale of *The Three Golden Hairs*, a poor woman gives birth to a son, of whom it is prophesied that he will be very fortunate and marry the king's daughter. The king, hearing of this, offers to take care of the boy. He puts him in a box and sets him adrift on the river; he floats down to the mill-dam and is rescued by the miller and brought up by him. Later, the king comes to know who the boy is, and again attempts to get rid of him, by sending him to the queen with a letter, ordering the bearer to be put to death at once. The youth is taken by robbers, who find the letter, and substitute another commanding that the bearer shall be married immediately to the king's daughter. An Indian variant, containing the marriage-motif and the substituted-letter motif, is *The King Who Would be Stronger than Fate*, and the substituted letter turns up again in a Serbian story, *The Three Wonderful Beggars*, where the place of the king is taken by a rich merchant, who tried to get rid of the Child of Fortune by throwing him over a cliff in a snow-storm. In the English folk-tale of *The Fish and the Ring* the child is a peasant-girl, fated to marry the son of the local baron, and the dénouement is once more brought about by means of the substituted letter.

In all these tales, the expected disaster is connected with some kind of usurpation, whether of wealth or power, though it by no means always involves the death of the person who has tried to cheat the oracle. There is nothing surprising about this. Autocrats have always lived in terror of being assassinated or deposed. It is one of the risks of their profession, and we need not invoke parricidal impulses to explain it. Even today, if a rich person dies in suspicious circumstances, the first question the police ask is: "Who comes in for the money?" On the other hand, in the Indian story of *Chandra's Vengeance*, which contains the "exposure by setting adrift in a box", the child is a Rajah's daughter, and the prophecy is that her hair will one day set her native country ablaze—some solar myth or fire-myth being presumably involved. In none of these stories is there any suggestion of incest.

Let us go back for a moment to Perseus. He, after many adventures, returns to his native land, and there competes in the games. A gust of wind seizes his quoit, which strikes the aged

King Acrisius and kills him. The prophecy is fulfilled by pure accident—or, more precisely, by direct interposition of the gods; the resulting pollution is purely formal and is purged by the usual ceremonies, since no evil intention was behind the slaying, neither did Perseus, like Oedipus, help to bring his doom upon himself either by taking steps to avert it, or by indulging in violent temper, or by unwittingly invoking a curse upon the slayer. This at once raises the question of the underlying morality of all these tales. The will of the gods must be done, that is certain; but how far is the *manner* of its accomplishment related to the attitude of the persons concerned? Did the Greeks feel it to be presumption to try and cheat the oracle? Supposing that Laius and Jocasta, and Oedipus himself, had resigned themselves to the divine will—would the prophecy have been fulfilled harmlessly? Would the slaying have been accidental as in the case of Perseus? Might Oedipus, succeeding peaceably to his father, and devoting himself to the well-being of Thebes, have been said to have "wedded himself to his mother-city", so that in that word the prophecy might be both broken and fulfilled?

Some such riddling fulfilment of dark prophecies is by no means unknown in classical folk-lore. In the Third Book of the *Aeneid*, the Harpy announces that before the voyagers reach the end of their adventures they will be reduced to "eating their trenchers". They come to Latium; they partake of a picnic meal of meat and fruit served on cakes of barley-bread, and end by thriftily eating the bread as well. The boy Iulus cries jestingly: "Why, we have eaten our trenchers!" and the fulfilment of the prophecy is accepted as a good omen.

Still more significant is the tale of Deucalion, the classical counterpart of Noah, as we find it in Ovid's *Metamorphoses*. Deucalion and his wife Pyrrha are the sole survivors of a flood which has drowned the whole world. They consult the oracle of Themis and are told to depart and, as they go, to "throw behind them the bones of their great mother". Pyrrha is horrified at the idea of so offending the spirit of an ancestress and at first refuses to obey. At length Deucalion says: "Either my wit is at fault, or else (for oracles are holy and never counsel guilt) our great mother is the earth, and I think that the bones which the goddess speaks of are the stones in the earth's body." This pious attitude is rewarded; the stones which they throw behind them are turned into men and women, and the earth is re-peopled. We notice here both the suggestion of an outrage offered to a parent, and also the insistence that the oracle must be obeyed and "cannot counsel guilt".

Twenty centuries of Christian tradition have so conditioned us to look upon the source of power as identical with the source of ethics that it is extremely difficult for us to enter into the mind of the Greeks in this matter. For them, sin and pollution, which for us are ethical terms, so often appear to have meant something merely extraneous and mechanical. One was "polluted" by even accidentally committing incest or parricide, just as one would be physically "polluted" by accidentally falling into a cess-pool. But in this story we recognize an explicit connection between the will of the gods and that which is right. In the form in which I have quoted it, the legend has passed through a Roman mind; and Roman religious feeling was always, I think, more consciously moral than that of the Greeks.

But not so emphatically so as that of another ancient race. It was the Jews who, from very early times, were most conscious of the will of God—not of "the gods" but of really-truly God, in the sense we attach to the word. A divine prophecy was fulfilled, not merely because it *had* to be, but because it *ought* to be. In their folk-literature, the great cheat-the-oracle story is the story of Joseph, and it is as unlike the Oedipus-story as Jehovah is unlike Apollo. Yet in outline it agrees with all the tales of its class. Joseph has two prophetic dreams which seem to indicate that his father and his eleven brothers will one day do homage to him (the usurpation-motif). The brothers attempt to get rid of him. At first they suggest killing him, but Reuben dissuades them, and they drop him into a dry well (the exposure-motif). Finally they sell him to some passing merchants (a variant of the rescue-theme). He is taken to Egypt and becomes Pharaoh's overseer. This leads to the story of the famine, and of how the ten elder brothers first and finally the youngest brother and the father himself have to come and beg for corn and bow before him as Pharaoh's representative. There is no killing and no incest; Joseph knows what he is doing, and amuses himself by playing tricks on his brothers. What is constant in this as in the other tales is the fact that the very means taken to confound the prophecy lead directly to its fulfilment. It is the gayest and most charming of all the cheat-the-oracle stories. I am bound to admit that many of the Old Testament worthies seem to me rather an unpleasant lot of people; but if anybody maintains that Jewish legend is entirely compact of gloomy ferocity, and that classical legend is unadulterated sweetness and light, let him compare the story of Oedipus with its corresponding story of Joseph, and he will see that the cheerful piety is not all on one side.

There is never any doubt in the Jewish mind that true prophecy is, in the most pregnant sense of the words, "of God"; whether it conveys a divine command or exhibits that pattern in the nature of things which reveals the shape of the future. Christendom is the heir to this tradition; it could scarcely be otherwise, founding itself as it does on Scriptures which resound from end to end with the phrase: "That it might be fulfilled which was spoken by the prophet." In those Scriptures, the historical events of the Gospel are consistently presented as an acceptance of prophecy, and a total obedience to the will of God, whatever apparent disasters that submission might entail.

This Judaeo-Christian concept has probably to some extent influenced and modified the European folk-lore of cheating the oracle, and has quite certainly influenced and modified the conscious handling of the theme in literature. It is to the literature that I now propose to turn. But I ought, perhaps, first of all to say a word about the whole idea of prophecy as such.

It has, I think, always been generally held that true prophecy, in so far as it involves the prediction of future events, is uttered unconsciously—that is, without any clear or detailed knowledge of the manner of its fulfilment. Sometimes, as in the case of the Delphic Sibyl, the prophet is held to speak in a trance—she is possessed by the god, and acts only as a mouthpiece or "medium" for the divine voice. Sometimes the prophet, though conscious, is aware that the words he utters are not his own: "The word of the Lord came to me." The poet—for every poet was once considered a *vates*—felt himself to be "inspired" by the Muse. (It is only in comparatively recent years that the poet has declined into mere self-expression; in his palmy days he expressed something a great deal more important than himself.) And nearly always—and this is the characteristic of true prophecy—his words were fulfilled in a manner which he could not and did not foresee. What he said in one sense came true in a totally different sense, and the thing he foretold was not in the least the thing he thought he was writing about. He was not like a man running a pin down a list of names to pick a Derby winner. He was more like a man picking "Jet-pilot" to win, who has all his windows blown out next day by a supersonic bang. He was right about the name, but greatly underestimated its significance. When a university professor solemnly writes that Virgil's Fourth Eclogue was—wrongly—accepted in the Middle Ages as a prophecy of Christ, the word "wrongly" has no meaning. If a prophecy is fulfilled, it is fulfilled; it does not matter in the least that Virgil supposed himself to be writing about a possible son of Octavian or Mark Antony—he is a prophet, not a tipster. No doubt the Harpy in the *Aeneid* supposed herself to be uttering not merely a prophecy but a curse; her words were fulfilled as she neither foresaw nor desired. At the bottom of all this lies that assumption to which I have already referred; that the poet or prophet has *insight*; he is a seer, who discerns the underlying pattern of things. It is in this sense that the unknown inventor of the Oedipus-legend may be said, if you like, to have been a prophet of the Oedipus Complex. That is one of the fulfilments of his pattern, though it is not what he discerned at the time.

The last folk-tale I will deal with is the Icelandic story of *Ingebjörg*. In this, the Queen, under the influence of an evil magician, becomes jealous of her own daughter and casts a spell upon her that she shall burn down the palace, kill her father, and marry a terrible giant. The machinery of the story is at this point a trifle confused; I have not seen a primitive version of it, and it looks as though there might originally have been some sort of incest-motive, though with complete inversion of the "Oedipus-complex" both as to sex and generation—i.e. mother jealous of daughter, instead of son jealous of father. In any case, the girl is good and virtuous, and, in order that she avert this doom, she runs away from home. However, she meets her fairy godmother, who instructs her that the evil is to be overcome with good : "The king's palace I cannot save", she says, "but neither your father nor your mother shall be hurt... neither need you fear the giant." When the king and his courtiers are out hunting, the fairy and the princess send the servants away, carry all the treasure into safety and set fire to the palace, thus fulfilling and breaking the spell. Subsequently, the girl meets the giant, who turns out to be a handsome young prince, who has been bespelled by the magician. She breaks the spell and duly marries him as prophesied. The interesting point here is the breaking of the original spell by deliberately setting out to implement it.

Let us now abandon Oedipus and folk-lore, and see what happens to the cheat-the-oracle theme when it is handled by a conscious artist, addressing a sophisticated audience. The literature of the subject is too vast to permit anything like a full examination. Fortunately, there is one very well-known work which provides in itself a handy compendium of almost all the possible ways of dealing with prophecies, favourable or unfavourable. The plot of *Macbeth*, as distinct from the study of criminal psychology which it carries, is that and nothing else.

The Witches in *Macbeth*, although directly dominated by the powers of evil, are represented as true prophets. In some manner the Divine Voice speaks through them. The atmosphere of the play can scarcely be called overtly Christian; but the writer and his audience were Christian people, and would doubtless have been prepared to accept the theological proposition that even the evil powers are ultimately the instruments of an over-ruling Providence bringing all things into subjection to itself. It is tacitly taken for granted, that is, that the scheme of things is Monarchist and not Dualist. The playwright does not obtrude this question on us: all that matters is that we should accept the Witches as telling the truth for evil ends—just as the Serpent in Genesis tells the truth for evil ends.

At the first meeting with Macbeth and Banquo on the blasted heath, the Witches make three prophecies—two about Macbeth and one about Banquo. Having shown that they know Macbeth, by hailing him as "Thane of Glamis", they go on: "All hail, Macbeth! hail to thee, thane of Cawdor!" "All hail, Macbeth, that shalt be king hereafter!" And of Banquo they prophesy: "Thou shalt get kings, though thou be none." Of these three predictions, two are welcome to Macbeth; the third comes to seem to him most unwelcome; on his manner of dealing with them the whole action of the play hinges.

About the first, "Hail to thee, thane of Cawdor!", he does nothing. He has not time to do anything, for it has already been fulfilled in the preceding scene, and the announcement that Cawdor has turned traitor and been deprived of his title and estates in Macbeth's favour follows immediately upon the prophecy. This might and should have shown Macbeth that the Witches knew what they were talking about, and that he had only to sit still and let things happen, to get everything he wanted. As we know, he does nothing of the sort. The oracle fits in too well with his own secret thoughts, and he is ready to be persuaded that it supplies a sanction for murder. So he proceeds to implement the prophecy: not, like the virtuous Icelandic princess, in order to break it in the fulfilment, and so purge out the evil, but simply to force the hand of destiny by his own efforts, and that in the most evil manner possible. Up to that point there is nothing to suggest that Macbeth might not, somehow, have succeeded peaceably to Duncan; it is by the will of Macbeth and his wife that the evil which is potential in the Witches is assented to and called, by that assent, into actual existence and operation.

Duncan is murdered and Macbeth seizes the throne. But now there is Banquo. Just before the murder he had said to Macbeth:

> I dreamt last night of the three weird sisters:
> To you they have show'd some truth.

The accent is on "you"; the implication is "and to me?" Macbeth suggests that he and Banquo should some time talk the matter over, adding:

> If you shall cleave to my consent,—when 'tis,
> It shall make honour for you.

Banquo replies:
> So I lose none
> In seeking to augment it, but still keep
> My bosom franchis'd, and allegiance clear,
> I shall be counsell'd.

It seems he is not to be tempted into implementing prophecy by murder and treason—though perhaps it was rash of him to say so. After Duncan's murder, he unburdens his mind in a soliloquy, and his tone is a little changed:

> Thou hast it now, King, Cawdor, Glamis, all,
> As the weird women promis'd, and I fear
> Thou play'dst most foully for't: yet it was said
> It should not stand in thy posterity,
> But that myself should be the root and father
> Of many kings. If there come truth from them,
> As upon thee, Macbeth, their speeches shine,
> May they not be my oracles as well
> And set me up in hope?

Now that the obstacle is no longer a legitimate king but a usurping and suspected murderer, is Banquo thinking, after all, of taking a hand in his own fate? We are not quite sure; but Macbeth has no doubts at all. We are now back in the classic myth of the threatened king and the child of destiny. As usual, the king plots to destroy the predestined heir, adding the murder of Banquo for good measure. As usual, though Banquo is murdered, the child of destiny escapes. Oddly enough, Fleance, the traditional linch-pin of the plot, appears only once and says nothing; the crown passes to Malcolm; nor are we ever told how Fleance becomes ancestor to a line of kings. But that he will in fact do so we are assured both by the fact of his escape, and also in the second prophecy-scene, when the Witches call up the spirits from the cauldron. This time there are four prophecies: the first: "Beware Macduff"; the second: "None of woman born shall harm Macbeth"; the third: "Macbeth shall never vanquished be until/Great Birnam wood to high Dunsinane hill/Shall come against him"; the fourth is the shadow-show of Banquo's royal issue.

Macbeth is now prepared to accept whatever the Witches tell him. The fourth prophecy merely fills him with a kind of helpless horror; he is unable at the moment to do anything useful about the first, for he hears that Macduff has fled to England, and he can only execute a savage butchery of his wife and children. But he receives the second and third prophecies with a credulous confidence. In the end they are fulfilled, but riddlingly, after the manner of the Harpy's curse, and their fulfilment brings about the fulfilment of the first prediction.

Thus we have four methods of dealing with prophecies. (1) To do nothing about them, with the result that they are fulfilled harmlessly in the ordinary course of things (the Cawdor prophecy, and Banquo's issue); (2) to implement them by crime (Duncan's murder) with disastrous consequences; (3) to try to escape them at all costs (Banquo's murder and the attempted murder of Fleance), altogether in vain; (4) to trust them (the riddling prophecies), and be betrayed by them.

We must now pass over much entertaining and profitable matter, to come quickly to modern times, in which a number of efforts have been made to examine the phenomena of precognition along scientific and statistical lines.

In 1927, J. W. Dunne published a book called *An Experiment* with *Time*, in which he put forward a theory about time and precognition, founded on the examination of a number of apparently veridical dreams. This book, which was succeeded by another called *The Serial Universe*, stimulated the imagination of more than one writer of fiction. J. B. Priestley used it as the basis of two plays—*I Have Been Here Before*, which postulates a cyclical or spiral time, returning upon and repeating itself at vast intervals, and *Time and the Conways*, which postulates a kind of spatial or simultaneous time. Neither of these directly concerns us, since they do not handle the question of fore-knowledge. But the same book suggested to John Buchan the plot of *A Gap in the Curtain*, which does, and which, like *Macbeth*, presents us with a kind of survey of the various methods of cheating, or otherwise manipulating, the oracle.

In this story, five men concentrate on visualizing a page of *The Times* newspaper for that day twelve-month. The first, who is a financier, sees headlines about a merger of two big industrial companies. He realizes that this means that a certain mineral will become very valuable, and sets about buying the controlling interest in a moribund mining venture. Many of the shareholders live in wild and inaccessible places, and his quest involves him in great risk and trouble. At the moment of his triumphant success, a new chemical discovery makes the shares worthless, and though the merger duly takes place, he cannot profit by it. He is a good gambler and takes the disappointment cheerfully, losing only a few thousands which he can well afford.

The second man is a Member of Parliament, and sees the name of a new Prime Minister. He too tries to profit by the information, and plans his political adherences accordingly. He is an egotistical, prudent and calculating man; but a sudden unexpected coalition upsets the whole political picture. He finds he has backed the right man, but the wrong policy. No party now wants him, and his parliamentary career is ruined for ever. "If he hadn't been so clever", says a colleague, "he would have been at No. 10 today ... He was shrewd enough to spot the winner, but not the race it would win."

The third story is pure comedy. A young man of the world sees an announcement that he has joined an exploring expedition to Yucatan. He is firmly resolved to do nothing of the sort—especially as his public-school education has left him with the notion that Yucatan is in the East, and he takes a poor view of the Orient. Unfortunately, he gets entangled with an overpowering young woman and, in order to escape marrying her, agrees to go at a moment's notice on a voyage with a friend who is an explorer. "But not East", he says, "I absolutely refuse to go East." The friend assures him that they are going in the opposite direction. The next morning he finds himself on the ship, sailing for Yucatan.

The fourth and fifth men see their own obituary notices. One of them becomes obsessed by this and, eventually, dies of sheer fright. The fifth makes a gallant struggle against fate, but is fighting a losing battle when he falls in love with a girl, and confides in her. The girl falls seriously ill about a month before the fatal date, and in his love and anxiety for her, the young man altogether loses his fear of death. "He saw all things in a new perspective. Death was only a stumble in the race, a brief halt in an immortal pilgrimage. He and Pamela had won something which could never be taken away." The girl recovers and they are married. On their wedding morning the obituary notice appears in *The Times*, and turns out to apply to another man of the same name.

Here again, the writer has run the whole gamut of possible reactions, emerging this time with the conclusions that to implement, resist, or submit to fate are all equally vain, and that the only safeguard against futurity is to fix one's heart upon that which is not subject to time.

Now it will be seen that our whole attitude to divination, whether in life or in literature, is paradoxical. We desire to know the future, in order to control it—for if we cannot control it *at all*, to know it would be at best a tedium and at worst a horror. But if we can control it so completely as to evade it, then it is not the future. We desire the prophecy to come true, otherwise the story is pointless; but unless the manner of its coming true is affected by human behaviour, there is no story to tell. A universe in which everything is determined from moment to moment reduces to nonsense not only every action but also every emotion; on the other hand a universality of randomness affronts our sense of order. And a universe in which every man's will was entirely free from restriction would be formless—a mere chaotic flux of incompatibles. What in fact we desire is that the will should be both bound and free; the future at the same time fixed and indeterminate, foreseeable and unexpected. This may be irrational, but it is artistically right, and in fact all good stories about true prophecy are so constructed as to content this paradoxical appetite for inevitablility combined with surprise. That is why such tales exercise so powerful a fascination, and why we are all, willy-nilly, enthralled by the palmist, the crystal-gazer, the astrologer, the gipsy with the Tarot pack, and the seventh son of a seventh son who has the gift of sight. "Of course", we say, "it is all nonsense, but—." And the moment we come to the word "but", a curious note of satisfaction creeps into our voice. True prophecy may be pure illusion; yet a tale about a prophecy which turned out to be merely false would afford us no entertainment at all, but only a sense of anti-climax. (In real life, of course, these futilities frequently occur.) Now, in order to enjoy and write oracle-stories we must find some consistent philosophy to which we can relate them, if we are to keep our intellectual self-respect, and avoid being called backward, unscientific, superstitious, escapist, adolescent and similar ugly epithets. What we need, to justify our artistic enjoyment, is a theory of time and fate that will combine necessity with freedom—necessity as to the end, and freedom as to the means. Such a theory we will now proceed to construct

I do not myself think we need to postulate, with Mr. Dunne, an infinite regress of observers, nor yet an infinite series of dimensions of time. All such "bad infinities" have something unsatisfactory and faintly nonsensical about them; moreover, they offend against Occam's razor, by needlessly multiplying entities. Neither do we really need the cumbrous concepts of cyclic or spiral time, both of which have the grave disadvantage of moving far too slowly to be handled. All we actually require is two observers: the infinite Observer to whom Mr. Dunne himself has to come in the end, and the experiencing self. These are enough, provided that each is tri-une, that is, subsisting in three hypostases, each a mode of the whole self, and in virtue of which the self is, acts, and knows its act and being. Neither do we need more than two kinds of time: real time and created time. This duality of time has the advantage of being empirically known to us. Every novelist, and every reader of a novel, takes it so much for granted that he never gives it a thought. Real time is the rhythm or dimension in which the author himself has his being; created time is the time which takes place inside the story— known to the characters in it as a linear movement in one direction, but to the author as a simultaneity in which all its moments are present at once. The two times have nothing in common, except that they are both known to the author: there is no sense in which it can be said that the time *inside* the story I am writing coincides with *my* time in which I am living—they are related as what *we* call "time" is related to what *we* call "eternity". I write "the next seven years passed happily": those years have extension for the people in the story, but they have none in mine: they are only a curve in a created pattern which I perceive simultaneously in all its parts. Further, the future of the characters is known to me simultaneously with their past; to them it appears future; but it may be the thing with which I began, and which, unknown to them, conditions their past. Every event in their world is governed by two chains of causation: the *created* causation known to them, which provides that each of their events shall develop logically from events in their past, and the *real* causation, known only to their author, which may work backwards in their time so that their acts are the consequences of their own effects. This sounds confusing; but in practice every author deals casually and competently with double time and double causation without the least hesitation or confusion in his own mind. The reader also, though he does not share the author's omniscience, is aware of the double time scheme. He says to himself: "Let's see—Henry must be about thirty-seven by now—isn't it getting on for teatime?"

But note that the author, though his is the only ultimately effective will and the only real time or causation concerned, is to some extent bound by the laws he has made for his own creation. He must not reverse or confuse the time-sequence within the story, neither must he make his created people behave otherwise than in accordance with the natures he has bestowed upon them. Even in an imagined story the characters have a certain simulacrum of free will which the author must needs respect; and this encourages us to suppose that in the actual created universe a measure of free will may be compatible in the creature with the infinite Author's knowledge of the pattern. I say "knowledge", not "foreknowledge"; to the author, human or divine, there is neither before nor after: each event is known in its own place. It is only in the creature that we can speak of "foreknowledge", if any such knowledge is available to him—as, for our purpose, we must assume that it is.

Given thus the created pattern, with its two operative wills, its double time-scheme, and its double network of causation, we have to find room in it for both necessity (that is to say the absolute and unconditioned will of the creator) and potentiality (that is to say the free but conditioned will of the creature). We shall also have to account for those moments of apparent foresight which, though at the time they seem to have the quality of true prophecy, yet remain unfulfilled, or are only partially fulfilled, or fulfilled in riddling and ambiguous ways.

Let us then picture the totality of things as a web spread out in as many dimensions of time and space as we may find it easy and convenient to imagine. We shall observe in it certain fixed points; these are the nodes of necessity, through which the lines *must* pass in order to make the pattern. The nodes are determined by the artist, but the lines are self-determined, and may take any direction they choose, subject to two limitations. (1) However they bend and turn—even if they start off in the opposite direction—they are bound eventually to go through the fixed points; (2) every movement they make modifies and is modified by the movements of the neighbouring lines. The will of the maker readily submits to all these modifications, since the necessity laid upon the lines to come to the nodes means that all the possible modifications can only in the end produce a conditioned necessity of their own—just as, in a game of croquet, the path of every ball, however wildly it may diverge under the impact of a bad shot, or the disturbing shot of the adversary, is governed by the absolute external necessity imposed on both sides alike of going through the right hoops in the right order.

Thus: Oedipus must kill his father; that is the fixed node through which the lines must pass. But the manner of their passing is tragically determined by the folly of Laius and Jocasta, by the sins of Oedipus himself, by the very virtues of the shepherd and Polybus. The lines which seemed to run away are brought home by the master-hand, the chain of primary causation always adapting itself, link by link, to the chain of secondary causation, as the concave curve follows the curve of the convex and is identical with it.

Let us take another example: the tale which, if it is not true history, is at any rate the greatest of all the myths. Most races have cherished the prophecy that, in some manner or another, the Divine should become human and share human experience.

Given that all men are mortal, it becomes necessary that the human experience should include the experience of bodily death. Birth and death are thus, presumably, the essential nodes of the pattern. But time, place, circumstances, and in particular the manner of the death are determined by the course of human history; for though all men must die, comparatively few die violent deaths, and fewer still by judicial murder. This was recognized by certain mediaeval thinkers, who pleased themselves with the fancy that if Christ had not been crucified, He would have laid down His life by a natural death at the age of eighty, which they considered to be the perfect age.

At the rim of the pattern, then, the lines of potentiality lie wide apart, and may take almost any course towards the node. But as they close in, the area of available choice becomes narrower and narrower: the decision of man in general becomes the decision of an Empire, of a nation, of a court of law, and eventually the decision of particular persons—all moving to one end, under pressure of the history of decisions in the past. But the element of personal choice remains to the last moment: "the Son of Man goeth indeed as it is written of Him, but woe unto that man by whom the Son of Man is betrayed." Some measure of indeterminism, though limited at length to Pilate's simple choice between Yes and No.

On this hypothesis, then, an inescapable prediction, like that of the Oedipus-story, will mean that the seer has been vouchsafed a sight of one of the nodes, though all the lines of potentiality are veiled. I would add that, in order to make a good story it is advisable to *keep* the lines veiled; otherwise one will not achieve the desired effect of inevitability combined with surprise. What makes the boding dreams or warning visions of fiction both dull and incredible is an excessive accumulation of veridical detail, as, for example, in the allegorical dreams so common in mediaeval moral tales, or the monstrously elaborate dream in Wilkie Collins's *Armadale,* which is punctiliously fulfilled in episode after episode. Both in real life and in fiction, it is, as we have seen, the mark of convincing prophecy to be fulfilled "all wrong" —that is, along lines of potentiality which neither the prophet nor his contemporaries ever foresaw or guessed at. Thus, Virgil's Fourth Eclogue is a convincing prophecy of Christ just *because,* not in spite of, the fact that he supposed himself to be writing about somebody quite different.

When, however, a vision which appears to have the quality of prophecy remains unfulfilled, or only partially fulfilled, we shall say (on the same hypothesis) that the seer has been looking along one of the lines of potentiality. He has seen the future, not as it will be but as it might be. The lines of potentiality may be modified, if we care to take the risk; but if what we have seen turns out to be one of the nodes, then we take liberties with it at our own peril. And it may be said on behalf of the more conscientious kind of fortune-tellers that, if closely pressed, they will not as a rule claim more for what is written in the stars or on the cards than a very high potential.

The trouble is, of course, that before we undertake to meddle with fate, we want to know whether we are looking at the nodes or one of the lines of potentiality. Unfortunately, no one can tell us that, except the Author of the pattern. When contact is established with the mind of the Author, then the vision is properly called, not foresight, but revelation, and as such it forms no part of our subject. For the ordinary person, it is wisest to leave the whole thing alone—a disappointing conclusion, in which the Church, the Law, and most of the writers of cheat-the-oracle stories unreservedly concur. So do most scientists, though not altogether for the same reason. The statistical experiments carried out by Professor Soal and others, being directed only to discovering whether veridical foresight does in fact take place, are as potentially harmless or harmful as other scientific experiments —with nuclear fission or what not. It is always interesting to know what lies within our power; it is when we begin to make use of the knowledge that the balloon is likely to go up.

At this point we come up against another type of prophecy altogether—the type which William Blake recognized, and which is founded, not on foresight, but on insight. It begins by saying: "The universe is so made that if you insist on doing so-and-so the consequences will be such-and-such"; and it frequently goes on to say: "and knowing you as I do, I can confidently predict that you *will* do it and the inevitable result will follow." The only objection to this kind of prophecy is that it seldom flatters our hopes, and cannot, by its nature, offer us much in the way of dramatic surprise. Yet it, too, may have its false prophets; for insight may be as unreliable as foresight: we are, for instance, less sure than we were of the inevitable evolution of human perfection. Moreover, the stories in which it figures are for the most part of a deadly serious and edifying kind, like the *Industrious Apprentice* and *Eric, or Little by Little*. We do not invite Jeremiah to entertain us at parties, or pay astrologers to inform us that by honest thrift we may gradually amass a genteel sufficiency. What we want to hear is something quite different: "I see a black man in the crystal"; "the eight of swords is a journey by water"; "your twenty-first year will be perilous—I see Mars and Venus opposed, and Saturn threatening the House of Life"; "Cross the gipsy's palm with silver";

> "I dreamed a dream, a weary dream
> Ayont the Isle of Skye;
> I saw a dead man win a fight,
> And I think that man was I."

But when it comes to taking action about them, we fall into perplexity. What is it expedient to do? and what is our moral duty? And here, the prophecy of insight casts a damper on our hopes of dealing with the prophecy of foresight. If I dream that the 9.30 to Liverpool Street is due to be wrecked tomorrow I can refrain from travelling by it. But is it my duty to rush to the station and dissuade other passengers from travelling? My knowledge of human nature suggests that I shall have but little success. Am I to ring up British Railways and peremptorily summon them to cancel the train? Alas! my knowledge of the way government departments work pronounces that this is a node which there is no untying. With a delicious shudder we may remember Max Beerbohm's A. V. Laider, who reads the hands of all the passengers in a railway compartment, and finds that all, except himself, are foredoomed to die in the same imminent catastrophe. He has not the courage to pull the communication cord—and the next thing he knows is waking up in hospital.

"Tell me", says the acquaintance to whom he narrates this painful episode, "was it marked in your hands that you were not going to pull that cord?"... "It was marked very clearly", he answered, "in *their* hands."

Until prediction becomes an exact science—and how dull life will be when it does—it is probably best to take the thrill and let the profit go. We do not know enough; and the gods have a sardonic sense of humour which it is rather rash to provoke.

CHAPTER XII

POETRY, LANGUAGE AND AMBIGUITY

I STAND BEFORE you this evening in a position which is both essentially false and empirically perilous. Of the practical peril to which I am exposing myself, the name of your Society[1] is sufficient warning. Socrates, like some other great men, was a public danger, and I am not surprised that the Athenians made him drink hemlock. It was perilous to disagree with Socrates, for he would immediately pounce upon your feeble protest, tear it to shreds, and expose you publicly as a fool and an ignoramus. But it was equally perilous to agree with him; for if you were rash enough to concede a single step he would lead you away up the garden, at the end of a string of leading questions, till the path ended in a blank wall; and his genial, "Well, now, aren't we both fools?" did little to reconcile you to this humiliating situation. The trouble with Socrates' friends was that they were all far too earnest and intelligent to cope with him. The only possible defence against Socrates would have been that impenetrable frivolity which conceals a scepticism far more profound than his own. It does not flourish in the Academy, but you may meet it any day in the village pub. To all temptations to commit one's self it opposes a resolute screen of ambiguity, replying only: "Depends what you mean by it"; or "Well, I do and I don't, if you see what I mean"; or "So *you* say"; or at most, with an indulgent grin: "Come on, I'll buy it." And I give notice here and now that if anybody, in discussion, opens with the Socratic formula: "Would the speaker agree that—?" I shall employ public-house tactics in my reply.

More seriously: my position is false, because yours is a philosophic society, and I am in no way qualified to meet you on your own ground. I am no philosopher, "not even of any kind"; at most I have picked up such scraps of scholastic philosophy as are indispensable for explaining the scholastic theology of the *Commedia* to the simple-minded Penguin. All subsequent

[1] The Oxford University Socratic Society.

philosophies are dark to my understanding—partly because I have not had occasion to study them, partly because very often I cannot admit their assumptions, so far as I understand them, and also largely because I am not properly acquainted with their terminologies.

This last point is a very important one, at any rate to me. My only excuse for being here is that I have perhaps some of that practical experience in the handling of words which any workman acquires in using the tools of his trade. I am not equipped to lecture, theoretically, on epistemology or semantics, and I certainly shall not attempt to execute the monstrous programme outlined for me in the title given—not by me—to this address. I only know about language what any craftsman knows about his own medium—that there are some things it does well, others which it can only make shift to do, and others again which, by its very nature, it cannot do at all. But you must make allowance for me if I deal more than you like in images and anecdotes and concrete examples, because I am not a philosopher, but what used to be called a "poet" and "maker" and is now called, more cumbrously, a "creative writer"; and therefore cannot think very readily in abstract terms.

The reason why so much attention has been directed of late to the question of language and its meaning is the plain and alarming fact that, as the field of human knowledge widens and the various branches of that knowledge become more specialized, and as (at the same time and as a direct result of this) the whole structure of human society becomes more tightly locked together in a reciprocal interdependence of all its parts, so it is rapidly becoming more and more difficult for individual men to understand each other. Whenever two persons attempt to converse on any subject more abstruse than the weather or the wearing properties of nylon, a point may be reached—and reached only too quickly—when the speakers cease to communicate, and merely utter mutually unintelligible sounds. I will not waste time proving this by examples: the trouble is only too familiar; it has achieved the dignity of a label all to itself, and is known as "the problem of communication". To label a difficulty is not the same thing as to overcome it, or even to understand it; but it shows that we are at least aware of it, and that is something gained.

For this failure to communicate there are various—but I must not say "causes", for the word "cause" has become suspect (you see how difficult it all is!). I will say that there are various factors in the situation which it is possible at least for the purposes of argument to distinguish and comment on separately. One very obvious factor is this: that every branch of knowledge as it develops tends to acquire a specialized vocabulary of its own, intelligible to its own practitioners, but not to the practitioners in other departments, nor to the common man. This would not matter if groups of specialists could live side by side in one civilization, like cows and hens in one field, feeding on the same ground without needing to exchange ideas or explain themselves, or discuss each other's specialities. But they cannot, since each group's speciality issues in practical results which affect the whole community. And when Group A tries to explain its work to the world, using its specialized A-vocabulary, it is inevitably misunderstood, because the technical terms it uses are either new formations, meaningless to all other groups, or else words familiar in common speech, which have acquired a limited and specialized connotation, so that they are readily misinterpreted. Indeed, all technical language which does not consist of new formations is made up of common words in a state of arrested development, or to which significations have been assigned subtly differing from those of common usage, and perhaps unjustified by their derivation. Or again, words and phrases which for many centuries have had a specialized significance for one group are taken over and used in a quite different specialized significance by another group—neither party realizing that the change has taken place.

Let me give a few examples. Some friends of mine—all students of the Humanities—once invited a physicist to improve their minds with a little information about modern physics. When he had been speaking for some time, they said: "Hold hard! you keep on talking about 'acceleration'; to us that means 'increasing speed'. But in your last sentence you seem to use it as though it meant 'decreasing speed', which we should call 'deceleration'." The physicist then explained that in *his* jargon "acceleration" meant *any* change of speed in either direction. To which they replied: "That's all right, so long as we know." In this case, the hearers had the sense to ask; and if the outrage on derivation annoyed them they were ready to smother their feelings. But I have known a theologian and a scientist argue interminably about transubstantiation without its occurring to either of them to ask in what sense the other was using the word "substance". The theologian was, of course, using it in its theological sense, which has remained fossilized, so to speak, in somewhere about the thirteenth century: a *substance* is an independently existing being—the entity underlying the phenomena. We still use it more or less in that sense when we say: "Never mind reading the whole document: give me the *substance* of it." The scientist was using it in the common modern sense, which has strayed far from either derivation or ancient usage: he conceived it to be more or less synonymous with "matter", or "solidity". In this case, since neither disputant had the wits to raise the point, no understanding was possible. A similar deadlock is reached when people chattering about science apply to the so-called "laws of nature" the theologians' phrase "natural law". The confusion this causes is increased when other people, chattering about theology, suppose that *in that context* the phrase "natural law" really does mean "the laws of nature". Actually, in theology, the "laws of nature" (meaning the observed behaviour of material objects) form a subdivision of the Divine Law (*lex divina*); and "Natural Law" (*lex naturalis*) is something totally different, having to do with man's acceptance of the Divine Will.

Or again. When a scientist says that something "does not exist", he merely means (if you press him for a definition) that the thing in question is "not observable by any methods of which science takes cognisance". An object, for example, moving at a speed exceeding that of light, is, scientifically speaking, non-existent. Various heavenly bodies are, it seems, engaged in receding from us at a rapidly increasing pace. When they pass the light-barrier they, scientifically speaking, cease to exist. At the same time, we ourselves presumably "cease to exist" for scientific observers on those bodies. Indeed, we must have scientifically ceased to exist a long time ago—unless we are so parochially minded as to suppose that scientific observation is confined to our own inconsiderable planet. Scientifically speaking, therefore, there is no very significant distinction between existing and not existing; and the expression "God does not exist" boils down, scientifically speaking, to "God is not observable by scientific methods"—a proposition which need not keep the most nervous theologian awake o' nights.

But this is not what the expression meant, for example, to a correspondent in *Picture Post* when he suggested that "modern research" had shown that God "did not exist". He attached some absolute meaning to the words, supposing that, if God existed, He would by this time have been caught, measured, and dissected. (Even so, he did not perhaps allow sufficiently for the notorious difficulty of proving a universal negative. The coelacanth, which modern research had written off as "extinct", turned up one day in the trawl of a common fisherman.)

But for the theologian, the term "existent" does not mean "observable by the methods of physical science", nor yet "observable by observers on this planet". He starts from quite different assumptions. For him, God alone can be said to exist unconditionally, and is the pre-supposition behind all being: "I AM hath sent me to thee." Whatever observables contingently exist do so in virtue of being sustained in God's mind. "God is" thus means exactly what it says, and no other subject can thus stand without predicate. "Socrates is" would be simply a shorthand way of saying "Socrates is known to God". In all other contexts, "is" has only the force of a copula, indicating a relation of subject to predicate, whether singular to singular, singular to class, or class to class.

Whether propositions about God or metaphysical propositions, as such, have any real significance is a different question. I am only concerned to point out that the word "is" or "exists" has different meanings for the scientist and the theologian. The common man's meaning lies on the whole nearer to the theologian's; and probably amounts to "observable by any observer or method", but, since he has grown accustomed to believing that "science" is the sole means to and repository of knowledge, he will inevitably fit the scientist's conclusion on the theologian's premisses, with the curious results to be studied in *Picture Post*.

I may say that theology is peculiarly exposed, nowadays, to the hazards of having its specialized scientific vocabulary misinterpreted, partly because so much of its vocabulary has passed into common speech, and partly—indeed consequently—because people have largely forgotten that it *is* a science and *has* a specialized vocabulary. People who would not dream of discussing engineering or electricity without finding out what its special terms meant, will cheerfully quarrel with theology, without taking any such precautions. The result is as though some student of antiquarian culture should madly disagree with an engineer under the impression that whenever the engineer mentioned "torque" he was referring to a particular kind of metal ornament for the neck. But theology is not the only sufferer. I remember how, many years ago, some author was reckless enough to write a book called *Apology for England*. This roused the fury of one of our brighter dailies, which came out with an indignant article, affirming that England needed no apology, and had nothing whatever to apologize for. This, naturally, brought out of their holes a wildernessful of grammarians, philologists, and literary men, who wrote heated letters pointing out the derivation and proper meaning of "Apology", and referring to Xenophon, Plato, Newman's *Apologia pro Vitâ Suâ* and other famous examples of a well-established usage. At the end of which, the *Daily Blank*, still bloody, but totally unbowed by all this learning, came back in another article which concluded triumphantly: "an apology is an *apology*, and there's an end of it." And since the Editor had complete control over his own column, that was indeed the end of it.

Let us now look at certain other words which, in course of a long and varied history, have become so battered by usage that they have come to have almost no definable meaning, and are used chiefly for their incantatory virtues: words like "democracy", for example, or "liberty". Some of these have never enjoyed any generally accepted definition. Others have been defined with care, and their various possible meanings solicitously distinguished—only to be submerged by the passage of time in a welter of indistinguishable emotion. When platform speakers orate about our "liberties", or when amateur psychologists argue about the "freedom of the will", who remembers the minute and careful distinctions made by the Schoolmen between the *libertas minor*, the *libertas major* and that *liberum arbitrium* which in English is rendered as "free will", but of which a more exact translation would be "the freeing of the judgement"? Or when, during the last war, politicians and journalists made play with the phrase "the peace-loving nations", who cared to recall that, fifteen centuries ago, St. Augustine had pointed out that the words were strictly meaningless? "All men seek peace by war, but none seek war by peace. For they that perturb the peace they live in, do it not for hate of it, but to show their power in alteration of it. They would not disannul it, but they want it on their own terms." (*Civitas Dei* xix. 12.)

And so from battered words and meaningless clichés we are led to words which, though they still possess perfectly clear and well-defined meanings as purely descriptive terms, are nevertheless currently used as mere incantations for the calling-up of passions, such as: mediaeval, romantic, intellectual, dogmatic, adolescent, emotive, mystical. The last word in particular is almost never used in its correct technical connotation, but is saddled with a surprising variety of meanings, from "obscurantist" and "cabbalistic" to "unpractical"—all pejorative and all equally incorrect.

We must also mention—though we need not, I hope, dwell upon a subject so distasteful—certain other jargons, much less respectable than the specialized jargons of the arts and sciences, whose general effect is to deprive language of any definition that it ever possessed—such as journalese, officialses, genteel periphrasis, advertising jargon, parliamentary language, B. B. Cedarianism, telegraphese, and the curious lingo of the newspaper headline, which consists of nothing but nouns. All these, damaging as they are, have at least this to be said for them, that most educated people know them to be bad, and that even those who use them are vaguely aware of their sinful ugliness. They are the publicans and harlots of the linguistic world, who, though indeed they tend to corrupt their associates, may be readily known for what they are, and are comparatively free from the sin of pride.

It has been truly said that real tragedy is not the conflict of good with evil, but the conflict of good with good. The really perilous conflict that is going on today is a struggle between two sets of virtuous and well-meaning people with totally opposed ideas about what language ought to be. One set believes that words ought to be emptied as far as possible of all associative meaning, and made to approximate as closely as possible to the conventional signs of mathematics: each word to have an exactly defined, impersonal connotation, saying the same thing in every context, awaking no overtones, and arousing no emotions. This point of view is taken by some scientists, and by certain philosophers who think that there is no knowledge except that obtained by means of "scientific" (i.e. inductive) methods of reasoning from material data supplied by the senses and measured by instruments. For brevity I will refer to all those who incline to think in this way about language as "philomaths"—an *ad hoc* coinage which I trust will obtain no currency beyond the present occasion.

The other set of people believe that words should have as rich and suggestive an associative content as possible, and that their function is not limited to the making of exact statements about measurable data, but to stimulating emotion and imagination as well as reason, and so expressing and communicating experiences which lie outside the range of purely scientific knowledge. These people I will refer to as "the poets"—and I include in this term not only the professional masters of language, but also that poet hidden in every common man, who by his daily use of words makes language what it is.

And it is here that we come to the tragicomedy which lies at the heart of the conflict. Both sides are deserving of our deepest sympathy, for both are in a desperate situation. Of the two, the philomaths are the worst off, for while both they and the poets are fighting against the general cussedness of human nature, the philomaths are fighting against the nature of language itself, and if their cries are sometimes shrill and vituperative, who shall blame them? The poets' troubles have been voiced, unforgettably, by one of their greatest living captains: "Here I am," says T. S. Eliot:

> Trying to learn to use words, and every attempt
> Is a wholly new start, and a different kind of failure
> Because one has only learnt to get the better of words
> For the thing one no longer has to say, or the way in which
> One is no longer disposed to say it. And so each venture
> Is a new beginning, a raid on the inarticulate
> With shabby equipment always deteriorating
> In the general mess of imprecision of feeling,
> Undisciplined squads of emotion. And what there is to conquer
> By strength and submission, has already been discovered
> Once or twice, or several times, by men whom one cannot hope
> To emulate—but there is no competition—
> There is only the fight to recover what has been lost
> And found and lost again and again: and now, under conditions
> That seems unpropitious. But perhaps neither gain nor loss.
> For us, there is only the trying. The rest is not our business.
>
> (*East Coker*)

The philomath has realized all this, or a great part of it. But he cannot accept it. He cannot bring himself to say: "the rest is not our business." He is angrily determined to put the matter right. But he is held in a cleft stick. If he restricts himself to the incorruptible language of mathematics, he will find that his audience, though doubtless fit, is very few indeed. If he tries to speak the language of the common poet, he will be plunged in precisely that "mess of imprecision" which he deprecates, and, less accustomed than the poet to handling words in an imaginative way, he will be only the more easily bogged and trapped in verbal pitfalls. And, worse still, if he invents for himself words and phrases to which he gives his own specialized definitions, the common poet will promptly lay hands on those verbal weapons which he has invented, and turn them into something totally different, which makes a mock of all his prudence. What is the use of devising terms like "allergy" and "fixation", merely to hear people say over the cocktails: "Darling, I'm hopelessly allergic to puppet-shows", or "My dog has developed a dustman-fixation"—or, still more irritatingly, "I've got an absolute *thing* about after-dinner speeches." For it is the common poet who makes the language and who, in the end, does what he likes with it: the technicalities of the most recent science are one with the technicalities of mediaeval theology, and all go the primrose path to the everlasting glory-hole. Where are the precisions of yester-year?

And, worst of all, there is no word in common use that does not, when carefully analysed, derive from some image or metaphor—dead, perhaps, in seeming, but capable, in an unexpected context, of being galvanized into a hideous and mocking resurrection. And there is nothing your philomath hates and distrusts so much as an image or metaphor.

Let us face the facts. A word or a phrase is not, and cannot be, an instrument of precision. Language is sometimes called "organic"—but that again is a metaphor. Let us say that it is one of those instruments which are altered by the mere act of using them. Infinitesimally, it may be, but none the less surely altered. The whole sea changes level for a stone. By every cut you make with a knife, the edge is ever so little thickened and blunted; every time you sharpen the edge to restore it, the entire bulk of the knife is by ever so little diminished. Every time you boil a kettle on the gas there is a trifling deposit of fur within, a trifling burning away of metal from without. And so, every time you use a word, however prudently, however precisely, in the mere act of using it you alter its content. You may enlarge or diminish, ennoble or debase, convert or pervert that content, but modify it one way or another you surely will. Do you think this is an exaggeration? Consider then that there was once a time when a man could speak, seriously and in compliment, of "a blooming girl". There must also have been a day when some lighthearted person unknown to history first used the word "blooming" as a slang intensive. Thereafter, for a period, the scales no doubt hung poised, each individual use of the word dropping imperceptibly into one pan or the other, until, at some unascertainable moment the pan of slang received the light word which overweighted it, and the other "flew up and kicked the beam". There is a somewhat disquieting text of Scripture which pronounces "that every idle word that men shall speak they shall give account thereof in the day of judgement". This may be true in a sense more literal than its context might suggest. It is not altogether for nothing that Dante banished to the filth of the Ditch of Flatterers the woman who said "miraculously" when "very much" would have sufficed. She had done her little part in corrupting the medium of communication.

Every word is an *event*. It is a sensitive point in history, containing in itself the whole of its own past and the seeds of its whole future. A phrase used by Dante not only contains and is illumined by the meanings it derived from Virgil or the Vulgate: it, in its turn, illuminates Virgil and the Vulgate and gives new meaning to them. It not only passes on those meanings, supercharged with Dante's own meaning, to Tennyson and Landor, to Rossetti and Yeats, to Williams and Eliot and Pound, but it receives back from them the reflected *splendore* of their own imaginative use of it. Poetic language is a web of light, the whole of which is spread through time and space, and quivers at every touch. Its behaviour is incalculable and unpredictable—not because it is in theory unamenable to the laws of statistics, but because the possible permutations and calculations are at once so astronomical in number and so infinitesimal in—so to call it—size. And also because not only the instrument but also the object itself is modified by the mere act of observation.

This being so, a certain pathos attends the efforts of all logicians to cage this peacock in an analytical net. Let us consider a sentence extracted, I think, from Professor A. J. Ayer's book, *Language, Truth, and Logic* : "A symbol"—and let me say, incidentally, that I wish people would be a little more careful how they use the word *symbol*; however, he proceeds to define what he means by it—"a symbol, that is, a word in use, is defined by showing how the sentences in which it significantly occurs can be translated into equivalent sentences, which contain neither the *definiendum* itself, nor any of its synonyms." Now, so far as such exercises as these are directed to ensuring that we shall not, intentionally or carelessly, use the same word with several different meanings in the course of the same argument, I could not more heartily applaud them. This is nothing new—it is what the handbooks of formal logic have been saying for centuries. What moves me is the touching confidence which assumes that there are such things as "synonyms" and "equivalent sentences". Alas !, a true synonym *in the same language* is the rarest thing in the world. Words have synonyms in other languages—I suppose that there is no serious difference of meaning between "the man is dead", "l'homme est mort", and "der Mann ist tot", for example. But if we look, in English, for a sentence precisely equivalent to "the man is dead", we at once find that each one we propose says less, or more, than this simple statement, or else complicates it with a good deal of information about the speaker which we did not intend to give. Suppose we say : "The man is lifeless", we immediately remember that when Louisa Musgrave so inconsiderately leapt off the steps on to the Lower Cobb at Lyme Regis, she "was taken up lifeless". Here Miss Austen is amusing herself with our fears, for Louisa was only rendered unconscious. The word is a true synonym, but liable to misinterpretation. We may fall back on medical detail : "The man has ceased to breathe; his heart has stopped; his pulse has failed", and so on. We then turn up Dixon Mann's *Forensic Medicine* and find : "When both heart and lungs have ceased to act, the tissues retain 'vitality' for some time, during the continuance of which it cannot be truly asserted that the individual is dead." It seems that we have said too little. If, on the other hand, we say that the man "has passed away", or "passed over", or "fallen asleep" or "is no more" we are saying too much, in that we are committing ourselves to various religious implications about which "the man is dead" says nothing. We might, of course, say : "the male individual is deceased"—but there are various reasons why we should refrain from this. Still, in its nasty way, it is an equivalent in sense, though not in dignity—it is we, not the meaning, that are betrayed by it. It would pass in a police report or a court of law, but scarcely anywhere else; whereas "he has kicked the bucket", "popped off", or "cashed in his checks" might pass anywhere else, but scarcely in a court of law. The sentences may be called "equivalent", but they are not in every respect equivalent.

Now let us take the thing another way. Does "the man is dead" always mean precisely what it says and not more? Indeed it does not: it depends upon the context. You may remember the *Ingoldsby* tale of Lord Tomnoddy and his friends who went to see a man hanged, but unhappily overslept themselves and missed the crucial moment.

> The man was dead,
> There was no more to be said;
> So my Lord Tomnoddy went home to bed.

The words are instinct with finality. This is one aspect of death, but not the only one. For example:

"As for John Doe, he always was a sneak and a liar and a bully."

"My dear, the man is dead."

Not the finality, but the defencelessness of death is here in question. *De mortuis nil nisi bonum.*

Or again; imagine this scene: the police have burst open the door of a gas-filled room and dragged out the lifeless (mark the word) bodies of a man, a woman, and a child. The doctor examines them and presently he says: "The man is dead." A message, not of finality, but of hope—for its implies that the woman and child are alive, and prompt action may restore them to health.

Or, once again: one of a party of people drinks his coffee and suddenly falls to the ground. He has fainted—he has been taken suddenly ill—he has succumbed, perhaps, to a stroke. Open the window, undo his collar, fetch water, give him some brandy, put him to bed with a hot-water bottle, send for the doctor! The person nearest him looks up and says: "The man is dead." Neither air nor water nor brandy nor medical care will serve him now—and behind the shadow of death a ghastlier shadow has loomed up. Ring up the police, notify the coroner, lock coffee and cups in a safe place, and keep the key, see to it that nobody leaves the house—for those words may mean not merely death but murder.

You will notice that in all these examples the literal meaning of the words is in no way altered. They are not used in any transferred or figurative sense. It is the context alone which lends them an acquired and additional significance.

"The sentences in which they significantly occur"—the operative word is "significantly", and God alone knows what any word may signify at any moment. For language is by its nature ambiguous. We receive it, loaded with all its accrued associations; we use it in varying contexts which modify its significance, as a colour shows modified by the colours which surround it; we alter it by our use of it; and we pass it on, thus altered and enriched—or, it may be, impoverished—by our treatment of it, to those who come after. All new ideas, all new systems of thought are compelled to communicate themselves, as best they can, not in a language fresh-minted for the occasion, but in this ancient currency. To the poet this is an advantage, for it makes of every word a storehouse of accumulated power. No one more than T. S Eliot, despite his moments of discouragement, has drawn upon the traditions of the past for his imagery and his art. But to the philomath it is an annoyance and a humiliation, unless he has in him enough of the poet and enough of the common man to accept the situation with cheerfulness.

Take, for example, Dr. H. J. Eysenck's little Penguin: *The Use and Abuse of Psychology,* which contains a section explaining that the old "faculty psychology" was unscientific and erroneous. The author then proceeds to enumerate the various "factors" involved in the process of doing intelligence tests and is suddenly reminded that he is in fact, and willy-nilly, using words like "memory", "numerical ability", and "inductive reasoning" which derive from the tainted vocabulary of an obsolete metaphysics. He hastens to exculpate himself in a footnote. "Faculties were posited on the basis of unsystematic observation and verbalization of certain stereotypes and prejudices current at the time; factors are carefully defined in terms of experimental and statistical procedures which follow the usual dictates of the scientific method." The tone and temper of this sentence, sweeping as it does into one contemptuous limbo every philosopher from Plato to Kant, is curiously reminiscent of a Christian bishop peevishly dismissing all natural religions, past and present, eastern and western, as "heathen superstition and mumbo-jumbo". It is entertaining to compare Jung's genial attitude in the face of the same verbal dilemma: "We are thus forced to resort to something which at first glance alarmingly resembles the old faculty psychology of the eighteenth century; in reality, however, we are only returning to current ideas in daily speech, perfectly accessible and comprehensible to everyone. When, for instance, I speak of 'thinking', it is only the philosopher who does not know what I mean; no layman will find it incomprehensible. He uses this word every day, and always in the same general sense, though it is true enough that he is not a little embarrassed if he is called upon suddenly to give an unequivocal definition of thinking. The same is true of 'memory' or 'feeling'." (*Modern Man in Search of a Soul*, p. 102.) It is perhaps this kind of thing which has earned for Jung the stigma of being "unscientific". Nevertheless, it is advisable for everyone who has something to communicate to come to terms with the inherited language of the common man. Otherwise, not only will he be unable to make himself understood, but he will be liable to error in every province outside his own. For every technician is a layman in another specialist's technique and, whether he knows it or not, will speak, in that context, only the language of the common man.

I have hitherto said little about the influence exercised on language by the poet in the more restricted and professional sense of the word. It is, indeed, hardly a subject to be dealt with summarily, without lengthy quotation and analysis. For the purposes of this paper I should like to approach it by a rather different road.

It is still frequently said that there is today a quarrel between science and religion. I do not think myself that this is where the real conflict lies. Pure religion has, in fact, a good deal in common with pure science—or with what used to be called, charmingly and in some ways more accurately, Natural Philosophy. What they have chiefly in common is humility. Science which is philosophic in the original meaning of the word—which desires only knowledge—calls for humility in the face of the facts. Religion—and poetry in so far as it is religious—calls for humility in the face of unconditioned reality. Both are the servants of truth, and they have no good reason to hate or fear one another.

The real conflict is between a kind of science, and a kind of poetry, which aim, not at truth, but at the exercise of power. Between these two there is an antagonism which is, at bottom, the jealousy of rival magicians. Modern applied science has inherited from the alchemist and the sorcerer the lust to power over the forces of irrational nature; and just so far as its aim is power, it is magical and dangerous and may be evil. Poetry—that is, the incantatory element in poetry—has inherited from the enchanter and the witch-doctor the lust to power over souls; and when we speak of oratory or poetic language as "spell-binding" we recognize its magical nature, which, again, is always dangerous and may be evil. The two lusts to domination meet, rather ominously, in the field of psychology, where rival practitioners use the technique perfected by science to exploit the magical images originally summoned up from the unconscious by the incantatory technique of the poet. Thus we find a stubborn and by no means silent struggle going on between the champions of *verstehende* psychology on the one hand and *erklärende* psychology on the other—each side claiming the right to bear upon their achievement of arms the sacred motto "Science". It is not that the *erklärende* kind—which postulates a total impersonality and statistical objectivity—renounces power over human affairs: on the contrary. It aims at the control of human beings by exterior methods, releasing persons into jobs and opinions into Gallup polls with the mechanical accuracy of a linotype machine distributing type. The other kind seeks to dominate and order the human situation from within; by direct action upon the individual psyche. The first group have probably the better claim to be called "scientific" psychologists, in the limited modern sense attached to the word "science"; the second ought perhaps rather to be called "poetic" psychologists—each according to the type of magical power which they employ.

I can now no longer postpone a brief consideration of poetry, whose power consists in so manipulating language that every word or phrase calls up images by which the mind and feelings of the reader are vividly affected. To this end, every latent ambiguity, arising out of derivation, history, association, context, hidden or open metaphor, and the suggestion of mere sound, is pressed into service. The images thus invoked are always in excess of the literal statement made by the words, and in modern poetry frequently take the place of literal statement, leaving the poem practically void of any content except the images themselves. Of these images, some are magical; others—those which belong to the poetry of religious inspiration—are prophetic or mystical. This is not the place to go deeply into the difference between them. I will only say briefly that the magical images are made by the poet as a means to the control of nature (in himself or in others); whereas the prophetic or mystical poet aims rather at interpreting the unconditioned Reality by means of those images which exist already and are *given* in Nature. That is, he looks upon Nature as the expression and visible form of that which sustains Nature, and on himself not as wielding power, but as the conduit by which a Power transcendent to Nature and himself is communicated. In other words, magic postulates a dualism, but religion a unity, between mind and nature. The two types of imagery tend, of course, to mingle and coalesce, even in the work of the same poet; but the distinction is there.

What may be profitable for the moment is to glance at the two chief ways in which, as I mentioned just now, poetry may evoke the images. The first example I will choose consists of a few lines from the seventh canto of the *Paradiso*. They occur in the course of a long passage of direct statement about Atonement Theology.

[The example from Dante which Dr. Sayers chose is a passage (*Paradiso*, vii. 109-120) which she also discusses in the second essay in this collection, *Dante the Maker*. As the analysis in the present essay was a repetition of the earlier one (p. 40, beginning: "Beatrice is explaining..."), we have omitted it here. It concludes with the words:

> Now, this great procession of imagery is not in the passage I have read: the images are *evoked* by Dante by the juxtaposition of two ambiguous words. They involve no alteration of the direct statement which those words convey in their context; yet univocal words, such as "method" and "operation", would have left the images unsummoned. With an astonishing economy of means, the poet simply speaks his two words of power and leaves the rest to our imagination. *He* makes the statement; *we* make the images.]

The modern poetic method is the direct opposite of this. I have chosen as example a poem by David Gascoigne; and I will leave the commentary to Professor Day Lewis, who has done it better and more succinctly than I could hope to do. The poem is called *Winter Garden*.

> The season's anguish, crashing whirlwind, ice,
> Have passed, and cleansed the trodden paths
> That silent gardeners have strewn with ash.
>
> The iron circles of the sky
> Are worn away by tempest;
> Yet in this garden there is no more strife:
> The Winter's knife is buried in the earth.
> Pure music is the cry that tears
> The birdless branches in the wind.
> No blossom is reborn. The blue
> Stare of the pond is blind.
> And no one sees
> A restless stranger through the morning stray
> Across the sodden lawn, whose eyes
> Are tired of weeping, in whose breast
> A savage sun consumes its hidden day.

Here is Professor Day Lewis's comment. "Nothing here is explicit. What *emerges from the sequences of images* of anguish, purification, peace and again anguish is a parallel between nature and man—a parallel which includes both likeness and antithesis. The 'restless stranger' is like the garden because he has passed through a storm of anguish, yet the opposite of it because he *is* restless, alive, while the garden is dead with winter's knife in its heart; the blue stare of the pond is blind and the stranger's eyes are tired of weeping; in the garden there is no more strife, whereas in his breast a savage sun consumes its hidden day: but in this last line likeness and antithesis are fused, for nature as well as man contains its contradictions, nature too has its sun, burning now unseen but still leading earth through the endless cycles of decay and purification, calm and storm, death and rebirth." (*The Poetic Image*, p. 132.)

In this poem, it is the *poet* who makes the images, with all their ambiguities of language and mood; there is no direct statement of "meaning" at all; it is left to the reader to elicit that from the movement of the images, so far as such a poem is susceptible of having its "meaning" directly stated.

Between these extremes lie many kinds of poetic presentation, in which the proportion of direct to indirect statement and direct to indirect evocation of images varies indefinitely, and we are confronted with innumerable types of linguistic ambiguity. Let me hasten to say that to my mind not all such types are desirable. I think, for example, that William Empson and his school tend to attach too much value to the ambiguity which arises out of mere looseness of syntax and failure to define one's terms. In a language like English, almost wholly uninflected, and having an immensely rich vocabulary, it is far too easy to achieve this kind of ambiguity by accident, or through clumsiness, laziness, or putting on pretentious airs of profundity. I did indeed compose for your pleasure and instruction an *ad hoc* specimen of verse, compressing into a single quatrain not only the whole of Dante's argument about the Atonement, but also almost every conceivable species of vicious ambiguity. Unhappily, I over-reached myself; for since almost every phrase in it is susceptible of at least three interpretations it would, I fear, take too much time to expound. But I succeeded in proving to myself the fatal ease with which that kind of thing could be written.

The right kind of ambiguity is that which, almost against the poet's will, imposes itself upon him when he is most earnestly striving to express with clarity that for which no verbal stereotypes exist—some apprehension of truth which is new to him, some subtlety of experience which has hitherto remained undefined. He cannot say: "it was thus", but only, "it was as though", seeking for his purpose such images and likenesses as he can discover in the conscious or unconscious part of his mind. Very often, indeed, it is only in an unconscious image that the experience can make itself known even to him—*a fortiori* be communicated by him to others.

Poetry, history, and theology are alike in this: that they involve a philosophy of singleness, because their chief concern is with unique events. They are therefore never wholly amenable to analysis by statistical methods, neither can their crucial experiments be reproduced in the laboratory. Wars, love-affairs, myths may bear a general resemblance to one another; but only once does Frankie Drake gun the Armada up the Channel; only once does Dante meet Beatrice in Florence; only once does the only God irrupt into terrestrial history, at Bethlehem in Jewry, in the reign of Caesar Augustus. All assessment of such events must depend, perilously, on the evidence of human witnesses and on argument by analogy; and since poetry is the language of analogy, there hangs about all such events a disconcerting aura of poetry. Yet we cannot reduce them altogether to poetry and so dismiss them. No one that I know of has endeavoured to dismiss the Armada as pure poetry (though they have done their best about Troy), but there have been stubborn attempts to dispose of Beatrice and of Christ. The trouble is that, in such cases, unless you can bring positive proof that something *else* happened, you just either accept the evidence or else deny it *a priori*; you cannot arrange a series of control experiments by which to estimate the probability or frequency of its occurrence. It is by hypothesis unique, and, being unique, neither probable nor improbable until it has happened. Once it has happened, the difficulty is to find out exactly *what* has happened. Since there is no ready-made vocabulary with which to define a thing *sui generis*, we have to set about and make one. And it will, inevitably, be a vocabulary of analogy.

"The Kingdom of Heaven", said the Lord Christ, "is among you." But what, precisely, is the Kingdom of Heaven? You cannot point to existing specimens, saying, "Lo, here!" or "Lo, there!" You can only experience it. But what is it *like*, so that when we experience it we may recognize it? Well, it is a change, like being born again and re-learning everything from the start. It is secret, living power—like yeast. It is something that grows, like seed. It is precious like buried treasure, like a rich pearl, and you have to pay for it. It is a sharp cleavage through the rich jumble of things which life presents: like fish and rubbish in a draw-net, like wheat and tares; like wisdom and folly; and it carries with it a kind of menacing finality; it is new, yet in a sense it was always there—like turning out a cupboard and finding there your own childhood as well as your present self; it makes demands, it is like an invitation to a royal banquet—gratifying, but not to be disregarded, and you have to live up to it; where it is equal, it seems unjust, where it is just it is clearly not equal—as with the single pound, the diverse talents, the labourers in the vineyard, you have what you bargained for; it knows no compromise between an uncalculating mercy and a terrible justice—like the unmerciful servant, you get what you give; it is helpless in your hands like the King's Son, but if you slay it, it will judge you; it was from the foundations of the world; it is to come; it is here and now; it is within you. It is recorded that the multitude sometimes failed to understand.

Explicit parabolic statement may fail to be understood; metaphorical statement may lead to positive misunderstanding. Nobody, so far as I know, has ever supposed that the Kingdom of God *was* a fishing-net, or a pearl, or a grain of mustard-seed. But it has happened sometimes that the image has been taken for the thing imaged; this results in a more serious type of error. Thus St. Augustine's City of God has been equated with the Visible Church: as, on the secular plane, the mathematics of the revolving Ptolemaic heavens, carrying the planets *as though* on concentric spheres, hardened into a popular conception of vitreous globes of crystal; or as, within living memory, Bohr's model of the atom haunted the mind with a space filled with little hard round balls.

Conspicuous theological offenders are the successive images made of the Atonement to fit the changing times. That the soul was in some sense "made free" by Christ was a fact of experience. But it was not, obviously, a historical fact, like His birth and death and resurrection. Those you could accept, or deny, on the evidence; the experience of atonement was somehow connected with them—but how? Images for this were needed. The long religious experience of the Jews produced the image of the vicarious sacrifice; the ram in the thicket, the scapegoat, the Passover lamb; the burnt-offering and the sin-offering and the trespass-offering. To the Gentiles of the Roman Empire another image was suggested: to them a literal slavery was a reality only too familiar; it produced the image of the ransom. The rising bourgeois civilization of the Mediaeval West tended to find itself in bondage to the usurer and harassed by suits in the civil courts; the dominant image became, as in the passage from the *Paradiso*, the image of the just debt, and gave rise to those miracle plays in which Christ, or more often Our Lady, haggles interminably with the Devil about the price of souls—frequently cheating him out of his lawful rights by some very dubious pleading. In the nineteenth century, the Evangelical movement, for some reason at present obscure to me, was much obsessed with dirt, and inclined in its imagery to gather at the river and to be washed in the Blood of the Lamb. Many of those images, excellent in themselves and all founded in Scripture, have from time to time tended to be taken with a disturbing literalism. Even the first, and most august, sanctified by Dominical authority and rooted in the solemn events of Holy Week, has in Western Christendom been so narrowly stressed as to limit the Atonement to Calvary rather than to the Incarnate Life as a whole, with enduring and unhappy effects upon the doctrine of the Eucharist. Even more unfortunate have been the results of so stressing legal and financial metaphor as to present the whole work of salvation as literally a kind of spiritual transaction, worked out in terms of imputed merit, quantitive satisfaction and the writing-off of bankrupt debts. Nor is it easy to disabuse the popular mind of an abominable fiction whereby a vindictive Jehovah is only induced to release sinners from eternal torment by "taking it out" upon His own Son, appointed whipping-boy to Adam for that purpose.

The peculiar *Angst* of our own age—socially and financially secure by comparison, aesthetically revolted by blood-baths and crimson fountains, and too dogmatically egalitarian to desire anybody's sacrificial charity—has taken a new form, predominantly morbid and medical. This has most interestingly produced an entirely new set of Atonement images, of which the central symbol is Christ the Healer. We have, for example, Eliot's:

> The wounded surgeon plies the steel
> That questions the distempered part;
> Beneath the bleeding hands we feel
> The sharp compassion of the healer's art
> Resolving the enigma of the fever chart—
> (*East Coker*)

with the Church as the "dying nurse" and the world as "our hospital" endowed by Adam, "the ruined millionaire". And at least one writer has worked out a complete re-presentation of Atonement doctrine in Freudian terms of trauma and transference (G. Sanders: *Christianity after Freud*). All such efforts seems to me entirely laudable, being wholly in the living tradition of an adaptable theological language and at the same time an escape from metaphors which no longer form part of living experience. They can, however, be equally perilous with their predecessors if image and reality are too literally equated. The Freudian assumptions, having imparted an indelible stamp to popular language and imagery, appear to be already on their way out, and may prove as unacceptable to the next generation as the assumptions of vicarious sacrifice are to ours.

Moreover, whether we are dealing with simile or metaphor, it has to be remembered that every image is true and helpful only at its relevant point. God is, in a manner, light: but He is not a succession of wave-lengths in the prime matter. My love is like a red, red rose: but it is not advisable to mulch her with manure. The common sense of mankind can usually be trusted to disentangle the relevant from the irrelevant—but not always. The great dispute that was fought out at Nicaea turned upon the relevant point of a metaphor. That the Divine Son was begotten of the Divine Father was common ground; the Arians, a literal-minded set of people, argued that He must therefore be subsequent to Him, like a bodily pro-creation. The Orthodox, more sensitively aware of the trap concealed in metaphor, rejected the temptation to enclose God in space-time, holding stubbornly to the paradox of the Son's co-eternity. Indeed, nearly all heresies arise from the pressing of a metaphor beyond the point where the image ceases to be relevant.

For these causes, unavoidable as imagery and analogy are, when dealing with what is unique, it is always well to bear in mind the warnings of those mystics who, going by the Negative Way, have perceived the Reality beyond the Images: "It is not soul or mind ... or number, or order, or greatness, or littleness, or equality, or inequality.... It is not power, or light, and does not live, and is not life; nor is It personal essence, or eternity, or time; nor can It be grasped by the understanding, since It is not knowledge or truth; nor is It kingship or wisdom; nor is It one, nor is It unity, nor is It Godhead or Goodness; nor is It a spirit as we understand the term ... nor Sonship nor Fatherhood; nor is It any other thing such as we or any other being can have knowledge of ... nor can any affirmation or negation apply to It ... inasmuch as It transcends all affirmation by being the perfect and unique Cause of all things, and transcends all negation by the pre-eminence of Its simple and absolute nature—free from every limitation and beyond them all." Thus (at considerably greater length) the Pseudo-Dionysius, maintaining not so much that these things cannot be truly affirmed of the Absolute as that It must not be identified with anything at all but Itself.

Having thus pursued language into the rarefied atmosphere of the Absolutely Singular, we must get back to earth as best we can.

I started out—rather disingenuously as you will see—by talking about "the problem of communication". It is generally expected that to any discourse with such a beginning the speaker will, after rambling for as long as he thinks his audience can endure him, annex a tailpiece, introduced by some coy phrase, such as "towards a solution", or "I would tentatively answer"— but, having digged this verbal pitfall, I shall disappoint your hopes of seeing me fall into it. The word "problem", originally pinched, I suppose, from Old Man Euclid, and now a journalistic commonplace of universal application, is a question-begger of the most deluding kind, for it carries with it a veiled assumption that every difficulty is susceptible of a single and complete resolution. This is true of problems in mathematics, logic, and detective fiction, for all these are mental constructs whose conclusions are implied in their premisses. But very few human situations are of this kind. Indeed, I sometimes think that if detective fiction is popular, and if it does harm by its popularity, it is not because blood is its argument but because it helps to suggest that logical solutions are always possible—at once deluding and flattering the delusion. In the field of practical action, this leads to the short cut and the doctrinaire panacea; in the field of speculation it may tempt the theologian, the philosopher, and even the poet, to abandon metaphysical method for methods appropriate only to the physical sciences, with results such as overtook Theology during the period of the Enlightenment. Then, without in the least realizing what they were doing, theologians insensibly came to accept the determinist assumptions of a knowledge based on mensuration, and so landed themselves either in a mechanistic Deism, or in a desperate attempt to locate God within the shrinking borders of indeterminacy. It will not do to listen to the siren-song of words like "problem" and "solution". We must bring imagination to the task of communicating thought. The task grows harder every day because of the multitude of techniques, because of the proliferation of meaningless verbiage, and also because the younger generations have been steadily deprived of the four great traditional safeguards: formal logic and the Latin Grammar, which were a negative defence against fallacy and slipshod syntax; a dogmatic theology and the habit of great verse, which were a positive education in the handling of the magical images.

Language is a living and a dangerous thing. It is coeval with humanity and aeviternal, so that a bullet in the heart is no remedy. If I am to offer you an image, it must be that of Hercules wrestling with Proteus. Hold on and squeeze hard, and, after it has changed shape a thousand times, language will tell you what you wish to know. But the answer you receive, Socrates, will depend on how you frame the question.

LIST OF SOURCES

The Poetry of Search and the Poetry of Statement; delivered to the Oxford University Spectator Club, October 30, 1956.

Dante the Maker; delivered to the Cambridge University Italian Society, May 8, 1956, under the title *Dante Faber: Structure in the Poetry of Statement.*

The Beatrician Vision in Dante and other Poets; delivered as the Herford Memorial Lecture to the Manchester Dante Society, March 14, 1956; published in Nottingham Mediaeval Studies, Volume II, 1958.

Charles Williams: Poet's Critic; delivered to a Conference held at Milland Place, Liphook, Hants., August 23, 1955.

On Translating the *Divina Commedia*; delivered at a course for Italian teachers of English organized by the British Council at Girton College, Cambridge, August, 1954; published in Nottingham Mediaeval Studies, Volume II, 1958.

The Translation of Verse; delivered to the Oxford University English Club, March 6, 1957.

The Lost Tools of Learning; delivered at a Vacation Course in Education, Oxford, 1947; published in the *Hibbert Journal*, October, 1947, and by Methuen, 1948.

The Teaching of Latin: a New Approach; delivered to the Association for the Reform of Latin Teaching, August 26, 1952; published in the *Journal* of the Association, October, 1952.

The Writing and Reading of Allegory; delivered as the second Sarah Walker Memorial Lecture, at the Training College, Darlington, November 10, 1954.

The Faust Legend and the Idea of the Devil; delivered to the English Goethe Society, February 22, 1945; Publications of the Society, Vol. XV, 1946.

Oedipus Simplex: Freedom and Fate in Folk-lore and Fiction; delivered to the Royal Institution of Great Britain, November 11, 1955; Proceedings of the Society, 36, No. 162, 1955.

Poetry, Language and Ambiguity; delivered to the Oxford University Socratic Society, June 3, 1954.

www.ingramcontent.com/pod-product-compliance
Lightning Source LLC
Chambersburg PA
CBHW050840230426
43667CB00012B/2088